SUPREME COURT WATCH 2006

*Highlights of the 2004 and 2005 Terms
Preview of the 2006 Term*

DAVID M. O'BRIEN
UNIVERSITY OF VIRGINIA

W·W· **NORTON & COMPANY** · NEW YORK · LONDON

W. W. Norton & Company has been independent since its founding in 1923, when William Warder Norton and Mary D. Herter Norton first published lectures delivered at the People's Institute, the adult education division of New York City's Cooper Union. The Nortons soon expanded their program beyond the Institute, publishing books by celebrated academics from America and abroad. By mid-century, the two major pillars of Norton's publishing program—trade books and college texts—were firmly established. In the 1950s, the Norton family transferred control of the company to its employees, and today—with a staff of four hundred and a comparable number of trade, college, and professional titles published each year—W. W. Norton & Company stands as the largest and oldest publishing house owned wholly by its employees.

Copyright © 2007 by W. W. Norton & Company, Inc.
All rights reserved.
Printed in the United States of America.

Composition by Cathy Lombardi.
Manufacturing by Victor Graphics, Inc.
Production Manager: Benjamin Reynolds.

ISBN-10: 0-393-92997-3 (pbk.)
ISBN-13: 978-0-393-92997-3

W. W. Norton & Company, Inc., 500 Fifth Avenue, New York, NY 10110
wwnorton.com

W. W. Norton & Company Ltd., Castle House, 75/76 Wells Street,
London W1T 3QT

Contents

Preface   ix

Volume One

Chapter 2 ■ *Law and Politics in the Supreme Court: Jurisdiction and Decision-Making Process*   1

A. Jurisdiction and Justiciable Controversies   7
  □ THE DEVELOPMENT OF LAW: Class Action Suits   7

B. The Court's Docket and Screening Cases   8
  □ INSIDE THE COURT: The Business of the Supreme Court in the 2005–2006 Term   8

H. Opinion Days and Communicating Decisions   9
  □ INSIDE THE COURT: Opinion Writing during the 2005–2006 Term   9

Chapter 3 ■ *Presidential Power, the Rule of Law, and Foreign Affairs*   10

D. War-Making and Emergency Powers   10
  [*Padilla v. Hanft*]   10
  Hamdan v. Rumsfeld   11
  □ IN COMPARATIVE PERSPECTIVE: The Supreme Court of Israel's Ruling Against the Use of Torture   28
  □ THE DEVELOPMENT OF LAW: The National Security Agency's Warrantless Electronic Surveillance   32
  □ IN COMPARATIVE PERSPECTIVE: The House of Lords Rules Against the Indefinite Detention of Terrorists   34

CHAPTER 4 ■ *The President as Chief Executive in Domestic Affairs* 36

☐ THE DEVELOPMENT OF LAW: Presidential Signing Statements and Legislative Powers 36

CHAPTER 6 ■ *Congress: Legislative, Taxing, and Spending Powers* 38

C. FROM THE NEW DEAL CRISIS TO THE ADMINISTRATIVE STATE 38
  [*Gonzales v. O Centro Espirita Beneficente Uniao do Vegetal*] 39
  Gonzales v. Raich 39
  Gonzales v. Oregon 50

CHAPTER 7 ■ *The States and American Federalism* 56

A. STATES' POWER OVER COMMERCE AND REGULATION 56
  ☐ THE DEVELOPMENT OF LAW: Other Rulings on State Regulatory Powers in Alleged Conflict with Federal Legislation 56
  ☐ THE DEVELOPMENT OF LAW: Other Rulings on State Regulation of Commerce in the Absence of Federal Legislation 57

B. THE TENTH AND ELEVENTH AMENDMENTS AND THE STATES 58
  ☐ THE DEVELOPMENT OF LAW: Other Recent Rulings on the Eleventh Amendment 58

CHAPTER 8 ■ *Representative Government, Voting Rights, and Electoral Politics* 59

B. VOTING RIGHTS AND THE REAPPORTIONMENT REVOLUTION 59
  League of United Latin American Citizens v. Perry 60

C. CAMPAIGNS AND ELECTIONS 74
  Garcetti v. Ceballos 74

Randall v. Sorrell 80
☐ THE DEVELOPMENT OF LAW: Other Rulings on Campaigns and Elections 89

CHAPTER 9 ■ *Economic Rights and American Capitalism* 90

C. THE "TAKINGS CLAUSE" AND JUST COMPENSATION 90
Kelo v. City of New London, Connecticut 91
☐ THE DEVELOPMENT OF LAW: Other Important Rulings on the Takings Clause 100

VOLUME TWO

CHAPTER 4 ■ *The Nationalization of the Bill of Rights* 103

B. THE RISE AND (PARTIAL) RETREAT OF THE "DUE PROCESS REVOLUTION" 103
[*Phillip Morris USA v. Williams*] 103
☐ THE DEVELOPMENT OF LAW: Other Recent Rulings on Substantive and Procedural Due Process 104

CHAPTER 5 ■ *Freedom of Expression and Association* 105

Rumsfeld v. Forum for Academic and Institutional Rights 105

C. LIBEL 110
☐ IN COMPARATIVE PERSPECTIVE: Blasphemy and Other Hate Speech 110

D. COMMERCIAL SPEECH 111
☐ THE DEVELOPMENT OF LAW: Other Recent Rulings on Commercial Speech and the First Amendment 111

E. FREEDOM OF THE PRESS 112
(2) INDIRECT PRIOR RESTRAINTS 112
[*Beard v. Banks*] 112

CHAPTER 6 ■ *Freedom from and of Religion*   113

A. THE (DIS)ESTABLISHMENT CLAUSE   113
   Cutter v. Wilkinson   114
   Van Orden v. Perry   117
   McCreary County v. American Civil Liberties Union of Kentucky   128

B. FREE EXERCISE OF RELIGION   137
   [*Gonzales v. O Centro Espirita Beneficente Uniao do Vegetal*]   137

CHAPTER 7 ■ *The Fourth Amendment Guarantee Against Unreasonable Searches and Seizures*   138

A. REQUIREMENTS FOR A WARRANT AND REASONABLE SEARCHES AND SEIZURES   138
   [*Muehler v. Mena*]   138
   [*United States v. Grubbs*]   138
   Georgia v. Randolph   139

B. EXCEPTIONS TO THE WARRANT REQUIREMENT   144
   [*Brigham City, Utah v. Stuart*]   145
   [*Samson v. California*]   145
   Illinois v. Caballes   145
   □ THE DEVELOPMENT OF LAW: The National Security Agency's Warrantless Electronic Surveillance (reprise)   149

F. THE EXCLUSIONARY RULE   149
   Hudson v. Michigan   150

CHAPTER 9 ■ *The Rights to Counsel and Other Procedural Guarantees*   157

A. THE RIGHT TO COUNSEL   157
   [*United States v. Gonzalez-Lopez*]   157

B. PLEA BARGAINING AND THE RIGHT TO EFFECTIVE COUNSEL   158
   □ THE DEVELOPMENT OF LAW: Rulings on Plea Bargaining and Effective Counsel   158

D. THE RIGHT TO AN IMPARTIAL JURY TRIAL   158
   [United States v. Booker]   159
   [Miller-El v. Dretke]   159
   [Johnson v. California]   159

F. THE RIGHT TO BE INFORMED OF CHARGES AND TO CONFRONT ACCUSERS   160
   [Davis v. Washington]   160

CHAPTER 10 ■ *Cruel and Unusual Punishment*   161

B. CAPITAL PUNISHMENT   161
   Roper v. Simmons   161
   □ THE DEVELOPMENT OF LAW: Other Recent Rulings on Capital Punishment   169

CHAPTER 11 ■ *The Right of Privacy*   170

A. PRIVACY AND REPRODUCTIVE FREEDOM   170
   [Gonzales v. Carhart]   170
   [Gonzales v. Planned Parenthood Federation of America]   170
   Ayotte v. Planned Parenthood of Northern New England   171

CHAPTER 12 ■ *The Equal Protection of the Laws*   174

A. RACIAL DISCRIMINATION AND STATE ACTION   174
   [Johnson v. California]   174

B. RACIAL DISCRIMINATION IN EDUCATION   175
   [Parents Involved in Community Schools v. Seattle School District No. 1]   175
   [Meredith v. Jefferson County Board of Education]   175

C. AFFIRMATIVE ACTION AND REVERSE DISCRIMINATION   176
   [Parents Involved in Community Schools v. Seattle School District No. 1] (reprise)   176
   [Meredith v. Jefferson County Board of Education] (reprise)   176

D. NONRACIAL CLASSIFICATIONS AND THE EQUAL PROTECTION OF THE LAW   177
   (4) ALIENAGE AND AGE   177
     □ THE DEVELOPMENT OF LAW: Rulings on the Classification of Aliens   177

INDEX OF CASES   179

PREFACE

Supreme Court Watch 2006 examines the changes and decisions made during the Supreme Court's 2004 and 2005 terms. In addition to highlighting the major constitutional rulings in excerpts from leading cases, I discuss in section-by-section introductions other important decisions and analyze recent developments in various areas of constitutional law. I also preview here the important cases that the Court has granted review and will decide in its 2006–2007 term. To offer even more information in an efficient format, special boxes titled "The Development of Law," "In Comparative Perspective," and "Inside the Court" are also included.

The favorable reception of previous editions of the *Watch* has been gratifying, and I hope that this sixteenth edition will further contribute to students' understanding of constitutional law, politics, and history, as well as to their appreciation for how the politics of constitutional interpretation turns on differing interpretations of constitutional politics and the role of the Supreme Court. I am most grateful to Brian Baker for doing a terrific and expeditious job in producing this edition.

D.M.O.
June 29, 2006

Supreme Court Watch 2006
Volume One

2

Law and Politics in the Supreme Court: Jurisdiction and Decision-Making Process

Continuing a decade-old trend, in its 2005–2006 term the Court granted and decided by written opinion less than 1 percent of its total docket of 9,608 cases, giving plenary consideration to 74 cases and summarily deciding with full opinions another nine cases (see the "Inside the Court" boxes in this chapter). As usual, the Court more often reversed than affirmed the decisions below, as indicated in the following table.

The Court's Disposition of Appeals in the 2005 Term

	AFFIRMED	REVERSED OR VACATED
First Circuit	1	1
Second Circuit	2	4
Third Circuit		3
Fourth Circuit	2	2
Fifth Circuit	1	2
Sixth Circuit	1	5
Seventh Circuit		2
Eighth Circuit	2	1
Ninth Circuit	2	16
Tenth Circuit	3	2
Eleventh Circuit	1	6
Federal Circuit		2
District of Columbia Circuit	1	1
Other Federal Courts		3
State Courts and Other	7	8
*Totals:	23	58

*Excludes cases decided on original jurisdiction or dismissed for lack of jurisdiction and remanded.

Throughout the 2004–2005 term, speculation mounted that Chief Justice William H. Rehnquist would retire. He had served on the Court for 33 years and as chief justice for 19 years. Undergoing treatment for thyroid cancer, he missed several months of the Court's oral argument sessions but participated in cases in which the other justices split four to four. But four days after the end of the term, Justice Sandra Day O'Connor sent President George W. Bush a letter informing him of her retirement upon the nomination and the Senate's confirmation of her successor. Appointed in 1981 by Republican President Ronald Reagan, who in his 1980 presidential campaign promised to name the first woman to the Court, Justice O'Connor served 24 years and in the last decade became the pivotal, "swing," vote on some of the most hotly contested social-civil rights issues. In the last decade, Justice O'Connor was in the majority in 148 out of 193 cases decided by a bare majority, and wrote the opinion for the Court in 25 of those decisions.

Justice O'Connor generally voted with other conservatives to limit congressional power, in defense of federalism. She delivered the Court's opinion in *New York v. United States*, 505 U.S. 144 (1992) (excerpted in Vol. 1, Ch. 7), and joined the majority in other leading rulings, including *United States v. Lopez*, 514 U.S. 549 (1995) (excerpted in Vol. 1, Ch. 6); *Printz v. United States*, 521 U.S. 898 (1997) (excerpted in Vol. 1, Ch. 7); and *United States v. Morrison*, 529 U.S. 598 (2000) (excerpted in Vol. 1, Ch. 6). Justice O'Connor also joined bare majorities in enforcing the Eleventh Amendment to limit congressional power in *Seminole Tribe of Florida v. Florida*, 517 U.S. 44 (1996) (excerpted in Vol. 1, Ch. 7), and *Alden v. Maine*, 527 U.S. 706 (1999) (excerpted in Vol. 1, Ch. 7), among other decisions. But she eventually voted to uphold Congress's power to abrogate states' sovereign immunity from private lawsuits brought under the Family and Medical Leave Act, in *Nevada Department of Human Resources v. Hibbs*, 538 U.S. 721 (2003) (excerpted in Vol. 1, Ch. 7); and under the Americans with Disabilities Act, in *Tennessee v. Lane*, 541 U.S. 509 (2004). Justice O'Connor also generally voted with conservatives in cases involving the rights of the accused and the death penalty, though she issued a bitter dissent from the bare majority's upholding of random drug tests for students in *Board of Education of Independent School District No. 92 of Pottawatomie City v. Earls*, 536 U.S. 822 (2002) (excerpted in Vol. 2, Ch. 7). Likewise, although generally voting with the conservative block to strike down most affirmative-action programs, Justice O'Connor ruled that race may be taken into consideration in order to achieve diverse student bodies in colleges and universities, in *Grutter v. Bollinger*, 539 U.S. 306 (2003) (excerpted in Vol. 2, Ch. 12); as well as in congressional redistricting, in *Hunt v. Cromartie*, 532 U.S. 234 (2001) (excerpted in Vol. 1, Ch. 8).

During her tenure, Justice O'Connor sided with liberal and left-of-center justices to affirm *Roe v. Wade*, 410 U.S. 113 (1973) (excerpted in Vol. 2, Ch. 11), in *Planned Parenthood of Southeastern Pennsylvania v. Casey*, 505 U.S. 833 (1992) (excerpted in Vol. 2, Ch. 11), and to strike down bans on "partial-birth abortions," in

Stenberg v. Carhart, 530 U.S. 914 (2000) (excerpted in Vol. 2, Ch. 11), as well as joined the majority to strike down laws criminalizing homosexual sodomy in *Lawrence v. Texas*, 539 U.S. 558 (2003) (excerpted in Vol. 2, Ch. 11). In the 2004–2005 term, Justice O'Connor voted to hold the First Amendment to bar state and local governments from posting the Ten Commandments in courthouses in *McCreary v. American Civil Liberties Union of Kentucky* (2005) (excerpted below in Vol. 2, Ch 5). Hence, despite her generally conservative record, including siding with the bare majority in *Bush v. Gore*, 531 U.S. 98 (2000), which ended the Florida election recount and effectively decided the presidential election, because of those and other votes Justice O'Connor remained a disappointment for "movement conservatives."

The last time a pivotal justice retired and the balance of the Court shifted was in 1987, when Justice Lewis F. Powell, Jr., stepped down. At the time, he also cast the crucial votes on abortion, affirmative action, and some other controversial issues. President Reagan's nomination to fill his seat of a hard-line conservative, Judge Robert H. Bork, sparked a bitter confirmation battle that resulted in defeat and led to the appointment of a more moderate conservative, Justice Anthony Kennedy.

A little over two weeks after Justice O'Connor announced her retirement, President Bush nominated Court of Appeals for the District of Columbia Circuit Judge John G. Roberts to fill her seat. In that time, conservatives mounted opposition to the possible nomination of the president's friend, Attorney General Alberto Gonzales, as the first Hispanic to sit on the Court. Liberal groups in turn raised funds to wage a media campaign against any hardline conservative nominee. Bush told both sides to tone down their rhetoric. Speculation grew that 80-year-old Chief Justice Rehnquist might still retire because of poor health and give Bush strategic opportunities to fill more vacancies, until the chief finally announced that he would stay as long as his health permitted.

But before the Senate Judiciary Committee could hold confirmation hearings, Chief Justice Rehnquist died, on September 3, 2005. After a few days of consultations and Justice O'Connor's agreeing to stay on the bench until the confirmation of her successor, President Bush renominated Judge Roberts, this time to fill his mentor's seat on the high bench.

In naming Judge Roberts, who was 50 years old, Bush satisfied his conservative base, which predicted that the Court's balance would shift to the right. On the other hand, the selection of Judge Roberts over others with longer, more hard-line judicial records, such as Judge Michael Luttig, made it more difficult for Democratic senators initially to voice staunch opposition. A graduate of Harvard College and Harvard Law School, Judge Roberts served on the appellate bench for just two years and had written few opinions. Following law school, he served as a law clerk to then-Associate Justice Rehnquist, before moving into the administration of President Ronald Reagan, first as special assistant to the attorney general and later as associate counsel to the president. After a few years in private practice, he became a deputy solicitor general in the administration of President George H. W. Bush, who nominated him in 1992 to the federal bench but a Senate confirmation vote was never taken. Subsequently, following another eight years in private practice, Roberts was nominated by President George W. Bush to the appellate bench in 2001; after the nomination was blocked by Senate Democrats, Bush renominated Roberts in 2003; he was then confirmed by the Senate without a roll call vote. Throughout his career (eleven years in government service and thirteen in private practice), Judge Roberts earned a reputation within Washington legal circles as a solid conservative and a skillful Supreme Court litigator, arguing 39 cases before the Court and winning 25 of them.

In anticipation of the Senate Judiciary's confirmation hearing in September 2005, interest groups for and against him mobilized supporters through emails, Web sites, and direct mail and television ads.

Yet the American Bar Association ranked him "well qualified"—its highest ranking—and his confirmation hearings proved relatively noncontroversial, largely because the balance on the Court would not shift. On Friday, September 30, 2005, just prior to the first Monday in October, when the Court begins its term, Roberts was confirmed by a Senate vote of 78 to 22, with all 55 Republicans and half of the 44 Democrats and independent senator James Jeffords voting in favor. Three hours later Roberts was sworn in as the 109th justice and 17th chief justice.

President Bush, then, faced competing pressures in selecting another nominee for Justice O'Connor's seat. Hispanic groups pressured for the elevation of Attorney General Gonzales, but conservatives opposed him. Women's groups pushed for the appointment of a woman, while liberal Democratic senators argued that the appointment should go to a moderate, in the mold of Justice O'Connor, since she cast the critical vote in several controversial areas and her replacement would shift the balance on the bench. By contrast, conservative groups insisted on the nomination of another solid conservative.

Shortly before the Court opened its 2005 term, with Chief Justice Roberts presiding, on October 3, President Bush nominated his long-time Texas friend and legal counselor, Harriet Miers. Within hours conservatives turned against her, contending that she was not a proven conservative and lacked qualifications since she had no prior judicial experience. In the weeks that followed, the criticisms grew and Miers's personal meetings with individual senators did not go well. Finally, on October 28, Miers withdrew from her nomination.

Subsequently, President Bush sought to satisfy his conservative base by nominating 55-year-old U.S. Court of Appeals for the Third Circuit judge Samuel Alito, Jr., who had been named to the federal bench in 1990 by President George H. W. Bush. Like Chief Justice Roberts, Judge Alito spent much of his early legal career working in the Reagan administration. As an attorney in the Department of Justice's Office of Legal Counsel and as an assistant to the solicitor general, according to memos released by the National Archives and the Reagan Presidential Library, on the one hand, he staked out positions opposing a woman's right to choose and affirmative action, and, on the other hand, supported expanding presidential powers and limits on congressional power. As an appellate judge, he established a mixed record, though a more conservative record than that of Justice O'Connor. In the weeks before his confirmation hearings in January 2006, women's and environmental groups, the Alliance for Justice, the People for the American Way, and the AFL-CIO, among other organizations, announced their opposition and vowed to fight his confirmation.

During four days of testimony before the Senate Judiciary Committee, in response to almost 700 questions, Alito proved humble, while refusing to further explain positions he had held as an attorney in the Reagan administration and as an appellate court judge, claiming that they were the views of his "client" or that he could not comment because the issues might come before him on the high bench. The Senate Judiciary Committee split along party lines in its recommendation, with all 10 Republicans voting for him and the eight Democrats in opposition. The full Senate confirmed Alito as the 110th justice by a vote of 58 to 42, with four Democrats voting with Republicans and one Republican—Lincoln Chafee (R.I.)—joining 40 Democrats and independent senator Jeffords voting against confirmation.

A | Jurisdiction and Justiciable Controversies

■ THE DEVELOPMENT OF LAW
Class Action Suits

In February 2005, President George W. Bush signed into law the Class Action Fairness Act, which moves from state courts to federal courts large, interstate class action lawsuits brought by consumers against businesses for fraud or faulty products. For over a decade business groups had lobbied for the legislation. They contended that business faced too many frivolous lawsuits, excessive punitive damage awards, and that lawyers filed such suits in states known to be more favorable to consumers. Consumer advocates, trial lawyers, and the U.S. Judicial Conference opposed the law. They countered that the law would burden the federal judiciary; that federal courts are ill equipped to deal with such suits, which usually involve the application of state consumer-protection laws; and that consumers would be discouraged from bringing such suits.

Under the law, class action suits seeking $5 million or more would remain in state courts only if the primary defendant and more than one-third of the plaintiffs are from the same state. If fewer than one-third of the plaintiffs are from the same state as the primary defendant, and more than $5 million is sought, the case would go to a federal court. In addition, the law also limits attorney fees when plaintiffs only receive discount coupons on products, instead of financial settlements, by linking the fees to the coupon's redemption rate or the actual hours spent working on the case.

B | The Court's Docket and Screening Cases

■ INSIDE THE COURT

The Business of the Supreme Court in the 2005–2006 Term

SUBJECT OF COURT OPINIONS*	SUMMARY	PLENARY
Admiralty		1
Antitrust		2
Bankruptcy		2
Bill of Rights (other than rights of accused) and Equal Protection		6
Commerce Clause		
1. Constitutionality and construction of federal regulation		
2. Constitutionality of state regulation		
Common Law		
Miscellaneous Statutory Construction	2	22
Due process		
1. Economic interests		1
2. Procedure and rights of accused	3	14
3. Substantive due process (noneconomic)		
Impairment of Contract and Just Compensation		1
International Law, War, and Peace		1
Jurisdiction, Procedure, and Practice	4	16
Land Legislation		
Native Americans		2
Patents, Copyright, and Trademarks		2
Other Suits against the Government		4
Suits by States		1
Taxation (federal and state)		
Totals	9	74

*Note: The classification of cases is that of the author and necessarily invites differences of opinion as to the dominant issue in some cases. The table includes opinions in cases whether decided summarily or given plenary consideration, but not cases summarily disposed of by simple orders, opinions dissenting from the denial of review, and those dismissing cases as improvidently granted.

H | Opinion Days and Communicating Decisions

- INSIDE THE COURT

Opinion Writing during the 2005–2006 Term*

OPINIONS	MAJORITY	CONCURRING	DISSENTING	SEPARATE	TOTALS
Per Curiam	16				16
Roberts	8	1	1	2	12
Stevens	7	6	13	1	27
O'Connor	3				3
Scalia	9	4	5	2	20
Kennedy	8	6	3		17
Souter	7	1	4	1	13
Thomas	8	2	7	1	18
Ginsburg	7	3	5		15
Breyer	7	4	9	2	22
Alito	3	3	2		8
Totals	83	30	49	9	171

*Note that court opinions disposing of two or more companion cases are counted only once here. In addition, this table includes opinions in cases disposed of either summarily or upon plenary consideration, but does not include cases summarily disposed of by simple orders or concurring or dissenting opinions from the denial of *certiorari*.

3

PRESIDENTIAL POWER, THE RULE OF LAW, AND FOREIGN AFFAIRS

D | *War-Making and Emergency Powers*

In its 2005–2006 term, the Court continued to confront issues growing out of the war against international terrorism and the Bush administration's detention and treatment of enemy combatants; for further discussion see the Constitutional History box in Volume 1, Chapter 3. The case of Jose Padilla, the so-called dirty bomber and only citizen captured within the U.S. and declared an enemy combatant and held in a Navy brig, returned to the Court. In *Rumsfeld v. Padilla*, 542 U.S. 426 (2004), the Court dismissed on jurisdictional grounds his *habeas corpus* petition challenging his detention. On remand, a district court sided with Padilla but the Court of Appeals for the Fourth Circuit reversed, holding that Congress's joint resolution on the Authorization of the Use of Military Force authorized the President to hold suspected terrorists as enemy combatants. Padilla appealed but the administration then switched positions and removed him from military detention to a jail and filed criminal charges against him. Subsequently, the Court denied his petition, in *Padilla v. Hanft*, 126 S.Ct. 1649 (2006). Justice Kennedy filed a concurring opinion to the denial of *certiorari*, joined by Chief Justice Roberts and Justice Stevens, explaining that the issue was now hypothetical, since he was now facing criminal charges and his status would not change even if the Court ruled in his favor. Justices Souter, Breyer, and Ginsburg dissented; the latter filed a dissenting opinion, arguing that the Court should decide the issue presented, namely, whether the President has the power to declare citizens enemy combatants and hold them in military detention.

In a historic ruling, the Court also rebuffed the Bush administration's position that it could try enemy combatants by military commissions, rather than in civilian courts or in courts-martial, and according to the Geneva Conventions, in *Hamdan v. Rumsfeld* (2006) (excerpted below). Within a month, the administration agreed to accord detained combatants certain guarantees of the Geneva Conventions. Congress considered legislation authorizing trials by military commissions, according to the procedures of the Uniform Code of Military Justice (UCMJ), but the administration opposed that.

Hamdan v. Rumsfeld
126 S.Ct. 2749 (2006)

Salim Ahmed Hamdan, a Yemeni who served as a bodyguard and driver for Osama bin Laden, was captured in 2001 in Afghanistan and then transferred in 2002 to the prison in Guantanamo Bay, Cuba. Over a year later, President George W. Bush decided to try him by military commission for then-unspecified crimes. In 2003, military counsel was appointed to represent Hamdan, and that attorney filed demands for a speedy trial and for the charges or accusations against Hamdan, according to the UCMJ. After another year passed, a legal authority for the commission ruled against those demands. Subsequently, Hamdan was charged with one count of conspiracy "to commit . . . offenses triable by military commission." In 2004, Hamdan filed a petition for a writ of *habeas corpus*, challenging the administration's use of a military commission to try him and the charge of conspiracy. He conceded that a court-martial constituted in accordance with the UCMJ would have authority to try him. But, he contended the military commission lacked authority for two principal reasons: First, neither a congressional act nor the common law of war supported trial by such a commission for the crime of conspiracy—an offense that is not a violation of the law of war. Second, the procedures of the military commission violate the most basic tenets of military and international law, including the principle that a defendant must be permitted to see and hear the evidence against him.

A federal district court granted Hamdan's request for a writ of *habeas corpus*, but it was reversed by the Court of Appeals for the District of Columbia Circuit. Hamdan appealed that decision and the Supreme Court granted *certiorari*.

The appellate court's decision was reversed by a five to three vote with Chief Justice Roberts not participating, because he had sat as a then judge on the appellate court deciding the case. Justice Stevens announced the opinion for the Court and parts of his opinion were joined by only a plurality—Justices Souter, Ginsburg, and Breyer. Justices Kennedy and Breyer filed concurring opinions. Justices Scalia, Thomas, and Alito filed dissenting opinions.

☐ *Justice STEVENS announced the judgment of the Court and delivered the opinion of the Court with respect to Parts I through IV, Parts VI through VI–D–iii, Part VI–D–v, and Part VII, and an opinion with respect to Parts V and VI–D–iv, in which Justice SOUTER, Justice GINSBURG, and Justice BREYER join.*

For the reasons that follow, we conclude that the military commission convened to try Hamdan lacks power to proceed because its structure and procedures violate both the [Uniform Code of Military Justice] UCMJ and the Geneva Conventions. Four of us also conclude that the offense [conspiracy] with which Hamdan has been charged is not an "offens[e] that by . . . the law of war may be tried by military commissions."

■ I

On September 11, 2001, agents of the al Qaeda terrorist organization hijacked commercial airplanes and attacked the World Trade Center in New York City and the national headquarters of the Department of Defense in Arlington, Virginia. Americans will never forget the devastation wrought by these acts. Nearly 3,000 civilians were killed.

Congress responded by adopting a Joint Resolution authorizing the President to "use all necessary and appropriate force against those nations, organizations, or persons he determines planned, authorized, committed, or aided the terrorist attacks . . . in order to prevent any future acts of international terrorism against the United States by such nations, organizations or persons." Authorization for Use of Military Force (AUMF). Acting pursuant to the AUMF, and having determined that the Taliban regime had supported al Qaeda, the President ordered the Armed Forces of the United States to invade Afghanistan. In the ensuing hostilities, hundreds of individuals, Hamdan among them, were captured and eventually detained at Guantanamo Bay.

On November 13, 2001, while the United States was still engaged in active combat with the Taliban, the President issued a comprehensive military order intended to govern the "Detention, Treatment, and Trial of Certain Non-Citizens in the War Against Terrorism." Those subject to the November 13 Order include any noncitizen for whom the President determines "there is reason to believe" that he or she (1) "is or was" a member of al Qaeda or (2) has engaged or participated in terrorist activities aimed at or harmful to the United States. Any such individual "shall, when tried, be tried by military commission for any and all offenses triable by military commission that such individual is alleged to have committed, and may be punished in accordance with the penalties provided under applicable law, including imprisonment or death."

[W]e granted *certiorari* to decide whether the military commission convened to try Hamdan has authority to do so, and whether Hamdan may rely on the Geneva Conventions in these proceedings.

II

On February 13, 2006, the Government filed a motion to dismiss the writ of *certiorari*. The ground cited for dismissal was the recently enacted Detainee Treatment Act of 2005 (DTA). We postponed our ruling on that motion pending argument on the merits, and now deny it.

The DTA, which was signed into law on December 30, 2005, addresses a broad swath of subjects related to detainees. It places restrictions on the treatment and interrogation of detainees in U. S. custody, and it furnishes procedural protections for U. S. personnel accused of engaging in improper interrogation. It also sets forth certain "procedures for status review of detainees outside the United States." Subsections (a) through (d) of Section 1005 direct the Secretary of Defense to report to Congress the procedures being used by [Combatant Status Review Tribunal] CSRTs to determine the proper classification of detainees held in Guantanamo Bay, Iraq, and Afghanistan, and to adopt certain safeguards as part of those procedures.

Subsection (e) of Section 1005, which is entitled "Judicial Review of Detention of Enemy Combatants," supplies the basis for the Government's jurisdictional argument. The subsection contains three numbered paragraphs. The first paragraph amends the judicial code as follows: "(1) In general.—Section 2241 of title 28, United States Code, is amended by adding at the end the following: "(e) Except as provided in section 1005 of the Detainee Treatment Act of 2005, no court, justice, or judge shall have jurisdiction to hear or consider—(1) an application for a writ of *habeas corpus* filed by or on behalf of an alien detained by the Department of Defense at Guantanamo Bay, Cuba; or (2) any other action against the United States or its agents relating to any aspect of the detention by the Department of Defense of an alien at Guantanamo Bay, Cuba, who—(A) is currently in military custody; or (B) has been determined by the United States Court of Appeals for the District of Columbia Circuit in accordance with the procedures set forth in section 1005(e) of the Detainee Treatment Act of 2005 to have been properly detained as an enemy combatant." . . .

Paragraph (3) mirrors paragraph (2) in structure, but governs judicial review of final decisions of military commissions, not CSRTs. It vests in the Court of Appeals for the District of Columbia Circuit "exclusive jurisdiction to determine the validity of any final decision rendered pursuant to Military Commission Order No. 1, dated August 31, 2005 (or any successor military order)." Review is as of right for any alien sentenced to death or a term of imprisonment of 10 years or more, but is at the Court of Appeals' discretion in all other cases. The scope of review is limited to the following inquiries: "(i) whether the final decision [of the military commission] was consistent with the standards and procedures specified in the military order referred to in subparagraph (A); and (ii) to the extent the Constitution and laws of the United States are applicable, whether the use of such standards and procedures to reach the final decision is consistent with the Constitution and laws of the United States."

Finally, Section 1005 contains an "effective date" provision, which reads as follows: "(1) In general.—This section shall take effect on the date of the enactment of this Act. (2) Review of Combatant Status Tribunal and Military Commission Decisions.—Paragraphs (2) and (3) of subsection (e) shall apply with respect to any claim whose review is governed by one of such paragraphs and that is pending on or after the date of the enactment of this Act." The Act is silent about whether paragraph (1) of subsection (e) "shall apply" to claims pending on the date of enactment.

The Government argues that [the DTA] had the immediate effect, upon enactment, of repealing federal jurisdiction not just over detainee *habeas* actions yet to be filed but also over any such actions then pending in any federal court—including this Court. Accordingly, it argues, we lack jurisdiction to review the Court of Appeals' decision below. . . .

We find it unnecessary to reach either of these arguments. Ordinary principles of statutory construction suffice to rebut the Government's theory—at least insofar as this case, which was pending at the time the DTA was enacted, is concerned. . . . [W]e deny the Government's motion to dismiss.

■ III

Relying on our decision in [*Schlesinger v.*] *Councilman*, 420 U.S. 738 [(1975)], the Government argues that, even if we have statutory jurisdiction, we should apply the "judge-made rule that civilian courts should await the final outcome of on-going military proceedings before entertaining an attack on those proceedings." Like the District Court and the Court of Appeals before us, we reject this argument.

In *Councilman*, an army officer on active duty was referred to a court-martial for trial on charges that he violated the UCMJ by selling, transferring, and possessing marijuana. Objecting that the alleged offenses were not "'service connected,'" the officer filed suit in Federal District Court to enjoin the proceedings. He neither questioned the lawfulness of courts-martial or their procedures nor disputed that, as a serviceman, he was subject to court-martial jurisdiction. His sole argument was that the subject matter of his case did not fall within the scope of court-martial authority. The District Court granted his request for injunctive relief, and the Court of Appeals affirmed.

We granted *certiorari* and reversed. We did not reach the merits of whether the marijuana charges were sufficiently "service connected" to place them within the subject-matter jurisdiction of a court-martial. Instead, we concluded that, as a matter of comity, federal courts should normally abstain from intervening in pending court-martial proceedings against members of the Armed Forces, and further that there was nothing in the particular circumstances of the officer's case to displace that general rule.

Councilman identifies two considerations of comity that together favor abstention pending completion of ongoing court-martial proceedings against service personnel. First, military discipline and, therefore, the efficient operation of the Armed Forces are best served if the military justice system acts without regular interference from civilian courts. Second, federal courts should respect the balance that Congress struck between military preparedness and fairness to individual service members when it created "an integrated system of military courts and review procedures, a critical element of which is the Court of Military Appeals, consisting of civilian judges 'completely removed from all military influence or persuasion . . . .'"

The same cannot be said here; indeed, neither of the comity considerations identified in *Councilman* weighs in favor of abstention in this case. First, Hamdan is not a member of our Nation's Armed Forces, so concerns about military discipline do not apply. Second, the tribunal convened to try Hamdan is not part of the integrated system of military courts, complete with independent review panels, that Congress has established. . . .

In sum, neither of the two comity considerations underlying our decision to abstain in *Councilman* applies to the circumstances of this case. . . .

IV

The military commission, a tribunal neither mentioned in the Constitution nor created by statute, was born of military necessity....

Exigency alone, of course, will not justify the establishment and use of penal tribunals not contemplated by Article I, Section 8 and Article III, Section 1 of the Constitution unless some other part of that document authorizes a response to the felt need. See *Ex parte Milligan*, 4 Wall. 2 (1866). And that authority, if it exists, can derive only from the powers granted jointly to the President and Congress in time of war.

The Constitution makes the President the "Commander in Chief" of the Armed Forces, Art. II, Section 2, clause 1, but vests in Congress the powers to "declare War . . . and make Rules concerning Captures on Land and Water," Art. I, Section 8, clause. 11, to "raise and support Armies," to "define and punish . . . Offences against the Law of Nations," and "To make Rules for the Government and Regulation of the land and naval Forces." . . .

[W]e held in [*Ex parte*] *Quirin* [317 U.S. 1 (1942)] that Congress had, through Article of War 15, sanctioned the use of military commissions in such circumstances. Article 21 of the UCMJ, the language of which is substantially identical to the old Article 15 and was preserved by Congress after World War II, reads as follows: "Jurisdiction of courts-martial not exclusive. The provisions of this code conferring jurisdiction upon courts-martial shall not be construed as depriving military commissions, provost courts, or other military tribunals of concurrent jurisdiction in respect of offenders or offenses that by statute or by the law of war may be tried by such military commissions, provost courts, or other military tribunals."

We have no occasion to revisit *Quirin*'s controversial characterization of Article of War 15 as congressional authorization for military commissions. Contrary to the Government's assertion, however, even *Quirin* did not view the authorization as a sweeping mandate for the President to "invoke military commissions when he deems them necessary." Rather, the *Quirin* Court recognized that Congress had simply preserved what power, under the Constitution and the common law of war, the President had had before 1916 to convene military commissions—with the express condition that the President and those under his command comply with the law of war. . . . The Government would have us dispense with the inquiry that the *Quirin* Court undertook and find in either the AUMF or the DTA specific, overriding authorization for the very commission that has been convened to try Hamdan. Neither of these congressional Acts, however, expands the President's authority to convene military commissions. First, while we assume that the AUMF activated the President's war powers, see *Hamdi v. Rumsfeld*, 542 U.S. 507 (2004), and that those powers include the authority to convene military commissions in appropriate circumstances, there is nothing in the text or legislative history of the AUMF even hinting that Congress intended to expand or alter the authorization set forth in Article 21 of the UCMJ.

Likewise, the DTA cannot be read to authorize this commission. Although the DTA, unlike either Article 21 or the AUMF, was enacted after the President had convened Hamdan's commission, it contains no language authorizing that tribunal or any other at Guantanamo Bay. [T]he statute also pointedly reserves judgment on whether "the Constitution and laws of the United States are applicable" in reviewing such decisions and whether, if they are, the "standards and procedures" used to try Hamdan and other detainees actually violate the "Constitution and laws." Together, the UCMJ, the AUMF, and the

DTA at most acknowledge a general Presidential authority to convene military commissions in circumstances where justified under the "Constitution and laws," including the law of war. Absent a more specific congressional authorization, the task of this Court is, as it was in *Quirin*, to decide whether Hamdan's military commission is so justified. It is to that inquiry we now turn.

■ V

Quirin is the model the Government invokes most frequently to defend the commission convened to try Hamdan. That is both appropriate and unsurprising. Since Guantanamo Bay is neither enemy-occupied territory nor under martial law, the law-of-war commission is the only model available. At the same time, no more robust model of executive power exists; *Quirin* represents the high-water mark of military power to try enemy combatants for war crimes.

The classic treatise penned by Colonel William Winthrop, whom we have called "the 'Blackstone of Military Law,'" *Reid v. Covert*, 354 U.S. 1 (1957), describes at least four preconditions for exercise of jurisdiction by a tribunal of the type convened to try Hamdan. First, "[a] military commission, (except where otherwise authorized by statute), can legally assume jurisdiction only of offenses committed within the field of the command of the convening commander." The "field of command" in these circumstances means the "theatre of war." Second, the offense charged "must have been committed within the period of the war." No jurisdiction exists to try offenses "committed either before or after the war." Third, a military commission not established pursuant to martial law or an occupation may try only "[i]ndividuals of the enemy's army who have been guilty of illegitimate warfare or other offences in violation of the laws of war" and members of one's own army "who, in time of war, become chargeable with crimes or offences not cognizable, or triable, by the criminal courts or under the Articles of war." Finally, a law-of-war commission has jurisdiction to try only two kinds of offense: "Violations of the laws and usages of war cognizable by military tribunals only," and "[b]reaches of military orders or regulations for which offenders are not legally triable by court-martial under the Articles of war."

All parties agree that Colonel Winthrop's treatise accurately describes the common law governing military commissions, and that the jurisdictional limitations he identifies were incorporated in Article of War 15 and, later, Article 21 of the UCMJ. It also is undisputed that Hamdan's commission lacks jurisdiction to try him unless the charge "properly set[s] forth, not only the details of the act charged, but the circumstances conferring jurisdiction." The question is whether the preconditions designed to ensure that a military necessity exists to justify the use of this extraordinary tribunal have been satisfied here.

The charge against Hamdan alleges a conspiracy extending over a number of years, from 1996 to November 2001. All but two months of that more than 5-year-long period preceded the attacks of September 11, 2001, and the enactment of the AUMF—the Act of Congress on which the Government relies for exercise of its war powers and thus for its authority to convene military commissions. Neither the purported agreement with Osama bin Laden and others to commit war crimes, nor a single overt act, is alleged to have occurred in a theater of war or on any specified date after September 11, 2001. None of the overt acts that Hamdan is alleged to have committed violates the law of war.

These facts alone cast doubt on the legality of the charge and, hence, the commission; the offense alleged must have been committed both in a theater of war and during, not before, the relevant conflict. But the deficiencies in the time and place allegations also underscore—indeed are symptomatic of—the most serious defect of this charge: The offense it alleges is not triable by law-of-war military commission.

There is no suggestion that Congress has, in exercise of its constitutional authority to "define and punish . . . Offences against the Law of Nations," U.S. Const., Art. I, Section 8, clause 10, positively identified "conspiracy" as a war crime. As we explained in *Quirin*, that is not necessarily fatal to the Government's claim of authority to try the alleged offense by military commission; Congress, through Article 21 of the UCMJ, has "incorporated by reference" the common law of war, which may render triable by military commission certain offenses not defined by statute. When, however, neither the elements of the offense nor the range of permissible punishments is defined by statute or treaty, the precedent must be plain and unambiguous. To demand any less would be to risk concentrating in military hands a degree of adjudicative and punitive power in excess of that contemplated either by statute or by the Constitution.

This high standard was met in *Quirin*; the violation there alleged was, by "universal agreement and practice" both in this country and internationally, recognized as an offense against the law of war. . . .

At a minimum, the Government must make a substantial showing that the crime for which it seeks to try a defendant by military commission is acknowledged to be an offense against the law of war. That burden is satisfied here. The crime of "conspiracy" has rarely if ever been tried as such in this country by any law-of-war military commission not exercising some other form of jurisdiction, and does not appear in either the Geneva Conventions or the Hague Conventions—the major treaties on the law of war. . . .

The Government cites three sources that it says show otherwise. First, it points out that the Nazi saboteurs in *Quirin* were charged with conspiracy. Second, it observes that Winthrop at one point in his treatise identifies conspiracy as an offense "prosecuted by military commissions." Finally, it notes that another military historian lists conspiracy "'to violate the laws of war by destroying life or property in aid of the enemy'" as an offense that was tried as a violation of the law of war during the Civil War. On close analysis, however, these sources at best lend little support to the Government's position and at worst undermine it. By any measure, they fail to satisfy the high standard of clarity required to justify the use of a military commission. . . .

Finally, international sources confirm that the crime charged here is not a recognized violation of the law of war. As observed above, none of the major treaties governing the law of war identifies conspiracy as a violation thereof. And the only "conspiracy" crimes that have been recognized by international war crimes tribunals (whose jurisdiction often extends beyond war crimes proper to crimes against humanity and crimes against the peace) are conspiracy to commit genocide and common plan to wage aggressive war, which is a crime against the peace and requires for its commission actual participation in a "concrete plan to wage war.". . .

In sum, the sources that the Government and Justice THOMAS rely upon to show that conspiracy to violate the law of war is itself a violation of the law of war in fact demonstrate quite the opposite. Far from making the requisite substantial showing, the Government has failed even to offer a "merely colorable" case for inclusion of conspiracy among those offenses cognizable by law-of-war military commission. Because the charge does not support the commission's jurisdiction, the commission lacks authority to try Hamdan. . . .

■ VI

Whether or not the Government has charged Hamdan with an offense against the law of war cognizable by military commission, the commission lacks power to proceed. The UCMJ conditions the President's use of military commissions on compliance not only with the American common law of war, but also with the rest of the UCMJ itself, insofar as applicable, and with the "rules and precepts of the law of nations," the four Geneva Conventions signed in 1949. The procedures that the Government has decreed will govern Hamdan's trial by commission violate these laws.

A

The commission's procedures are set forth in Commission Order No. 1, which was amended most recently on August 31, 2005—after Hamdan's trial had already begun. Every commission established pursuant to Commission Order No. 1 must have a presiding officer and at least three other members, all of whom must be commissioned officers. The presiding officer's job is to rule on questions of law and other evidentiary and interlocutory issues; the other members make findings and, if applicable, sentencing decisions. The accused is entitled to appointed military counsel and may hire civilian counsel at his own expense so long as such counsel is a U.S. citizen with security clearance "at the level SECRET or higher."

The accused also is entitled to a copy of the charge(s) against him, both in English and his own language (if different), to a presumption of innocence, and to certain other rights typically afforded criminal defendants in civilian courts and courts-martial. These rights are subject, however, to one glaring condition: The accused and his civilian counsel may be excluded from, and precluded from ever learning what evidence was presented during, any part of the proceeding that either the Appointing Authority or the presiding officer decides to "close."

Once all the evidence is in, the commission members (not including the presiding officer) must vote on the accused's guilt. A two-thirds vote will suffice for both a verdict of guilty and for imposition of any sentence not including death (the imposition of which requires a unanimous vote). Any appeal is taken to a three-member review panel composed of military officers and designated by the Secretary of Defense, only one member of which need have experience as a judge. The review panel is directed to "disregard any variance from procedures specified in this Order or elsewhere that would not materially have affected the outcome of the trial before the Commission." Once the panel makes its recommendation to the Secretary of Defense, the Secretary can either remand for further proceedings or forward the record to the President with his recommendation as to final disposition. The President then, unless he has delegated the task to the Secretary, makes the "final decision." He may change the commission's findings or sentence only in a manner favorable to the accused.

B

Hamdan raises both general and particular objections to the procedures set forth in Commission Order No. 1. His general objection is that the procedures' admitted deviation from those governing courts-martial itself renders the commission illegal. Chief among his particular objections are that he may, under the Commission Order, be convicted based on evidence he has not seen or heard, and that any evidence admitted against him need not comply with the admissibility or relevance rules typically applicable in criminal trials and court-martial proceedings. . . .

C

In part because the difference between military commissions and courts-martial originally was a difference of jurisdiction alone, and in part to protect against abuse and ensure evenhandedness under the pressures of war, the procedures governing trials by military commission historically have been the same as those governing courts-martial.

There is a glaring historical exception to this general rule. The procedures and evidentiary rules used to try General Yamashita near the end of World War II deviated in significant respects from those then governing courts-martial. The force of that precedent, however, has been seriously undermined by post-World War II developments.

Yamashita, from late 1944 until September 1945, was Commanding General of the Fourteenth Army Group of the Imperial Japanese Army, which had exercised control over the Philippine Islands. On September 3, 1945, after American forces regained control of the Philippines, Yamashita surrendered. Three weeks later, he was charged with violations of the law of war. A few weeks after that, he was arraigned before a military commission convened in the Philippines. He pleaded not guilty, and his trial lasted for two months. On December 7, 1945, Yamashita was convicted and sentenced to hang. This Court upheld the denial of his petition for a writ of *habeas corpus*. . . .

At least partially in response to subsequent criticism of General Yamashita's trial, the UCMJ's codification of the Articles of War after World War II expanded the category of persons subject thereto to include defendants in Yamashita's (and Hamdan's) position, and the Third Geneva Convention of 1949 extended prisoner-of-war protections to individuals tried for crimes committed before their capture.

Article 36 places two restrictions on the President's power to promulgate rules of procedure for courts-martial and military commissions alike. First, no procedural rule he adopts may be "contrary to or inconsistent with" the UCMJ—however practical it may seem. Second, the rules adopted must be "uniform insofar as practicable." That is, the rules applied to military commissions must be the same as those applied to courts-martial unless such uniformity proves impracticable.

Hamdan argues that Commission Order No. 1 violates both of these restrictions; he maintains that the procedures described in the Commission Order are inconsistent with the UCMJ and that the Government has offered no explanation for their deviation from the procedures governing courts-martial, which are set forth in the Manual for Courts-Martial. Among the inconsistencies Hamdan identifies is that between Section 6 of the Commission Order, which permits exclusion of the accused from proceedings and denial of his access to evidence in certain circumstances, and the UCMJ's requirement that "[a]ll ... proceedings" other than votes and deliberations by courts-martial "shall be made a part of the record and shall be in the presence of the accused." Hamdan also observes that the Commission Order dispenses with virtually all evidentiary rules applicable in courts-martial....

Without reaching the question whether any provision of Commission Order No. 1 is strictly "contrary to or inconsistent with" other provisions of the UCMJ, we conclude that the "practicability" determination the President has made is insufficient to justify variances from the procedures governing courts-martial. Subsection (b) of Article 36 was added after World War II, and requires a different showing of impracticability from the one required by subsection (a). Subsection (a) requires that the rules the President promulgates for courts-martial, provost courts, and military commissions alike conform to those that govern procedures in Article III courts, "so far as he considers practicable." Subsection (b), by contrast, demands that the rules applied in courts-martial, provost courts, and military commissions—whether or not they conform with the Federal Rules of Evidence—be "uniform insofar as practicable." Under the latter provision, then, the rules set forth in the Manual for Courts-Martial must apply to military commissions unless impracticable.

The President here has determined, pursuant to subsection (a), that it is impracticable to apply the rules and principles of law that govern "the trial of criminal cases in the United States district courts" to Hamdan's commission. We assume that complete deference is owed that determination. The President has not, however, made a similar official determination that it is impracticable to apply the rules for courts-martial. And even if subsection (b)'s requirements may be satisfied without such an official determination, the requirements of that subsection are not satisfied here.

Nothing in the record before us demonstrates that it would be impracticable to apply court-martial rules in this case....

D

The procedures adopted to try Hamdan also violate the Geneva Conventions. The Court of Appeals dismissed Hamdan's Geneva Convention challenge on three independent grounds: (1) the Geneva Conventions are not judicially enforceable; (2) Hamdan in any event is not entitled to their protections; and (3) even if he is entitled to their protections, *Councilman* abstention is appropriate. Judge Williams, concurring, rejected the second ground but agreed with the majority respecting the first and the last. As we explained in Part III, the abstention rule applied in *Councilman* is not applicable here. And for the reasons that follow, we hold that neither of the other grounds the Court of Appeals gave for its decision is persuasive....

iii

Common Article 3, then, is applicable here and, as indicated above, requires that Hamdan be tried by a "regularly constituted court affording all the judicial guarantees which are recognized as indispensable by civilized peoples." While the term "regularly constituted court" is not specifically defined in either Common Article 3 or its accompanying commentary, other sources disclose its core meaning. The commentary accompanying a provision of the Fourth Geneva Convention, for example, defines "'regularly constituted'" tribunals to include "ordinary military courts" and "definitely exclud[e] all special tribunals."...

iv

Inextricably intertwined with the question of regular constitution is the evaluation of the procedures governing the tribunal and whether they afford "all the judicial guarantees which are recognized as indispensable by civilized peoples." Like the phrase "regularly constituted court," this phrase is not defined in the text of the Geneva Conventions. But it must be understood to incorporate at least the barest of those trial protections that have been recognized by customary international law. Many of these are described in Article 75 of Protocol I to the Geneva Conventions of 1949, adopted in 1977 (Protocol I). Although the United States declined to ratify Protocol I, its objections were not to Article 75 thereof. Indeed, it appears that the Government "regard[s] the provisions of Article 75 as an articulation of safeguards to which all persons in the hands of an enemy are entitled." Among the rights set forth in Article 75 is the "right to be tried in [one's] presence."

We agree with Justice KENNEDY that the procedures adopted to try Hamdan deviate from those governing courts-martial in ways not justified by any "evident practical need," and for that reason, at least, fail to afford the requisite guarantees. . . .

v

Common Article 3 obviously tolerates a great degree of flexibility in trying individuals captured during armed conflict; its requirements are general ones, crafted to accommodate a wide variety of legal systems. But requirements they are nonetheless. The commission that the President has convened to try Hamdan does not meet those requirements. . . .

- **VII**

[I]n undertaking to try Hamdan and subject him to criminal punishment, the Executive is bound to comply with the Rule of Law that prevails in this jurisdiction.

The judgment of the Court of Appeals is reversed, and the case is remanded for further proceedings.

☐ *Justice KENNEDY, with whom Justice SOUTER, Justice GINSBURG, and Justice BREYER join as to Parts I and II, concurring in part.*

Military Commission Order No. 1, which governs the military commission established to try petitioner Salim Hamdan for war crimes, exceeds limits that certain statutes, duly enacted by Congress, have placed on the President's authority to convene military courts. This is not a case, then, where the Executive can assert some unilateral authority to fill a void left by congressional inaction. It is a case where Congress, in the proper exercise of its powers as an independent branch of government, and as part of a long tradition of legislative involvement in matters of military justice, has considered the subject of military tribunals and set limits on the President's authority. Where a statute provides the conditions for the exercise of governmental power, its requirements are the result of a deliberative and reflective process engaging both of the political branches. Respect for laws derived from the customary operation of the Executive and Legislative Branches gives some assurance of stability in time of crisis. The Constitution is best preserved by reliance on standards tested over time and insulated from the pressures of the moment.

These principles seem vindicated here, for a case that may be of extraordinary importance is resolved by ordinary rules. The rules of most relevance here are those pertaining to the authority of Congress and the interpretation of its enactments. . . .

If Congress, after due consideration, deems it appropriate to change the controlling statutes, in conformance with the Constitution and other laws, it has the power and prerogative to do so. . . .

☐ *Justice BREYER, with whom Justice KENNEDY, Justice SOUTER, and Justice GINSBURG join, concurring.*

The dissenters say that today's decision would "sorely hamper the President's ability to confront and defeat a new and deadly enemy." They suggest that it undermines our Nation's ability to "preven[t] future attacks" of the grievous sort that we have already suffered. That claim leads me to state briefly what I believe the majority sets forth both explicitly and implicitly at greater length. The Court's conclusion ultimately rests upon a single ground: Congress has not issued the Executive a "blank check." Cf. *Hamdi v. Rumsfeld*, 542 U.S. 507 (2004). Indeed, Congress has denied the President the legislative authority to create military commissions of the kind at issue here. Nothing prevents the President from returning to Congress to seek the authority he believes necessary.

Where, as here, no emergency prevents consultation with Congress, judicial insistence upon that consultation does not weaken our Nation's ability to deal with danger. To the contrary, that insistence strengthens the Nation's ability to determine—through democratic means—how best to do so. The Constitution places its faith in those democratic means. Our Court today simply does the same.

☐ *Justice SCALIA, with whom Justice THOMAS and Justice ALITO join, dissenting.*

On December 30, 2005, Congress enacted the Detainee Treatment Act (DTA). It unambiguously provides that, as of that date, "no court, justice, or judge" shall have jurisdiction to consider the *habeas* application of a Guantanamo Bay detainee. Notwithstanding this plain directive, the Court today concludes that, on what it calls the statute's most natural reading, every "court, justice, or judge" before whom such a habeas application was pending on December 30 has jurisdiction to hear, consider, and render judgment on it. This conclusion is patently erroneous. And even if it were not, the jurisdiction supposedly retained should, in an exercise of sound equitable discretion, not be exercised. . . .

☐ *Justice THOMAS, with whom Justice SCALIA joins, and with whom Justice ALITO joins in all but Parts I, II–C–1, and III–B–2, dissenting.*

■ I

Our review of petitioner's claims arises in the context of the President's wartime exercise of his commander-in-chief authority in conjunction with the complete support of Congress. Accordingly, it is important to take measure of the respective roles the Constitution assigns to the three branches of our Government in the conduct of war.

As I explained in *Hamdi v. Rumsfeld*, 542 U.S. 507 (2004), the structural advantages attendant to the Executive Branch—namely, the decisiveness, "'activity, secrecy, and dispatch'" that flow from the Executive's "'unity,'"— led the Founders to conclude that the "President ha[s] primary responsibility— along with the necessary power—to protect the national security and to conduct the Nation's foreign relations." Consistent with this conclusion, the Constitution vests in the President "[t]he executive Power," Art. II, Section 1, provides that he "shall be Commander in Chief" of the Armed Forces, Section 2, and places in him the power to recognize foreign governments, Section 3. This Court has observed that these provisions confer upon the President broad constitutional authority to protect the Nation's security in the manner he deems fit. . . .

When "the President acts pursuant to an express or implied authorization from Congress," his actions are "'supported by the strongest of presumptions and the widest latitude of judicial interpretation, and the burden of persuasion rest[s] heavily upon any who might attack it.'" Accordingly, in the very context that we address today, this Court has concluded that "the detention and trial of petitioners—ordered by the President in the declared exercise of his powers as Commander in Chief of the Army in time of war and of grave public danger—are not to be set aside by the courts without the clear conviction that they are in conflict with the Constitution or laws of Congress constitutionally enacted." *Ex parte Quirin*, 317 U.S. 1 (1942).

Under this framework, the President's decision to try Hamdan before a military commission for his involvement with al Qaeda is entitled to a heavy measure of deference. In the present conflict, Congress has authorized the President "to use all necessary and appropriate force against those nations, organizations, or persons he determines planned, authorized, committed, or aided the terrorist attacks that occurred on September 11, 2001 in order to prevent any future acts of international terrorism against the United States by such nations, organizations or persons." Authorization for Use of Military Force (AUMF). As a plurality of the Court observed in *Hamdi*, the "capture, detention, and trial of unlawful combatants, by 'universal agreement and practice,' are 'important incident[s] of war,'" and are therefore "an exercise of the 'necessary and appropriate force' Congress has authorized the President to use." . . .

Although the Court concedes the legitimacy of the President's use of military commissions in certain circumstances, it suggests that the AUMF has no bearing on the scope of the President's power to utilize military commissions in the present conflict. Nothing in the language of Article 21, however, suggests that it outlines the entire reach of congressional authorization of military commissions in all conflicts—quite the contrary, the language of Article 21 presupposes the existence of military commissions under an independent basis of authorization. [C]ongressional authorization for military commissions pertaining to the instant conflict derives not only from Article 21 of the UCMJ, but also from the more recent, and broader, authorization contained in the AUMF. . . .

■ II

The plurality accurately describes some aspects of the history of military commissions and the prerequisites for their use. Thus, I do not dispute that military commissions have historically been "used in three [different] situations," and that the only situation relevant to the instant case is the use of military commissions "'to seize and subject to disciplinary measures those enemies who have violated the law of war.'" Similarly, I agree with the plurality that Winthrop's treatise sets forth the four relevant considerations for determining the scope of a military commission's jurisdiction, considerations relating to the (1) time and (2) place of the offense, (3) the status of the offender, and (4) the nature of the offense charged. The Executive has easily satisfied these considerations here. The plurality's contrary conclusion rests upon an incomplete accounting and an unfaithful application of those considerations. . . .

C

In one key respect, the plurality departs from the proper framework for evaluating the adequacy of the charge against Hamdan under the laws of war. The plurality holds that where, as here, "neither the elements of the offense nor the range of permissible punishments is defined by statute or treaty, the precedent [establishing whether an offense is triable by military commission] must be plain and unambiguous." This is a pure contrivance, and a bad one at that. It is contrary to the presumption we acknowledged in *Quirin*, namely, that the actions of military commissions are "not to be set aside by the courts without the clear conviction that they are" unlawful. . . .

The plurality's newly minted clear-statement rule is also fundamentally inconsistent with the nature of the common law which, by definition, evolves and develops over time and does not, in all cases, "say what may be done." Similarly, it is inconsistent with the nature of warfare, which also evolves and changes over time, and for which a flexible, evolutionary common-law system is uniquely appropriate. . . . Ultimately, the plurality's determination that Hamdan has not been charged with an offense triable before a military commission rests not upon any historical example or authority, but upon the plurality's raw judgment of the "inability on the Executive's part here to satisfy the most basic precondition for establishment of military commissions: military necessity." This judgment starkly confirms that the plurality has appointed itself the ultimate arbiter of what is quintessentially a policy and military judgment, namely, the appropriate military measures to take against those who "aided the terrorist attacks that occurred on September 11, 2001." AUMF. The plurality's suggestion that Hamdan's commission is illegitimate because it is not dispensing swift justice on the battlefield is unsupportable. Even a cursory review of the authorities confirms that law-of-war military commissions have wide-ranging jurisdiction to try offenses against the law of war in exigent and nonexigent circumstances alike. Traditionally, retributive justice for heinous war crimes is as much a "military necessity" as the "demands" of "military efficiency" touted by the plurality, and swift military retribution is precisely what Congress authorized the President to impose on the September 11 attackers in the AUMF.

Today a plurality of this Court would hold that conspiracy to massacre innocent civilians does not violate the laws of war. This determination is unsustainable. The judgment of the political branches that Hamdan, and others like him, must be held accountable before military commissions for their involvement with and membership in an unlawful organization dedicated to inflicting massive civilian casualties is supported by virtually every relevant authority, including all of the authorities invoked by the plurality today. It is also supported by the nature of the present conflict. We are not engaged in a traditional battle with a nation-state, but with a worldwide, hydra-headed enemy, who lurks in the shadows conspiring to reproduce the atrocities of September 11, 2001, and who has boasted of sending suicide bombers into civilian gatherings, has proudly distributed videotapes of beheadings of civilian workers, and has tortured and dismembered captured American soldiers. . . .

■ III

The Court holds that even if "the Government has charged Hamdan with an offense against the law of war cognizable by military commission, the commission lacks power to proceed" because of its failure to comply with the terms of the UCMJ and the four Geneva Conventions signed in 1949. This position is untenable.

As with the jurisdiction of military commissions, the procedure of such commissions "has [not] been prescribed by statute," but "has been adapted in each instance to the need that called it forth." Indeed, this Court has concluded that "[i]n the absence of attempts by Congress to limit the President's power, it appears that, as Commander in Chief of the Army and Navy of the United States, he may, in time of war, establish and prescribe the jurisdiction and procedure of military commissions." This conclusion is consistent with this Court's understanding that military commissions are "our common-law war courts." As such, "[s]hould the conduct of those who compose martial-law tribunals become [a] matter of judicial determination subsequently before the civil courts, those courts will give great weight to the opinions of the officers as to what the customs of war in any case justify and render necessary." . . .

The Court contends that Hamdan's military commission is also unlawful because it violates Common Article 3 of the Geneva Conventions. Furthermore, Hamdan contends that his commission is unlawful because it violates various provisions of the Third Geneva Convention. These contentions are untenable.

As an initial matter, and as the Court of Appeals concluded, both of Hamdan's Geneva Convention claims are foreclosed by *Johnson v. Eisentrager*, 339 U.S. 763 (1950). . . .

In addition to being foreclosed by *Eisentrager*, Hamdan's claim under Common Article 3 of the Geneva Conventions is meritless. Common Article 3 applies to "armed conflict not of an international character occurring in the territory of one of the High Contracting Parties." "Pursuant to [his] authority as Commander in Chief and Chief Executive of the United States," the President has "accept[ed] the legal conclusion of the Department of Justice that common Article 3 of Geneva does not apply to al Qaeda detainees, because, among other reasons, the relevant conflicts are international in scope and common Article 3 applies only to 'armed conflict not of an international character.'" . . .

The President's interpretation of Common Article 3 is reasonable and should be sustained. The conflict with al Qaeda is international in character in the sense that it is occurring in various nations around the globe. Thus, it is also "occurring in the territory of" more than "one of the High Contracting Parties." . . . For these reasons, I would affirm the judgment of the Court of Appeals.

☐ *Justice ALITO, with whom Justices SCALIA and THOMAS join in Parts I–III, dissenting.*

For the reasons set out in Justice Scalia's dissent, which I join, I would hold that we lack jurisdiction. I add the following comments to provide a further explanation of my reasons for disagreeing with the holding of the Court.

The holding of the Court, as I understand it, rests on the following reasoning. A military commission is lawful only if it is authorized by 10 U.S.C. Section 821; this provision permits the use of a commission to try "offenders or offenses" that "by statute or by the law of war may be tried by" such a commission; because no statute provides that an offender such as petitioner or an offense such as the one with which he is charged may be tried by a military commission, he may be tried by military commission only if the trial is authorized by "the law of war"; the Geneva Conventions are part of the law of war; and Common Article 3 of the Conventions prohibits petitioner's trial because the commission before which he would be tried is not "a regularly constituted court." I disagree with this holding because petitioner's commission is "a regularly constituted court." . . .

Common Article 3 . . . imposes three requirements. Sentences may be imposed only by (1) a "court" (2) that is "regularly constituted" and (3) that affords "all the judicial guarantees which are recognized as indispensable by civilized peoples."

I see no need here to comment extensively on the meaning of the first and third requirements. The first requirement is largely self-explanatory, and, with respect to the third, I note only that on its face it imposes a uniform international standard that does not vary from signatory to signatory.

The second element ("regularly constituted") is the one on which the Court relies, and I interpret this element to require that the court be appointed or established in accordance with the appointing country's domestic law. I agree with the Court that, as used in Common Article 3, the term "regularly" is synonymous with "properly." The term "constitute" means "appoint," "set up," or "establish," and therefore "regularly constituted" means properly appointed, set up, or established. Our cases repeatedly use the phrases "regularly constituted" and "properly constituted" in this sense.

In order to determine whether a court has been properly appointed, set up, or established, it is necessary to refer to a body of law that governs such matters. I interpret Common Article 3 as looking to the domestic law of the appointing country because I am not aware of any international law standard regarding the way in which such a court must be appointed, set up, or established, and because different countries with different government structures handle this matter differently. Accordingly, "a regularly constituted court" is a court that has been appointed, set up, or established in accordance with the domestic law of the appointing country.

In contrast to this interpretation, the opinions supporting the judgment today hold that the military commission before which petitioner would be tried is not "a regularly constituted court" (a) because "no evident practical need explains" why its "structure and composition . . . deviate from conventional court-martial standards"; and (b) because the procedures specified for use in the proceeding before the military commission impermissibly differ from those provided under the Uniform Code of Military Justice (UCMJ) for use by courts-martial. I do not believe that either of these grounds is sound.

I see no basis for the Court's holding that a military commission cannot be regarded as "a regularly constituted court" unless it is similar in structure and composition to a regular military court or unless there is an "evident practical need" for the divergence. There is no reason why a court that differs in structure or composition from an ordinary military court must be viewed as having been improperly constituted. Tribunals that vary significantly in structure, composition, and procedures may all be "regularly" or "properly" constituted. Consider, for example, a municipal court, a state trial court of general jurisdiction, an Article I federal trial court, a federal district court, and an international court, such as the International Criminal Tribunal for the Former Yugoslavia. Although these courts are "differently constituted" and differ substantially in many other respects, they are all "regularly constituted." . . .

I also disagree with the Court's conclusion that petitioner's military commission is "illegal," because its procedures allegedly do not . . . impose at least a limited uniformity requirement amongst the tribunals contemplated by the UCMJ. . . .

Returning to the three elements of Common Article 3—(1) a court, (2) that is appointed, set up, and established in compliance with domestic law, and (3) that respects universally recognized fundamental rights—I conclude that all of these elements are satisfied in this case.

First, the commissions qualify as courts.

Second, the commissions were appointed, set up, and established pursuant to an order of the President, just like the commission in *Ex parte Quirin*, 317 U. S. 1 (1942).

Finally, the commission procedures, taken as a whole, and including the availability of review by a United States Court of Appeals and by this Court, do not provide a basis for deeming the commissions to be illegitimate. The Court questions the following two procedural rules: the rule allowing the Secretary of Defense to change the governing rules "'from time to time'" (which does not rule out mid-trial changes); and the rule that permits the admission of any evidence that would have "'probative value to a reasonable person'." Neither of these two rules undermines the legitimacy of the commissions.

Surely the entire commission structure cannot be stricken merely because it is possible that the governing rules might be changed during the course of one or more proceedings. If a change is made and applied during the course of an ongoing proceeding and if the accused is found guilty, the validity of that procedure can be considered in the review proceeding for that case. After all, not every midtrial change will be prejudicial. A midtrial change might amend the governing rules in a way that is inconsequential or actually favorable to the accused.

As for the standard for the admission of evidence at commission proceedings, the Court does not suggest that this rule violates the international standard incorporated into Common Article 3 . . . .

It seems clear that the commissions at issue here meet this standard. Whatever else may be said about the system that was created by Military Commission Order No. 1 and augmented by the Detainee Treatment Act, this system—which features formal trial procedures, multiple levels of administrative review, and the opportunity for review by a United States Court of Appeals and by this Court—does not dispense "summary justice." For these reasons, I respectfully dissent.

■ IN COMPARATIVE PERSPECTIVE

The Supreme Court of Israel's Ruling Against the Use of Torture

The disclosure of the abuse of prisoners by U.S. soldiers at the Abu Ghraib prison in Iraq, and the further revelations in 2006 that torture continues in some Iraqi jails, fueled the controversy over the application of international human rights standards to interrogations for military intelligence purposes during wartime. Torture and other cruel, inhuman, or degrading treatment and punishment violates the Third Geneva Convention of 1949, the Convention Against Torture and Other Cruel, Inhuman or Degrading Treatment or Punishment, and the International Covenant on Civil and Political Rights; all of which the U.S. joined. In addition, a 1994 federal law makes the use of torture by U.S. officials abroad a criminal offense.

The Supreme Court of Israel, in the 1999 *Judgment Concerning the Interrogation Methods Implied [sic] by the General Security Services*, ruled against the use of certain techniques involving inhuman treatment and torture used when interrogating Palestinians suspected of terrorism.

> President [Chief Justice Aharon] Barak:
>
> The General Security Service (hereinafter, the "GSS") investigates individuals suspected of committing crimes against Israel's security.... The interrogations are conducted on the basis of directives regulating interrogation methods. These directives equally authorize investigators to apply physical means against those undergoing interrogation (for instance, shaking the suspect and the "*Shabach*" position [the cuffing of the suspect, seating him on a low chair, covering his head with an opaque sack (head covering) and playing powerfully loud music in the area]. The basis for permitting such methods is that they are deemed immediately necessary for saving human lives....
>
> The State of Israel has been engaged in an unceasing struggle for both its very existence and security, from the day of its founding. Terrorist organizations have established as their goal Israel's annihilation. Terrorist acts and the general disruption of order are their means of choice. In employing such methods, these groups do not distinguish between civilian and military targets. They carry out terrorist attacks in which scores are murdered in public areas, public transportation, city squares and centers, theaters and coffee shops....
>
> In order to fulfill this function, the GSS also investigates those suspected of hostile terrorist activities. The purpose of these interrogations is, among others, to gather information regarding terrorists

and their organizing methods for the purpose of thwarting and preventing them from carrying out these terrorist attacks. . . .

We asked the applicants' attorneys whether the "ticking time bomb" rationale was not sufficiently persuasive to justify the use of physical means, for instance, when a bomb is known to have been placed in a public area and will undoubtedly explode causing immeasurable human tragedy if its location is not revealed at once. This question elicited a variety of responses from the various applicants before the Court. There are those convinced that physical means are not to be used under any circumstances; the prohibition on such methods to their mind is absolute, whatever the consequences may be. On the other hand, there are others who argue that even if it is perhaps acceptable to employ physical means in most exceptional "ticking time bomb" circumstances, these methods are in practice used even in absence of the "ticking time bomb" conditions. The very fact that, in most cases, the use of such means is illegal provides sufficient justification for banning their use altogether, even if doing so would inevitably absorb those rare cases in which physical coercion may have been justified. . . .

[A] reasonable investigation is necessarily one free of torture, free of cruel, inhuman treatment of the subject and free of any degrading handling whatsoever. There is a prohibition on the use of "brutal or inhuman means" in the course of an investigation. Human dignity also includes the dignity of the suspect being interrogated. This conclusion is in perfect accord with (various) International Law treaties-to which Israel is a signatory-which prohibit the use of torture, "cruel, inhuman treatment" and "degrading treatment." These prohibitions are "absolute." . . .

We shall now turn from the general to the particular. Plainly put, shaking is a prohibited investigation method. It harms the suspect's body. It violates his dignity. It is a violent method which does not form part of a legal investigation. It surpasses that which is necessary. . . .

It was argued before the Court that one of the investigation methods employed consists of the suspect crouching on the tips of his toes for five minute intervals. The State did not deny this practice. This is a prohibited investigation method. It does not serve any purpose inherent to an investigation. It is degrading and infringes upon an individual's human dignity.

The "*Shabach*" method is composed of a number of cumulative components: the cuffing of the suspect, seating him on a low chair, covering his head with an opaque sack (head covering) and playing powerfully loud music in the area. [W]e accept that the suspect's cuffing, for the purpose of preserving the investigators' safety, is an action included in the general power to investigate. Provided the suspect is cuffed for this purpose, it is within the investigator's authority to cuff him. . . . Notwithstanding, the cuffing associated with the "*Shabach*" position is unlike routine cuffing. The suspect is cuffed with his hands tied behind his back. One hand is placed inside the gap between the chair's seat and back support, while the other is tied behind him, against the chair's back support. This is a distorted and unnatural position. The investigators' safety does not require it. Therefore, there is no relevant justification for handcuffing the suspect's hands with particularly small handcuffs, if this is in fact the practice. The use of these methods is prohibited. . . .

This is the law with respect to the method involving seating the suspect in question in the "*Shabach*" position. We accept that seating a man is inherent to the investigation. This is not the case when the chair upon which he is seated is a very low one, tilted forward facing the ground, and when he is sitting in this position for long hours. This sort of seating is not encompassed by the general power to interrogate. . . . [Such] methods do not fall within the sphere of a "fair" interrogation. They are not reasonable. They impinge upon the suspect's dignity, his bodily integrity and his basic rights in an excessive manner (or beyond what is necessary). . . .

We accept that there are interrogation related considerations concerned with preventing contact between the suspect under interrogation and other suspects and his investigators, which require means capable of preventing the said contact. The need to prevent contact may, for instance, flow from the need to safeguard the investigators' security, or that of the suspects and witnesses. It can also be part of the "mind game" which pins the information possessed by the suspect, against that found in the hands of his investigators. For this purpose, the power to interrogate-in principle and according to the circumstances of each particular case-includes preventing eye contact with a given person or place. In the case at bar, this was the explanation provided by the State for covering the suspect's head with an opaque sack, while he is seated in the "*Shabach*" position. From what was stated in the declarations before us, the suspect's head is covered with an opaque sack throughout his "wait" in the "*Shabach*" position. It was argued that the sack (head covering) is entirely opaque, causing the suspect to suffocate. The edges of the sack are long, reaching the suspect's shoulders.

All these methods are not inherent to an interrogation. They do not confirm the State's position, arguing that they are meant to prevent eye contact between the suspect being interrogated and other suspects. Indeed, even if such contact should be prevented, what is the purpose of causing the suspect to suffocate? Employing this method is not connected to the purpose of preventing the said contact and is consequently forbidden. . . .

A similar-though not identical-combination of interrogation methods were discussed in the case of *Ireland v. United Kingdom* (1978) 2 EHRR 25. In that case, the Court probed five interrogation methods used by England for the purpose of investigating detainees suspected of terrorist activities in Northern Ireland. The methods were as follows: protracted standing against the wall on the tip of one's toes; covering of the suspect's head throughout the detention (except during the actual interrogation); exposing the suspect to powerfully loud noise for a prolonged period and deprivation of sleep, food and drink. The Court held that these methods did not constitute "torture." However, since they treated the suspect in an "inhuman and degrading" manner, they were nonetheless prohibited. . . .

This decision opens with a description of the difficult reality in which Israel finds herself security wise. We shall conclude this judgment by re-addressing that harsh reality. We are aware that this decision does not ease dealing with that reality. This is the destiny of democracy, as not all means are acceptable to it, and not all practices employed by its enemies are open before it. Although a democracy must often fight with one hand tied behind its back, it nonetheless has the upper hand. Preserving the Rule of Law and recognition of an individual's liberty constitutes an important component in its understanding of security. At the end of the day, they strengthen its spirit and its strength and allow it to overcome its difficulties. This having been said, there are those who argue that Israel's security problems are too numerous, thereby requiring the authorization to use physical means. If it will nonetheless be decided that it is appropriate for Israel, in light of its security difficulties to sanction physical means in interrogations (and the scope of these means which deviate from the ordinary investigation rules), this is an issue that must be decided by the legislative branch which represents the people. We do not take any stand on this matter at this time. It is there that various considerations must be weighed. The pointed debate must occur there. It is there that the required legislation may be passed, provided, of course, that a law infringing upon a suspect's liberty "befitting the values of the State of Israel," is enacted for a proper purpose, and to an extent no greater than is required.(Article 8 to the Basic Law: Human Dignity and Liberty). . .

■ The Development of Law
The National Security Agency's Warrantless Electronic Surveillance

In 2005, a controversy erupted over the revelation that after the September 11, 2001, terrorist attacks President George W. Bush issued a secret executive order authorizing the National Security Agency (NSA) to conduct warrantless electronic surveillance of "communications where one . . . party to the communication is outside of the United States" and there is "a reasonable basis to conclude that one party" is a member of or supporting al Qaeda or other terrorists. The surveillance involves monitoring emails, through Google-like searches, and tracking cell phone calls and other Internet and satellite communications.

Foreign intelligence surveillance was supposed to be governed by the Foreign Intelligence Surveillance Act (FISA) of 1978 (see The Development of Law: The USA Patriot Act of 2001 box in Vol. 1, Ch.3, and Vol. 2, Ch. 7). Under that law, the government must seek a warrant from a special FISA court, though in emergencies warrantless searches may be conducted for three days prior to requesting a warrant. The law also makes it a crime for government officials to conduct "electronic surveillance under color of law except as authorized by statute." The USA Patriot Act amended the FISA to require a "significant purpose" for an investigation of foreign intelligence information; in 2006 the major provisions of the USA Patriot Act were extended and made permanent.

The Bush administration defended the NSA's warrantless surveillance on three grounds. First, the President has the inherent power and power as Commander in Chief to do so during times of war. Prior presidents made similar claims. President Abraham Lincoln ordered the warrantless wiretapping of telegraph wires during the Civil War. Likewise, during World Wars I and II Presidents Woodrow Wilson and Franklin D. Roosevelt ordered the interception of international communications. Similar claims to presidential power were made by subsequent administrations, including those of Presidents Jimmy Carter and Bill Clinton.

Second, the joint resolution for the Authorization for the Use of Military Force (AUMF) of 2001 provides for the use of "all necessary and appropriate" force to combat terrorists, and thus justifies the President's action. Third, the AUMF justifies not complying with the provisions of the FISA, since it superseded FISA. In addition, *Smith v. Maryland*, 442 U.S. 735 (1979), upheld the use of pen registers, which record the telephone numbers called from phones but not the conversations. Accordingly, by extension the NSA's collection of "meta-data"—the time and to and from of Internet and satellite communications—was permissible.

By contrast, some members of Congress and civil liberties groups countered that the President has no inherent power to authorize warrantless domestic security surveillance; that neither the AUMF nor the FISA permit such a program; and that *United States v. United States District Court*, 407 U.S. 297 (1972), the so-called "Keith case," held that domestic intelligence surveillance requires prior judicial approval of a warrant in order to satisfy the Fourth Amendment's guarantee against unreasonable searches and seizures, though the decision left open the matter of warrantless foreign surveillance. After months of negotiations, in 2006 Congress enacted legislation reasserting the authority of the FISA court, while permitting wiretapping without a warrant for up to 45 days but requiring the attorney general to certify and explain why such warrantless surveillance is necessary to a subcommittee of the Senate Intelligence Committee.

Subsequently, in 2006 it was also revealed that the NSA had in the aftermath of the 9/11 terrorist attacks been monitoring the phone numbers dialed by millions of U.S. citizens in order to search for telephone calling patterns and possible links to terrorists, as well as that the Central Intelligence Agency and the Department of Treasury had been mining the transactions of 7,800 financial institutions worldwide. A Belgian cooperative routes daily about $6 trillion international transactions. And its database is monitored to find customers' names, account numbers, and other information that establishes links to al Qaeda and other terrorist organization.

In response to criticisms and pending lawsuits filed by civil liberties groups challenging the constitutionality of the NSA's warrantless surveillance, President Bush agreed to legislation that would consolidate the cases and give jurisdiction to the FISA court. But he also exacted concessions permitting in emergency situations warrantless surveillance for up to a week (instead of the pervious 72 hours) before requesting a warrant.

For further reading, see U.S. Department of Justice, "Legal Authorities Supporting the Activities of the National Security Agency Described by the President" (Washington, D.C.: Department of Justice, January 19, 2006), and compare Congressional Research Service, "Memorandum: Presidential Authority to Conduct Warrantless Electronic Surveillance to Gather Foreign Intelligence Information" (Washington, D.C.: Congressional Research Service, January 5, 2006). See also Eric Lichtblau and James Risen, "Bank Data is Sifted by U.S. in Secret to Block Terror," *The New York Times* (June 23, 2006), A1.

■ IN COMPARATIVE PERSPECTIVE
The House of Lords Rules Against the Indefinite Detention of Terrorists

As a result of the continued conflicts in North Ireland, the United Kingdom enacted the Terrorism Act of 2000, which broadened the definition of terrorism, prohibited fundraising for terrorist organizations, and expanded law enforcement powers to stop, search, arrest, and detain suspected terrorists. But, after the international terrorist attacks on September 11, 2001, on the Twin Towers and the Pentagon, the Parliament enacted the Anti-Terrorism, Crime, and Security Act of 2001, which, among other things, derogated obligations under Article 5 of the European Convention on Human Rights that prohibit detention without trial.

The provisions of the Anti-Terrorism, Crime, and Security Act were subsequently challenged and the House of Lords, in an eight-to-one decision, in *A(FC) and others (FC) v. Secretary of State for the Home Department*, [2004] UKHL 56, held that indefinite detention of suspected terrorists without charge or trial violates Articles 5 and 14 of the European Convention on Human Rights, issuing a "declaration of incompatibility" (since English courts have no power to invalidate legislation), and referring the matter back to Parliament. Lord Bingham issued the lead opinion and found that the flaw in the detention policy was the way it discriminated against foreign nations. In his words:

> The appellants share certain common characteristics which are central to their appeals. All are foreign (non-UK) nationals. None has been subject of any criminal charge. In none of their cases is a criminal trial in prospect. All challenge the lawfulness of their detention. More specifically, they all contend that such detention was inconsistent with obligations binding on the United Kingdom under the European Convention on Human Rights....
>
> The appellants were treated differently from both suspected international terrorists who were not UK nationals but could be removed and also from suspected international terrorists who were UK nationals and could not be removed. There can be no doubt but that the difference in treatment was on grounds of nationality or immigration status (one of the proscribed grounds under Article 14).

Lord Walker, the lone dissenter, countered that:

> The appropriate intensity of scrutiny of decisions in this crucial area—involving both national security and individual rights—presents a dilemma.... The court should show a high degree of respect for the Secretary of State's appreciation, based on secret intelligence

sources, of the security risks; but at the same time the court should subject to a very close scrutiny the practical effect which derogating measures have on human rights, the importance of the rights affected, and the robustness of any safeguards intended to minimize the impact of the derogating measures on individual human rights.

In 2005, Parliament enacted a new anti-terrorism act that authorizes judges to impose a range of restrictions on terrorist suspects, short of imprisonment, including placing them under house arrest, imposing nighttime curfews, requiring electronic tagging, and barring their use of cell phones and computers. The law, however, remained controversial and in 2006 a high court judge held the house arrest provisions were unfair and incompatible with human rights law. A high court judge affirmed that decision and the controversy continues.

4

THE PRESIDENT AS CHIEF EXECUTIVE IN DOMESTIC AFFAIRS

■ THE DEVELOPMENT OF LAW
Presidential Signing Statements and Legislative Powers

President George W. Bush opposed an amendment to an appropriations bill, sponsored by Senator John McCain (R-Az) and supported overwhelmingly in the House of Representatives, prohibiting the "cruel, inhuman, or degrading" treatment of detainees in U.S. custody. Although Bush eventually signed the bill in 2006, he issued a presidential signing statement declaring that the provision, among others, was only "advisory." He thus renewed debate over the uses of presidential signing statements and the assertion of greater presidential power in domestic and foreign affairs.

Presidential signing statements, issued when a President signs a bill into law, have served four functions. First, they explain to the public the potential impact or significance of the legislation. Second, they may direct subordinate officials in the executive branch on how to interpret and implement the law. Third, they may inform Congress and the public that the President deems a particular provision unconstitutional. However, some Presidents and scholars have maintained that such bills should not be signed into law and instead returned to Congress, although four justices—Justices O'Connor, Scalia, Kennedy, and Souter—noted in a concurring opinion, in *Freytag v. C.I.R.*,

501 U.S. 868 (1991), observing that the President may "disregard [laws] when they are unconstitutional." Fourth, and most controversial, is the use of presidential signing statements to add an "executive history" to the legislative history on which courts may draw when reviewing the executive branch's implementation of the law.

Prior to the 1980s administration of Ronald Reagan, the use of presidential signing statements was infrequent and limited to the first three functions. Only some sixteen times did thirteen different Presidents issue them, ranging from Andrew Jackson to John Tyler, Abraham Lincoln, Andrew Johnson, Theodore Roosevelt, Woodrow Wilson, Franklin D. Roosevelt, Harry Truman, Dwight D. Eisenhower, Richard M. Nixon, Gerald Ford, and Jimmy Carter.

During the Reagan administration extensive use of presidential signing statements was made to establish an "executive history" of legislation for the use of the executive branch and the judiciary. Notably, as a young attorney then in the administration, Justice Samuel Alito, Jr. championed their use for establishing presidential intent in signing legislation and for maintaining "a unitary executive." While Presidents George H. W. Bush and Bill Clinton also issued such statements, George W. Bush has made extensive use of them, even though federal courts have yet to give them much weight.

For further reading, see Walter Dellinger, Memorandum for Bernard N. Nussbaum, counsel to the President, "The Legal Significance of Presidential Signing Statements" (November 3, 1993), available at www.usdoj.gov:/olc/signing.htm; Phillip Cooper, "George W. Bush, Edgar Allan Poe, and the Use and Abuse of Presidential Signing Statements," 35 *Presidential Studies Quarterly* 525–532 (2005).

6

CONGRESS: LEGISLATIVE, TAXING, AND SPENDING POWERS

C | From the New Deal Crisis to the Administrative State

In *Gonzales v. Raich* (excerpted below), the Court upheld congressional power and the federal prosecution of users of medicinal marijuana over a challenge that Congress exceeded its powers and the boundaries of federalism. Ten states have legalized the medicinal use of marijuana, but writing for the Court Justice Stevens upheld congressional power to criminalize such use. Chief Justice Rehnquist and Justices O'Connor and Thomas dissented.

However, in a related controversy during its 2005–2006 term the Court split six to three in holding that the Attorney General's directive barring physician-assisted suicide exceeded his authority under the Controlled Substances Act (CSA) of 1970, and in *Gonzales v. Oregon* (excerpted below) upheld Oregon's Death with Dignity Act, permitting doctors to prescribe certain lethal substances to assist in the painless death of competent but terminally-ill individuals.

In addition, the Court unanimously ruled, without Justice Alito participating, that a religious sect could not be barred under the CSA from importing *hoasca* (pronounced "wass-ca"), used in sacramental tea by a sect originating in the Amazon Rainforest, even though the CSA bans all use of the hallucinogen, under the Religious Freedom Restoration

Act (RFRA). In *City of Boerne v. Flores*, 521 U.S. 507 (1997) (excerpted in Vol. 1, Ch. 6, and Vol. 2, Ch. 6), the Court ruled that the RFRA's application to state laws exceeded Congress's power. But in *Gonzales v. O Centro Espirita Beneficente Uniao do Vegetal*, 126 S.Ct. 1211 (2006), the Court unanimously held that the RFRA permitted federal courts to make exceptions on a case-by-case basis from that generally applicable law for the importation of drugs to be used in a "sincere exercise of religion." Writing for the Court, Chief Justice Roberts noted that peyote, another hallucinogen, had been made an exception to the CSA for the use by Native Americans for 35 years, observing that: "If such use is permitted . . . for hundreds of thousands of Native Americans practicing their faith, it is difficult to see how those same findings alone can preclude any consideration of a similar exception for the 130 or so American members of the [O Centro Espirita Beneficente Uniao] who want to practice theirs." In so holding, Chief Justice Roberts rejected the Bush administration's arguments that it had compelling governmental interests in forbidding the importation of *hoasca* based on (1) protecting the health of users, (2) preventing the diversion of the drug to recreational users, and (3) complying with the 1971 U.N. Convention on Psychotropic Substances.

Gonzales v. Raich
545 U.S. 1, 125 S.Ct. 2195 (2005)

Two seriously ill Californians, Angel McClary Raich and Diane Monson, use marijuana for medicinal purposes. Under California's Compassionate Use Act of 1996, they could legally do so; nine other states have similar laws. Raich received her marijuana free of charge from her caregivers, while Monson cultivated her own in the backyard. In 2002, deputies from the Butte County sheriff's department and federal Drug Enforcement Agency (DEA) agents arrived at Monson's home. The sheriff's deputies determined that Monson's cultivation and use of marijuana was legal under state law. But the DEA agents and the U.S. Attorney for the Eastern District of California contended that Monson was in violation of the federal Controlled Substances Act (CSA), which designates marijuana as a Schedule I "controlled substance" and makes it unlawful to possess, manufacture, or distribute such substances. After a three-hour standoff between the Butte County district attorney and the U.S. attorney, the DEA agents seized and destroyed Monson's cannabis plants. Subsequently, Raich and Monson filed a lawsuit and sought an injunction against the enforcement of the federal statute. A federal district court denied the motion but, on appeal before a three-judge panel, the U.S.

Court of Appeals for the Ninth Circuit reversed that decision, holding that, based on rulings in *United States v. Lopez*, 514 U.S. 549 (1995) (excerpted in Vol. 1, Ch. 6) and *United States v. Morrison*, 529 U.S. 598 (2000) (excerpted in Vol. 1, Ch. 6), the application of the CSA to Raich and Monson exceeded Congress's regulatory power under the Commerce Clause, and rejected the government's argument that the "aggregation principle" upheld in *Wickard v. Filburn*, 317 U.S. 111 (1942) (excerpted in Vol. 1, Ch. 6), applied, ruling instead that the principle was inapplicable to the activities of Raich and Monson. The Department of Justice appealed that decision and the Supreme Court granted review.

The appellate court's decision was reversed on a vote of six to three. Justice Stevens delivered the opinion of the Court and Justice Scalia filed a concurring opinion. Chief Justice Rehnquist and Justices O'Connor and Thomas dissented.

☐ *Justice STEVENS delivered the opinion of the Court.*

California is one of at least nine States that authorize the use of marijuana for medicinal purposes. The question presented in this case is whether the power vested in Congress by Article I, Section 8, of the Constitution "[t]o make all Laws which shall be necessary and proper for carrying into Execution" its authority to "regulate Commerce with foreign Nations, and among the several States" includes the power to prohibit the local cultivation and use of marijuana in compliance with California law. . . .

The obvious importance of the case prompted our grant of *certiorari*. The case is made difficult by respondents' strong arguments that they will suffer irreparable harm because, despite a congressional finding to the contrary, marijuana does have valid therapeutic purposes. The question before us, however, is not whether it is wise to enforce the statute in these circumstances; rather, it is whether Congress's power to regulate interstate markets for medicinal substances encompasses the portions of those markets that are supplied with drugs produced and consumed locally. Well-settled law controls our answer. The CSA is a valid exercise of federal power, even as applied to the troubling facts of this case. We accordingly vacate the judgment of the Court of Appeals.

Shortly after taking office in 1969, President Nixon declared a national "war on drugs." As the first campaign of that war, Congress set out to enact legislation that would consolidate various drug laws on the books into a comprehensive statute, provide meaningful regulation over legitimate sources of drugs to prevent diversion into illegal channels, and strengthen law enforcement tools against the traffic in illicit drugs. That effort culminated in the passage of the Comprehensive Drug Abuse Prevention and Control Act of 1970. . . .

In enacting the CSA, Congress classified marijuana as a Schedule I drug. This preliminary classification was based, in part, on the recommendation of the Assistant Secretary of HEW "that marihuana be retained within schedule I at least until the completion of certain studies now underway." Schedule I drugs are categorized as such because of their high potential for abuse, lack of any accepted medical use, and absence of any accepted safety for use in medically supervised treatment. . . .

Respondents in this case do not dispute that passage of the CSA, as part of the Comprehensive Drug Abuse Prevention and Control Act, was well within Congress's commerce power. Nor do they contend that any provision or section of the CSA amounts to an unconstitutional exercise of congressional authority. Rather, respondents' challenge is actually quite limited; they argue that the CSA's categorical prohibition of the manufacture and possession of marijuana as applied to the intrastate manufacture and possession of marijuana for medical purposes pursuant to California law exceeds Congress's authority under the Commerce Clause.

In assessing the validity of congressional regulation, none of our Commerce Clause cases can be viewed in isolation. As charted in considerable detail in *United States v. Lopez*, [514 U.S. 549 (1995)], our understanding of the reach of the Commerce Clause, as well as Congress's assertion of authority thereunder, has evolved over time. The Commerce Clause emerged as the Framers' response to the central problem giving rise to the Constitution itself: the absence of any federal commerce power under the Articles of Confederation. For the first century of our history, the primary use of the Clause was to preclude the kind of discriminatory state legislation that had once been permissible. Then, in response to rapid industrial development and an increasingly interdependent national economy, Congress "ushered in a new era of federal regulation under the commerce power," beginning with the enactment of the Interstate Commerce Act in 1887, and the Sherman Antitrust Act in 1890. Cases decided during that "new era," which now spans more than a century, have identified three general categories of regulation in which Congress is authorized to engage under its commerce power. First, Congress can regulate the channels of interstate commerce. *Perez v. United States*, 402 U.S. 146 (1971). Second, Congress has authority to regulate and protect the instrumentalities of interstate commerce, and persons or things in interstate commerce. Third, Congress has the power to regulate activities that substantially affect interstate commerce. *NLRB v. Jones & Laughlin Steel Corp.*, 301 U.S. 1 (1937). Only the third category is implicated in the case at hand.

Our case law firmly establishes Congress's power to regulate purely local activities that are part of an economic "class of activities" that have a substantial effect on interstate commerce. See, e.g., *Perez*; *Wickard v. Filburn*, 317 U.S. 111 (1942). As we stated in *Wickard*, "even if appellee's activity be local and though it may not be regarded as commerce, it may still, whatever its nature, be reached by Congress if it exerts a substantial economic effect on interstate commerce." We have never required Congress to legislate with scientific exactitude. When Congress decides that the "'total incidence'" of a practice poses a threat to a national market, it may regulate the entire class. In this vein, we have reiterated that when "'a general regulatory statute bears a substantial relation to commerce, the *de minimis* character of individual instances arising under that statute is of no consequence.'"

Our decision in *Wickard* is of particular relevance. In *Wickard*, we upheld the application of regulations promulgated under the Agricultural Adjustment Act of 1938, which were designed to control the volume of wheat moving in interstate and foreign commerce in order to avoid surpluses and consequent abnormally low prices. The regulations established an allotment of 11.1 acres for Filburn's 1941 wheat crop, but he sowed 23 acres, intending to use the excess by consuming it on his own farm. Filburn argued that even though we had sustained Congress's power to regulate the production of goods for commerce, that power did not authorize "federal regulation [of] production not intended in any part for commerce but wholly for consumption on the farm." Justice JACKSON's opinion for a unanimous Court rejected this submission. *Wickard* thus establishes that Congress can regulate purely intrastate activity that is not itself "commercial," in that it is not produced for sale, if it concludes that failure to regulate that class of activity would undercut the regulation of the interstate market in that commodity.

The similarities between this case and *Wickard* are striking. Like the farmer in *Wickard*, respondents are cultivating, for home consumption, a fungible commodity for which there is an established, albeit illegal, interstate market. Just as the Agricultural Adjustment Act was designed "to control the volume [of wheat] moving in interstate and foreign commerce in order to avoid surpluses . . ." and consequently control the market price, a primary purpose of the CSA is to control the supply and demand of controlled substances in both lawful and unlawful drug markets. In *Wickard*, we had no difficulty concluding that Congress had a rational basis for believing that, when viewed in the aggregate, leaving home-consumed wheat outside the regulatory scheme would have a substantial influence on price and market conditions. Here too, Congress had a rational basis for concluding that leaving home-consumed marijuana outside federal control would similarly affect price and market conditions.

More concretely, one concern prompting inclusion of wheat grown for home consumption in the 1938 Act was that rising market prices could draw such wheat into the interstate market, resulting in lower market prices. The parallel concern making it appropriate to include marijuana grown for home consumption in the CSA is the likelihood that the high demand in the interstate market will draw such marijuana into that market. While the diversion of homegrown wheat tended to frustrate the federal interest in stabilizing prices by regulating the volume of commercial transactions in the interstate market, the diversion of homegrown marijuana tends to frustrate the federal interest in eliminating commercial transactions in the interstate market in their entirety. In both cases, the regulation is squarely within Congress's commerce power because production of the commodity meant for home consumption, be it wheat or marijuana, has a substantial effect on supply and demand in the national market for that commodity.

Nonetheless, respondents suggest that *Wickard* differs from this case in three respects: (1) the Agricultural Adjustment Act, unlike the CSA, exempted small farming operations; (2) *Wickard* involved a "quintessential economic activity"—a commercial farm—whereas respondents do not sell marijuana; and (3) the *Wickard* record made it clear that the aggregate production of wheat for use on farms had a significant impact on market prices. Those differences, though factually accurate, do not diminish the precedential force of this Court's reasoning.

The fact that Wickard's own impact on the market was "trivial by itself" was not a sufficient reason for removing him from the scope of federal regulation. That the Secretary of Agriculture elected to exempt even smaller farms from regulation does not speak to his power to regulate all those whose aggregated production was significant, nor did that fact play any role in the Court's analysis. Moreover, even though Wickard was indeed a commercial farmer, the activity he was engaged in—the cultivation of wheat for home consumption—was not treated by the Court as part of his commercial farming operation. And while it is true that the record in the *Wickard* case itself established the causal connection between the production for local use and the national market, we have before us findings by Congress to the same effect. . . .

In assessing the scope of Congress's authority under the Commerce Clause, we stress that the task before us is a modest one. We need not determine whether respondents' activities, taken in the aggregate, substantially affect interstate commerce in fact, but only whether a "rational basis" exists for so concluding.

Given the enforcement difficulties that attend distinguishing between marijuana cultivated locally and marijuana grown elsewhere, and concerns about diversion into illicit channels, we have no difficulty concluding that Congress had a rational basis for believing that failure to regulate the intrastate manufacture and possession of marijuana would leave a gaping hole in the CSA. Thus, as in *Wickard*, when it enacted comprehensive legislation to regulate the interstate market in a fungible commodity, Congress was acting well within its authority to "make all Laws which shall be necessary and proper" to "regulate Commerce . . . among the several States." That the regulation ensnares some purely intrastate activity is of no moment. As we have done many times before, we refuse to excise individual components of that larger scheme.

To support their contrary submission, respondents rely heavily on two of our more recent Commerce Clause cases. In their myopic focus, they overlook the larger context of modern-era Commerce Clause jurisprudence preserved by those cases. Moreover, even in the narrow prism of respondents' creation, they read those cases far too broadly. Those two cases, of course, are *Lopez* and [*United States v.*] *Morrison*, 529 U.S. 598 [(2000)]. As an initial matter, the statutory challenges at issue in those cases were markedly different from the challenge respondents pursue in the case at hand. Here, respondents ask us to excise individual applications of a concededly valid statutory scheme. In contrast, in both *Lopez* and *Morrison*, the parties asserted that a particular statute or provision fell outside Congress's commerce power in its entirety. This distinction is pivotal for we have often reiterated that "[w]here the class of activities is regulated and that class is within the reach of federal power, the courts have no power 'to excise, as trivial, individual instances' of the class." *Perez*. . . .

Unlike those at issue in *Lopez* and *Morrison*, the activities regulated by the CSA are quintessentially economic. "Economics" refers to "the production, distribution, and consumption of commodities." The CSA is a statute that regulates the production, distribution, and consumption of commodities for which there is an established, and lucrative, interstate market. Prohibiting the intrastate possession or manufacture of an article of commerce is a rational (and commonly utilized) means of regulating commerce in that product. Such prohibitions include specific decisions requiring that a drug be withdrawn from the market as a result of the failure to comply with regulatory requirements as well as decisions excluding Schedule I drugs entirely from the market. Because the CSA is a statute that directly regulates economic, commercial activity, our opinion in *Morrison* casts no doubt on its constitutionality.

The Court of Appeals was able to conclude otherwise only by isolating a "separate and distinct" class of activities that it held to be beyond the reach of federal power, defined as "the intrastate, noncommercial cultivation, possession and use of marijuana for personal medical purposes on the advice of a physician and in accordance with state law." The court characterized this class as "different in kind from drug trafficking." The differences between the members of a class so defined and the principal traffickers in Schedule I substances might be sufficient to justify a policy decision exempting the narrower class from the coverage of the CSA. The question, however, is whether Congress's contrary policy judgment, i.e., its decision to include this narrower "class of activities" within the larger regulatory scheme, was constitutionally deficient. We have no difficulty concluding that Congress acted rationally in determining that none of the characteristics making up the purported class, whether viewed individually or in the aggregate, compelled an exemption from the CSA; rather, the subdivided class of activities defined by the Court of Appeals was an essential part of the larger regulatory scheme.

First, the fact that marijuana is used "for personal medical purposes on the advice of a physician" cannot itself serve as a distinguishing factor. The CSA designates marijuana as contraband for any purpose; in fact, by characterizing marijuana as a Schedule I drug, Congress expressly found that the drug has no acceptable medical uses. . . .

Second, limiting the activity to marijuana possession and cultivation "in accordance with state law" cannot serve to place respondents' activities beyond congressional reach. The Supremacy Clause unambiguously provides that if there is any conflict between federal and state law, federal law shall prevail. It is beyond peradventure that federal power over commerce is "'superior to that of the States to provide for the welfare or necessities of their inhabitants,'" however legitimate or dire those necessities may be. Just as state acquiescence to federal regulation cannot expand the bounds of the Commerce Clause, so too state action cannot circumscribe Congress's plenary commerce power.

So, from the "separate and distinct" class of activities identified by the Court of Appeals (and adopted by the dissenters), we are left with "the intrastate, noncommercial cultivation, possession and use of marijuana." Thus the case for the exemption comes down to the claim that a locally cultivated product that is used domestically rather than sold on the open market is not subject to federal regulation. Given the findings in the CSA and the undisputed magnitude of the commercial market for marijuana, our decisions in *Wickard v. Filburn* and the later cases endorsing its reasoning foreclose that claim. . . .

☐ *Justice SCALIA, concurring in the judgment.*

I write separately because my understanding of the doctrinal foundation on which that holding rests is, if not inconsistent with that of the Court, at least more nuanced.

Since *Perez v. United States*, 402 U.S. 146 (1971), our cases have mechanically recited that the Commerce Clause permits congressional regulation of three categories: (1) the channels of interstate commerce; (2) the instrumentalities of interstate commerce, and persons or things in interstate commerce; and (3) activities that "substantially affect" interstate commerce. The first two categories are self-evident, since they are the ingredients of interstate commerce itself. See *Gibbons v. Ogden*, 9 Wheat. 1 (1824). The third category, however, is different in kind, and its recitation without explanation is misleading and incomplete.

It is misleading because, unlike the channels, instrumentalities, and agents of interstate commerce, activities that substantially affect interstate commerce are not themselves part of interstate commerce, and thus the power to regulate them cannot come from the Commerce Clause alone. Rather, as this Court has acknowledged since at least *United States v. Coombs*, 12 Pet. 72 (1838), Congress's regulatory authority over intrastate activities that are not themselves part of interstate commerce (including activities that have a substantial effect on interstate commerce) derives from the Necessary and Proper Clause. And the category of "activities that substantially affect interstate commerce" is incomplete because the authority to enact laws necessary and proper for the regulation of interstate commerce is not limited to laws governing intrastate activities that substantially affect interstate commerce. Where necessary to make a regulation of interstate commerce effective, Congress may regulate even those intrastate activities that do not themselves substantially affect interstate commerce.

Our cases show that the regulation of intrastate activities may be necessary to and proper for the regulation of interstate commerce in two general circumstances. Most directly, the commerce power permits Congress not only to devise rules for the governance of commerce between States but also to facilitate interstate commerce by eliminating potential obstructions, and to restrict it by eliminating potential stimulants. See *NLRB v. Jones & Laughlin Steel Corp.*, 301 U.S. 1 (1937). That is why the Court has repeatedly sustained congressional legislation on the ground that the regulated activities had a substantial effect on interstate commerce. *Lopez* and *Morrison* recognized the expansive scope of Congress's authority in this regard: "[T]he pattern is clear. Where economic activity substantially affects interstate commerce, legislation regulating that activity will be sustained." *Lopez*.

This principle is not without limitation. In *Lopez* and *Morrison*, the Court—conscious of the potential of the "substantially affects" test to "'obliterate the distinction between what is national and what is local,'"—rejected the argument that Congress may regulate noneconomic activity based solely on the effect that it may have on interstate commerce through a remote chain of inferences. Thus, although Congress's authority to regulate intrastate activity that substantially affects interstate commerce is broad, it does not permit the Court to "pile inference upon inference" in order to establish that noneconomic activity has a substantial effect on interstate commerce. As we implicitly acknowledged in *Lopez*, however, Congress's authority to enact laws necessary and proper for the regulation of interstate commerce is not limited to laws directed against economic activities that have a substantial effect on interstate commerce. Though the conduct in *Lopez* was not economic, the Court nevertheless recognized that it could be regulated as "an essential part of a larger regulation of economic activity, in which the regulatory scheme could be undercut unless the intrastate activity were regulated." This statement referred to those cases permitting the regulation of intrastate activities "which in a substantial way interfere with or obstruct the exercise of the granted power."

Although this power "to make . . . regulation effective" commonly overlaps with the authority to regulate economic activities that substantially affect interstate commerce, and may in some cases have been confused with that authority, the two are distinct. The regulation of an intrastate activity may be essential to a comprehensive regulation of interstate commerce even though the intrastate activity does not itself "substantially affect" interstate commerce. Moreover, as the passage from *Lopez* quoted above suggests, Congress may regulate even noneconomic local activity if that regulation is a necessary part of a more general regulation of interstate commerce. The relevant question is simply whether the means chosen are "reasonably adapted" to the attainment of a legitimate end under the commerce power. . . .

As the Court said in the *Shreveport Rate Cases*, [234 U.S. 342 (1914)], the Necessary and Proper Clause does not give "Congress . . . the authority to regulate the internal commerce of a State, as such," but it does allow Congress "to take all measures necessary or appropriate to" the effective regulation of the interstate market, "although intrastate transactions . . . may thereby be controlled."

Today's principal dissent objects that, by permitting Congress to regulate activities necessary to effective interstate regulation, the Court reduces *Lopez* and *Morrison* to "little more than a drafting guide." (O'CONNOR, J.). I think that criticism unjustified. Unlike the power to regulate activities that have a substantial effect on interstate commerce, the power to enact laws enabling effective regulation of interstate commerce can only be exercised in conjunction with congressional regulation of an interstate market, and it extends only to those measures necessary to make the interstate regulation effective. As *Lopez* itself states, and the Court affirms today, Congress may regulate noneconomic intrastate activities only where the failure to do so "could . . . undercut" its regulation of interstate commerce. This is not a power that threatens to obliterate the line between "what is truly national and what is truly local." . . .

Lopez and *Morrison* affirm that Congress may not regulate certain "purely local" activity within the States based solely on the attenuated effect that such activity may have in the interstate market. But those decisions do not declare noneconomic intrastate activities to be categorically beyond the reach of the Federal Government. Neither case involved the power of Congress to exert control over intrastate activities in connection with a more comprehensive scheme of regulation. . . .

The application of these principles to the case before us is straightforward. In the CSA, Congress has undertaken to extinguish the interstate market in Schedule I controlled substances, including marijuana. The Commerce Clause unquestionably permits this. The power to regulate interstate commerce "extends not only to those regulations which aid, foster and protect the commerce, but embraces those which prohibit it." To effectuate its objective, Congress has prohibited almost all intrastate activities related to Schedule I substances—both economic activities (manufacture, distribution, possession with the intent to distribute) and noneconomic activities (simple possession). That simple possession is a noneconomic activity is immaterial to whether it can be prohibited as a necessary part of a larger regulation. Rather, Congress's authority to enact all of these prohibitions of intrastate controlled-substance activities depends only upon whether they are appropriate means of achieving the legitimate end of eradicating Schedule I substances from interstate commerce.

By this measure, I think the regulation must be sustained. . . .

☐ *Justice O'CONNOR, with whom THE CHIEF JUSTICE and Justice THOMAS join as to all but Part III, dissenting.*

We enforce the "outer limits" of Congress's Commerce Clause authority not for their own sake, but to protect historic spheres of state sovereignty from excessive federal encroachment and thereby to maintain the distribution of power fundamental to our federalist system of government. One of federalism's chief virtues, of course, is that it promotes innovation by allowing for the possibility that "a single courageous State may, if its citizens choose, serve as a laboratory; and try novel social and economic experiments without risk to the rest of the country." *New State Ice Co. v. Liebmann*, 285 U.S. 262 (1932) (BRANDEIS, J., dissenting).

This case exemplifies the role of States as laboratories. The States' core police powers have always included authority to define criminal law and to protect the health, safety, and welfare of their citizens. Exercising those powers, California (by ballot initiative and then by legislative codification) has come to its own conclusion about the difficult and sensitive question of whether marijuana should be available to relieve severe pain and suffering. Today the Court sanctions an application of the federal Controlled Substances Act that extinguishes that experiment, without any proof that the personal cultivation, possession, and use of marijuana for medicinal purposes, if economic activity in the first place, has a substantial effect on interstate commerce and is therefore an appropriate subject of federal regulation. In so doing, the Court announces a rule that gives Congress a perverse incentive to legislate broadly pursuant to the Commerce Clause—nestling questionable assertions of its authority into comprehensive regulatory schemes—rather than with precision. That rule and the result it produces in this case are irreconcilable with our decisions in *Lopez* and *United States v. Morrison*, 529 U.S. 598 (2000). Accordingly I dissent.

Our decision [in *Lopez*] about whether gun possession in school zones substantially affected interstate commerce turned on four considerations. First, we observed that our "substantial effects" cases generally have upheld federal regulation of economic activity that affected interstate commerce, but that Section 922(q) was a criminal statute having "nothing to do with 'commerce' or any sort of economic enterprise." Second, we noted that the statute contained no express jurisdictional requirement establishing its connection to interstate commerce.

Third, we found telling the absence of legislative findings about the regulated conduct's impact on interstate commerce. We explained that while express legislative findings are neither required nor, when provided, dispositive, findings "enable us to evaluate the legislative judgment that the activity in question substantially affect[s] interstate commerce, even though no such substantial effect [is] visible to the naked eye." Finally, we rejected as too attenuated the Government's argument that firearm possession in school zones could result in violent crime which in turn could adversely affect the national economy. The Constitution, we said, does not tolerate reasoning that would "convert congressional authority under the Commerce Clause to a general police power of the sort retained by the States." Later in *Morrison*, we relied on the same four considerations to hold that Section 40302 of the Violence Against Women Act of 1994 exceeded Congress's authority under the Commerce Clause.

In my view, the case before us is materially indistinguishable from *Lopez* and *Morrison* when the same considerations are taken into account. . . .

Today's decision allows Congress to regulate intrastate activity without check, so long as there is some implication by legislative design that regulating intrastate activity is essential (and the Court appears to equate "essential" with "necessary") to the interstate regulatory scheme. Seizing upon our language in *Lopez* that the statute prohibiting gun possession in school zones was "not an essential part of a larger regulation of economic activity, in which the regulatory scheme could be undercut unless the intrastate activity were regulated," the Court appears to reason that the placement of local activity in a comprehensive scheme confirms that it is essential to that scheme. If the Court is right, then *Lopez* stands for nothing more than a drafting guide: Congress should have described the relevant crime as "transfer or possession of a firearm anywhere in the nation"—thus including commercial and noncommercial activity, and clearly encompassing some activity with assuredly substantial effect on interstate commerce. Had it done so, the majority hints, we would have sustained its authority to regulate possession of firearms in school zones. Furthermore, today's decision suggests we would readily sustain a congressional decision to attach the regulation of intrastate activity to a pre-existing comprehensive (or even not-so-comprehensive) scheme. If so, the Court invites increased federal regulation of local activity even if, as it suggests, Congress would not enact a new interstate scheme exclusively for the sake of reaching intrastate activity.

I cannot agree that our decision in *Lopez* contemplated such evasive or overbroad legislative strategies with approval. Until today, such arguments have been made only in dissent. *Lopez* and *Morrison* did not indicate that the constitutionality of federal regulation depends on superficial and formalistic distinctions. Likewise I did not understand our discussion of the role of courts in enforcing outer limits of the Commerce Clause for the sake of maintaining the federalist balance our Constitution requires, as a signal to Congress to enact legislation that is more extensive and more intrusive into the domain of state power. If the Court always defers to Congress as it does today, little may be left to the notion of enumerated powers.

The hard work for courts, then, is to identify objective markers for confining the analysis in Commerce Clause cases.... A number of objective markers are available to confine the scope of constitutional review here. Both federal and state legislation—including the CSA itself, the California Compassionate Use Act, and other state medical marijuana legislation—recognize that medical and nonmedical (i.e., recreational) uses of drugs are realistically distinct and can be segregated, and regulate them differently. Moreover, because fundamental structural concerns about dual sovereignty animate our Commerce Clause cases, it is relevant that this case involves the interplay of federal and state regulation in areas of criminal law and social policy, where "States lay claim by right of history and expertise." *Lopez*. California, like other States, has drawn on its reserved powers to distinguish the regulation of medicinal marijuana. To ascertain whether Congress's encroachment is constitutionally justified in this case, then, I would focus here on the personal cultivation, possession, and use of marijuana for medicinal purposes.

Having thus defined the relevant conduct, we must determine whether, under our precedents, the conduct is economic and, in the aggregate, substantially affects interstate commerce. Even if intrastate cultivation and possession of marijuana for one's own medicinal use can properly be characterized as economic, and I question whether it can, it has not been shown that such activity substantially affects interstate commerce. Similarly, it is neither self-evident nor demonstrated that regulating such activity is necessary to the interstate drug control scheme.

The Court's definition of economic activity is breathtaking. It defines as economic any activity involving the production, distribution, and consumption of commodities. And it appears to reason that when an interstate market for a commodity exists, regulating the intrastate manufacture or possession of that commodity is constitutional either because that intrastate activity is itself economic, or because regulating it is a rational part of regulating its market. Putting to one side the problem endemic to the Court's opinion—the shift in focus from the activity at issue in this case to the entirety of what the CSA regulates—the Court's definition of economic activity for purposes of Commerce Clause jurisprudence threatens to sweep all of productive human activity into federal regulatory reach....

The Court suggests that *Wickard*, which we have identified as "perhaps the most far reaching example of Commerce Clause authority over intrastate activity," established federal regulatory power over any home consumption of a commodity for which a national market exists. I disagree. *Wickard* involved a challenge to the Agricultural Adjustment Act of 1938 (AAA), which directed the Secretary of Agriculture to set national quotas on wheat production, and penalties for excess production. The AAA itself confirmed that Congress made an explicit choice not to reach—and thus the Court could not possibly have approved of federal control over—small-scale, noncommercial wheat farming. . . .

Even assuming that economic activity is at issue in this case, the Government has made no showing in fact that the possession and use of homegrown marijuana for medical purposes, in California or elsewhere, has a substantial effect on interstate commerce. Similarly, the Government has not shown that regulating such activity is necessary to an interstate regulatory scheme. Whatever the specific theory of "substantial effects" at issue (i.e., whether the activity substantially affects interstate commerce, whether its regulation is necessary to an interstate regulatory scheme, or both), a concern for dual sovereignty requires that Congress's excursion into the traditional domain of States be justified.

That is why characterizing this as a case about the Necessary and Proper Clause does not change the analysis significantly. Congress must exercise its authority under the Necessary and Proper Clause in a manner consistent with basic constitutional principles. Congress cannot use its authority under the Clause to contravene the principle of state sovereignty embodied in the Tenth Amendment. Likewise, that authority must be used in a manner consistent with the notion of enumerated powers—a structural principle that is as much part of the Constitution as the Tenth Amendment's explicit textual command. Accordingly, something more than mere assertion is required when Congress purports to have power over local activity whose connection to an intrastate market is not self-evident. Otherwise, the Necessary and Proper Clause will always be a back door for unconstitutional federal regulation. Cf. *Printz v. United States,* 521 U.S. 898 (1997) (the Necessary and Proper Clause is "the last, best hope of those who defend *ultra vires* congressional action"). . . .

There is simply no evidence that homegrown medicinal marijuana users constitute, in the aggregate, a sizable enough class to have a discernable, let alone substantial, impact on the national illicit drug market—or otherwise to threaten the CSA regime. Explicit evidence is helpful when substantial effect is not "visible to the naked eye." And here, in part because common sense suggests that medical marijuana users may be limited in number and that California's Compassionate Use Act and similar state legislation may well isolate activities relating to medicinal marijuana from the illicit market, the effect of those activities on interstate drug traffic is not self-evidently substantial. . . .

Relying on Congress's abstract assertions, the Court has endorsed making it a federal crime to grow small amounts of marijuana in one's own home for one's own medicinal use. This overreaching stifles an express choice by some States, concerned for the lives and liberties of their people, to regulate medical marijuana differently. If I were a California citizen, I would not have voted for the medical marijuana ballot initiative; if I were a California legislator I would not have supported the Compassionate Use Act. But whatever the wisdom of California's experiment with medical marijuana, the federalism principles that have driven our Commerce Clause cases require that room for experiment be protected in this case. For these reasons I dissent.

☐ *Justice THOMAS, dissenting.*

As I explained at length in *United States v. Lopez*, 514 U.S. 549 (1995), the Commerce Clause empowers Congress to regulate the buying and selling of goods and services trafficked across state lines. The Clause's text, structure, and history all indicate that, at the time of the founding, the term "'commerce' consisted of selling, buying, and bartering, as well as transporting for these purposes." Commerce, or trade, stood in contrast to productive activities like manufacturing and agriculture. Throughout founding-era dictionaries, Madison's notes from the Constitutional Convention, *The Federalist Papers*, and the ratification debates, the term "commerce" is consistently used to mean trade or exchange—not all economic or gainful activity that has some attenuated connection to trade or exchange. The term "commerce" commonly meant trade or exchange (and shipping for these purposes) not simply to those involved in the drafting and ratification processes, but also to the general public.

Even the majority does not argue that respondents' conduct is itself "Commerce among the several States." Monson and Raich neither buy nor sell the marijuana that they consume. They cultivate their cannabis entirely in the State of California—it never crosses state lines, much less as part of a commercial transaction. Certainly no evidence from the founding suggests that "commerce" included the mere possession of a good or some purely personal activity that did not involve trade or exchange for value. In the early days of the Republic, it would have been unthinkable that Congress could prohibit the local cultivation, possession, and consumption of marijuana.

On this traditional understanding of "commerce," the Controlled Substances Act (CSA) regulates a great deal of marijuana trafficking that is interstate and commercial in character. The CSA does not, however, criminalize only the interstate buying and selling of marijuana. Instead, it bans the entire market—intrastate or interstate, noncommercial or commercial—for marijuana. Respondents are correct that the CSA exceeds Congress's commerce power as applied to their conduct, which is purely intrastate and noncommercial....

The majority prevents States like California from devising drug policies that they have concluded provide much-needed respite to the seriously ill. It does so without any serious inquiry into the necessity for federal regulation or the propriety of "displac[ing] state regulation in areas of traditional state concern." Our federalist system, properly understood, allows California and a growing number of other States to decide for themselves how to safeguard the health and welfare of their citizens. I would affirm the judgment of the Court of Appeals. I respectfully dissent.

Gonzales v. Oregon
126 S.Ct. 904 (2006)

In 1994, Oregon voters approved a ballot initiative and enacted the Death with Dignity Act, permitting doctors to legally prescribe certain lethal substances to assist in the death of competent but terminally-ill individuals. However, in November 2001 former U.S. Attorney General John Ashcroft took the position that physician-assisted suicide violates the Controlled Substances Act (CSA) of 1970, because assisting in suicide is not a "legitimate medical purpose" that justifies the dispensing of any controlled substance. He issued what became known as the "Ashcroft Directive," under which doctors who distribute controlled substances to assist suicide may have their registration to distribute controlled substances under the act revoked and may be criminally prosecuted for violating federal law. In 2002, a doctor, a pharmacist, a group of terminally-ill patients, and the state of Oregon challenged the Directive in federal district court. That court ruled that the Directive was invalid and enjoined its enforcement. Subsequently, a divided three-judge panel of the U.S. Court of Appeals for the Ninth Circuit agreed, holding that the Directive was unenforceable because it violated the plain language of the CSA, undermined Congress's intent, and overstepped the attorney general's authority. The court also emphasized the issue of "states' rights," observing that: "The principle that state governments bear the primary responsibility for evaluating physician assisted suicide follows from our concept of federalism, which requires that state lawmakers, not the federal government are the primary regulators of professional [medical] conduct." The Department of Justice appealed that decision and the Supreme Court granted review.

The appellate court's decision was affirmed by a six to three vote. Justice Kennedy delivered the opinion of the Court. Justice Scalia, joined by Chief Justice Roberts, and Justice Thomas filed dissenting opinions.

☐ *Justice KENNEDY delivered the opinion of the Court.*

The question before us is whether the Controlled Substances Act allows the United States Attorney General to prohibit doctors from prescribing regulated drugs for use in physician-assisted suicide, notwithstanding a state law permitting the procedure. As the Court has observed, "Americans are engaged in an earnest and profound debate about the morality, legality, and practicality of physician-assisted suicide." *Washington v. Glucksberg*, 521 U.S. 702 (1997). The dispute before us is in part a product of this political and moral debate, but its resolution requires an inquiry familiar to the courts: interpreting a federal statute to determine whether Executive action is authorized by, or otherwise consistent with, the enactment. . . .

We turn first to the text and structure of the CSA. Enacted in 1970 with the main objectives of combating drug abuse and controlling the legitimate and illegitimate traffic in controlled substances, the CSA creates a comprehensive, closed regulatory regime criminalizing the unauthorized manufacture, distribution, dispensing, and possession of substances classified in any of the Act's five schedules. *Gonzales v. Raich*, 545 U.S. 1 (2005). The Act places substances in one of five schedules based on their potential for abuse or dependence, their accepted medical use, and their accepted safety for use under medical supervision. Schedule I contains the most severe restrictions on access and use, and Schedule V the least. Congress classified a host of substances when it enacted the CSA, but the statute permits the Attorney General to add, remove, or reschedule substances. He may do so, however, only after making particular findings, and on scientific and medical matters he is required to accept the findings of the Secretary of Health and Human Services (Secretary).

The present dispute involves controlled substances listed in Schedule II, substances generally available only pursuant to a written, nonrefillable prescription by a physician. A 1971 regulation promulgated by the Attorney General requires that every prescription for a controlled substance "be issued for a legitimate medical purpose by an individual practitioner acting in the usual course of his professional practice." . . .

Executive actors often must interpret the enactments Congress has charged them with enforcing and implementing. The parties before us are in sharp disagreement both as to the degree of deference we must accord the Interpretive Rule's substantive conclusions and whether the Rule is authorized by the statutory text at all. Although balancing the necessary respect for an agency's knowledge, expertise, and constitutional office with the courts' role as interpreter of laws can be a delicate matter, familiar principles guide us. An administrative rule may receive substantial deference if it interprets the issuing agency's own ambiguous regulation. *Auer v. Robbins*, 519 U.S. 452 (1997). An interpretation of an ambiguous statute may also receive substantial deference. *Chevron U. S. A. Inc. v. Natural Resources Defense Council, Inc.*, 467 U.S. 837 (1984). Deference in accordance with Chevron, however, is warranted only "when it appears that Congress delegated authority to the agency generally to make rules carrying the force of law, and that the agency interpretation claiming deference was promulgated in the exercise of that authority." *United States v. Mead Corp.*, 533 U.S. 218 (2001). Otherwise, the interpretation is "entitled to respect" only to the extent it has the "power to persuade." *Skidmore v. Swift & Co.*, 323 U.S. 134 (1944).

In our view *Auer* and the standard of deference it accords to an agency are inapplicable here. *Auer* involved a disputed interpretation of the Fair Labor Standards Act of 1938 as applied to a class of law enforcement officers. Under regulations promulgated by the Secretary of Labor, an exemption from overtime pay depended, in part, on whether the employees met the "salary basis" test. In this Court the Secretary of Labor filed an *amicus* brief explaining why, in his view, the regulations gave exempt status to the officers. We gave weight to that interpretation, holding that because the applicable test was "a creature of the Secretary's own regulations, his interpretation of it is, under our jurisprudence, controlling unless plainly erroneous or inconsistent with the regulation."

In *Auer*, the underlying regulations gave specificity to a statutory scheme the Secretary was charged with enforcing and reflected the considerable experience and expertise the Department of Labor had acquired over time with respect to the complexities of the Fair Labor Standards Act. Here, on the other hand, the underlying regulation does little more than restate the terms of the statute itself. The language the Interpretive Rule addresses comes from Congress, not the Attorney General, and the near-equivalence of the statute and regulation belies the Government's argument for *Auer* deference. . . .

Just as the Interpretive Rule receives no deference under *Auer*, neither does it receive deference under *Chevron*. If a statute is ambiguous, judicial review of administrative rulemaking often demands *Chevron* deference; and the rule is judged accordingly. All would agree, we should think, that the statutory phrase "legitimate medical purpose" is a generality, susceptible to more precise definition and open to varying constructions, and thus ambiguous in the relevant sense. *Chevron* deference, however, is not accorded merely because the statute is ambiguous and an administrative official is involved. To begin with, the rule must be promulgated pursuant to authority Congress has delegated to the official.

The Attorney General has rulemaking power to fulfill his duties under the CSA. The specific respects in which he is authorized to make rules, however, instruct us that he is not authorized to make a rule declaring illegitimate a medical standard for care and treatment of patients that is specifically authorized under state law.

The starting point for this inquiry is, of course, the language of the delegation provision itself. In many cases authority is clear because the statute gives an agency broad power to enforce all provisions of the statute. The CSA does not grant the Attorney General this broad authority to promulgate rules.

The CSA gives the Attorney General limited powers, to be exercised in specific ways. His rulemaking authority under the CSA is described in two provisions: (1) "The Attorney General is authorized to promulgate rules and regulations and to charge reasonable fees relating to the registration and control of the manufacture, distribution, and dispensing of controlled substances and to listed chemicals," and (2) "The Attorney General may promulgate and enforce any rules, regulations, and procedures which he may deem necessary and appropriate for the efficient execution of his functions under this subchapter." As is evident from these sections, Congress did not delegate to the Attorney General authority to carry out or effect all provisions of the CSA. Rather, he can promulgate rules relating only to "registration" and "control" [of drugs] and "for the efficient execution of his functions" under the statute....

The structure of the CSA, then, conveys unwillingness to cede medical judgments to an Executive official who lacks medical expertise....

The Government contends the Attorney General's decision here is a legal, not a medical, one. This generality, however, does not suffice. The Attorney General's Interpretive Rule, and the Office of Legal Counsel memo it incorporates, place extensive reliance on medical judgments and the views of the medical community in concluding that assisted suicide is not a "legitimate medical purpose."...

The idea that Congress gave the Attorney General such broad and unusual authority through an implicit delegation in the CSA's registration provision is not sustainable. "Congress, we have held, does not alter the fundamental details of a regulatory scheme in vague terms or ancillary provisions—it does not, one might say, hide elephants in mouseholes." *Whitman v. American Trucking Assns., Inc.*, 531 US. 457 (2001)....

In deciding whether the CSA can be read as prohibiting physician-assisted suicide, we look to the statute's text and design. The statute and our case law amply support the conclusion that Congress regulates medical practice insofar as it bars doctors from using their prescription-writing powers as a means to engage in illicit drug dealing and trafficking as conventionally understood. Beyond this, however, the statute manifests no intent to regulate the practice of medicine generally. The silence is understandable given the structure and limitations of federalism, which allow the States "'great latitude under their police powers to legislate as to the protection of the lives, limbs, health, comfort, and quiet of all persons.'" *Medtronic, Inc. v. Lohr*, 518 U.S. 470 (1996)....

In the face of the CSA's silence on the practice of medicine generally and its recognition of state regulation of the medical profession it is difficult to defend the Attorney General's declaration that the statute impliedly criminalizes physician-assisted suicide. . . .

☐ *Justice SCALIA, with whom CHIEF JUSTICE ROBERTS and Justice THOMAS join, dissenting.*

Contrary to the Court's analysis, this case involves not one but three independently sufficient grounds for reversing the Ninth Circuit's judgment. First, the Attorney General's interpretation of "legitimate medical purpose" is clearly valid, given the substantial deference we must accord it under *Auer v. Robbins* and his two remaining conclusions follow naturally from this interpretation. Second, even if this interpretation of the Regulation is entitled to lesser deference or no deference at all, it is by far the most natural interpretation of the Regulation—whose validity is not challenged here. Third, even if that interpretation of the Regulation were incorrect, the Attorney General's independent interpretation of the statutory phrase "public interest" and his implicit interpretation of the statutory phrase "public health and safety" are entitled to deference under *Chevron U. S. A. Inc. v. Natural Resources Defense Council, Inc.*, and they are valid under *Chevron*. For these reasons, I respectfully dissent. . . .

☐ *Justice THOMAS dissenting.*

When Angel Raich and Diane Monson challenged the application of the Controlled Substances Act (CSA) to their purely intrastate possession of marijuana for medical use as authorized under California law, a majority of this Court determined that the CSA effectively invalidated California's law because "the CSA is a comprehensive regulatory regime specifically designed to regulate which controlled substances can be utilized for medicinal purposes, and in what manner." *Gonzales v. Raich*, 545 U.S. 1 (2005). The majority employed unambiguous language, concluding that the "manner" in which controlled substances can be utilized "for medicinal purposes" is one of the "core activities regulated by the CSA." And, it described the CSA as creating a comprehensive framework for regulating the production, distribution, and possession of . . . 'controlled substances,'" including those substances that "'have a useful and legitimate medical purpose,'" in order to "foster the beneficial use of those medications" and "to prevent their misuse."

Today the majority beats a hasty retreat from these conclusions. . . . The majority does so based on its conclusion that the CSA is only concerned with the regulation of "medical practice insofar as it bars doctors from using their prescription-writing powers as a means to engage in illicit drug dealing and trafficking as conventionally understood." In other words, in stark contrast to *Raich*'s broad conclusions about the scope of the CSA as it pertains to the medicinal use of controlled substances, today this Court concludes that the CSA is merely concerned with fighting "'drug abuse'" and only insofar as that abuse leads to "addiction or abnormal effects on the nervous system."

The majority's newfound understanding of the CSA as a statute of limited reach is all the more puzzling because it rests upon constitutional principles that the majority of the Court rejected in *Raich*. Notwithstanding the States' "'traditional police powers to define the criminal law and to protect the health, safety, and welfare of their citizens,'" the *Raich* majority concluded that the CSA applied to the intrastate possession of marijuana for medicinal purposes authorized by California law because "Congress could have rationally" concluded that such an application was necessary to the regulation of the "larger interstate marijuana market." Here, by contrast, the majority's restrictive interpretation of the CSA is based in no small part on "the structure and limitations of federalism, which allow the States 'great latitude under their police powers to legislate as to the protection of the lives, limbs, health, comfort, and quiet of all persons.'" According to the majority, these "background principles of our federal system . . . belie the notion that Congress would use . . . an obscure grant of authority to regulate areas traditionally supervised by the States' police power."

Of course there is nothing "obscure" about the CSA's grant of authority to the Attorney General. And, the Attorney General's conclusion that the CSA prohibits the States from authorizing physician assisted suicide is admittedly "at least reasonable," and is therefore entitled to deference. While the scope of the CSA and the Attorney General's power thereunder are sweeping, and perhaps troubling, such expansive federal legislation and broad grants of authority to administrative agencies are merely the inevitable and inexorable consequence of this Court's Commerce Clause and separation-of-powers jurisprudence.

I agree with limiting the applications of the CSA in a manner consistent with the principles of federalism and our constitutional structure. *Raich* (THOMAS, J., dissenting). But that is now water over the dam. The relevance of such considerations was at its zenith in *Raich*, when we considered whether the CSA could be applied to the intrastate possession of a controlled substance consistent with the limited federal powers enumerated by the Constitution. Such considerations have little, if any, relevance where, as here, we are merely presented with a question of statutory interpretation, and not the extent of constitutionally permissible federal power. . . . The Court's reliance upon the constitutional principles that it rejected in *Raich*—albeit under the guise of statutory interpretation—is perplexing to say the least. Accordingly, I respectfully dissent.

7

THE STATES AND AMERICAN FEDERALISM

A | *States' Power over Commerce and Regulation*

■ THE DEVELOPMENT OF LAW

Other Rulings on State Regulatory Powers in Alleged Conflict with Federal Legislation

CASE	RULING
Bates v. Dow Agrosciences, 544 U.S. 431 (2005)	Writing for the Court, Justice Stevens held that the Federal Insecticide Fungicide and Rodenticide Act (FIFRA) does not preempt state laws and tort relief lawsuits in state courts against manufacturers for negligently designed and manufactured products. Because the FIFRA does not provide for suits in federal courts, the ruling was significant since a contrary ruling would have denied consumers any opportunity to sue manufacturers. However, Justice Stevens also emphasized that not all state lawsuits under federal statutes are permitted. Preemption of each federal statute must be determined in light of its own statutory language, legislative history, and the history of litigation over a regulated product. Justices Scalia and Thomas dissented.

Mid-Con Freight Systems, Inc. v. Michigan Public Service Commission, 545 U.S. 440 (2005)

Federal law requires interstate truckers to obtain a federal permit and by 1991 some 39 states also demanded such proof. Because of differences in the states, Congress created a Single State Registration System (SSRS), which allows companies to file one set of state and federal registration forms, and prohibits states from imposing additional registration fees. Michigan imposed an annual $100 fee for state-licensed trucks and its law was challenged. Writing for the Court, Justice Breyer held that the federal law did not preempt Michigan's law because the federal statute only applies to the SSRS registration and does not preclude additional state regulations. Justice Kennedy, joined by Chief Justice Rehnquist and Justice O'Connor, dissented.

■ THE DEVELOPMENT OF LAW

Other Rulings on State Regulation of Commerce in the Absence of Federal Legislation

CASE	RULING
Granholm v. Heald, 544 U.S. 460 (2005)	A bare majority struck down Michigan and New York laws that forbid wineries located out of state from shipping wine directly to consumers. The ruling will have wide-ranging consequences for alcohol sales on the Internet and affect laws in 18 other states. Writing for the Court, Justice Kennedy noted that there was a "patchwork of laws," with some states banning all direct shipments, others only out-of-state shipments, and some requiring reciprocity. That amounted to "an ongoing, low-level trade war" that discriminated against interstate commerce. Such discrimination, Justice Kennedy ruled, was "neither authorized nor permitted by the Twenty-first Amendment," which gives states the authority to regulate the importation of liquor. In reversing the lower courts, Justice Kennedy emphasized that the Twenty-first Amendment "should not be subordinated to the dormant Commerce Clause," and noted that numerous previous decisions had rejected the "argument that the Twenty-first Amendment has somehow operated to 'repeal' the Commerce Clause for alcoholic beverages." In sum, "in all but the narrowest circumstances, state laws violate the Commerce Clause if they mandate differential treatment of in-state and out-of-state economic interests that benefits the former and burdens the later." Justices Stevens and Thomas issued dissenting opinions, which Chief Justice Rehnquist and Justice O'Connor joined.

| American Trucking Associations, Inc. v. Michigan Public Service Commission, 545 U.S. 429 (2005) | Writing for the Court, Justice Breyer ruled that the dormant Commerce Clause does not preclude Michigan from imposing a $100 annual fee on trucks engaged in intrastate commercial hauling, and does not discriminate against interstate commerce. Justices Scalia and Thomas filed concurring opinions. |

B | The Tenth and Eleventh Amendments and the States

■ THE DEVELOPMENT OF LAW

Other Recent Rulings on the Eleventh Amendment

CASE	VOTE	RULING
United States v. Georgia, 126 S.Ct. 877 (2006)	9:0	Writing for the Court, Justice Scalia held that Title II of the Americans with Disabilities Act (ADA) of 1990 created a private cause of action to sue state officials for monetary damages for violating constitutional rights and that Section 5 of the Fourteenth Amendment, which gives Congress the power to enact legislation to enforce the amendment, includes the power to abrogate Eleventh Amendment state immunity. The case, involving a paraplegic prison inmate claiming that prison officials violate his Eight Amendment rights, was remanded for reconsideration of whether the state had violated the inmate's rights.
Central Virginia Community College et al. v. Katz, 126 S.Ct. 990 (2006)	5:4	Writing for the majority, Justice Stevens held that states are not immune from bankruptcy proceedings and, like other creditors, are bound to a bankruptcy court's orders. After reviewing the history of the bankruptcy clause in Article I, Section 8, Justice Stevens concluded that the Constitution create a national uniform bankruptcy system. Justice Thomas filed a dissent, which was joined by Chief Justice Roberts and Justices Scalia and Kennedy.
Northern Insurance Co. v. Chatham County, Georgia, 126 S.Ct. 1689 (2006)	9:0	Writing for the Court, Justice Thomas held that the Eleventh Amendment does not bar Admiralty suits againsts counties that do not qualify as an "arm of the state" in such cases.

8

Representative Government, Voting Rights, and Electoral Politics

B | *Voting Rights and the Reapportionment Revolution*

In a complex and highly controversial case growing out of the Texas Republicans' mid-decennial redistricting and gerrymandering of congressional districts, the Court was sharply fragmented. Traditionally, redistricting has taken place after each census and partisan gerrymandering remains controversial. The Republican-dominated legislature redrew district lines in order to disadvantage Democrats, increase the size of the Republican majority in the House of Representatives, and to preserve the seat of an incumbent—Representative Henry Bonilla, who was losing support among the Latino majority in his district.

As discussed below, the Court's decision, in *League of United Latin American Citizens v. Perry* (2006) (excerpted below), Justice Kennedy's opinion announcing the Court's ruling commanded only a plurality. Chief Justice Roberts and Justices Stevens, Scalia, Souter, and Breyer each issued separate opinions in part concurring and in part dissenting.

League of United Latin American Citizens v. Perry
126 S.Ct. 2594 (2006)

The 1990 census resulted in a three-seat increase over the 27 seats previously allotted the Texas congressional delegation. Although the Democratic party then controlled 19 of those seats, the Republican Party had received 47 percent of the 1990 statewide vote, and Democrats only 51 percent. Faced with a possible Republican ascent to majority status, the legislature drew a congressional redistricting plan that favored Democrats. Republicans unsuccessfully challenged the 1991 redistricting as an unconstitutional partisan gerrymander.

The 2000 census authorized two additional seats for the Texas delegation. By then Republicans controlled the governorship and the state senate, but not the state house of representatives. As a result, the legislature was unable to pass a redistricting scheme and subsequent litigation led to a court-ordered plan to comply with the Fourteenth Amendment's one-person, one-vote requirement. A three-judge district court sought to apply only "neutral" redistricting standards when drawing up Plan 1151C, placing the two new seats in high-growth areas and following county and precinct lines. Under that redistricting plan, the 2002 congressional elections resulted in a 17 to 15 Democratic majority in the state's congressional delegation, compared to a 59 percent to 40 percent Republican majority in votes for statewide office in 2000, thus leaving the 1991 Democratic gerrymander largely in place.

In 2003, however, Republicans won control of both houses of the legislature and set out to increase their representation in the congressional delegation. After a protracted struggle, the Republican-controlled legislature enacted a new congressional districting map, Plan 1374C. That redistricting was immediately challenged for running afoul of the Fourteenth Amendment and provisions of the Voting Rights Act of 1965. In contention were a number of issues: (1) Whether political gerrymanders are justiciable and, if so, constitutional. (2) Whether mid-decennial redistricting for partisan reasons violates the Fourteenth Amendment. (3) Whether Plan 1374C's redrawing of District 23, which was created out of a district that had an effective Latino majority (but no longer does even though it has a Latino majority) in order to preserve an incumbant's seat, violates Section 2 of the Voting Rights Act. (4) Was the creation of another Latino majority district, District 25, because of concerns that the new District 23 diluted the voting strength of Latinos and, thus, violated Section 5 of the Voting Rights Act, sufficient? (5) Finally, the case challenged the statewide redistricting and specifically whether the redrawn District 24 diluted the votes of African Americans.

A three-judge district court rejected the challenges to the redistricting, but the Supreme Court vacated that decision and remanded the case for reconsideration in light of *Vieth v. Jubelirer*, 541 U.S. 267 (2004) (excerpted in Vol. 2, Ch. 8), in which a plurality took the position that partisan gerrymandering is justiciable. On remand, the district court limited its decision to issue of political gerrymandering and again rejected the challenge to Texas's redistricting plan.

On appeal, that decision was affirmed in part, reserved in part, vacated in part, and remanded by a sharply fragmented Court. Justice Kennedy delivered the opinion for the Court, but only a plurality joined sections and subsections. Justice Kennedy declined (1) to revisit the issue of justiciability. He held, on the one hand, (2) that Texas's redrawing of District 23's lines diluted the weight of Latino voters, in violation of Section 2 of the Voting Rights Act; and on the other hand, (3) that the new District 25 did not remedy the Latino vote dilution in District 23; as well as (4) rejected the challenge to redraw District 24. Chief Justice Roberts and Justices Stevens, Scalia, Souter, and Breyer each filed separate opinions in part concurring and in part dissenting.

☐ *Justice KENNEDY announced the judgment of the Court and delivered the opinion of the Court with respect to Parts II–A and III, an opinion with respect to Parts I and IV, in which THE CHIEF JUSTICE and Justice ALITO join, an opinion with respect to Parts II–B and II–C, and an opinion with respect to Part II–D, in which Justice SOUTER and Justice GINSBURG join.*

We affirm the District Court's dispositions on the statewide political gerrymandering claims and the Voting Rights Act claim against District 24. We reverse and remand on the Voting Rights Act claim with respect to District 23. Because we do not reach appellants' race-based equal protection claim or the political gerrymandering claim as to District 23, we vacate the judgment of the District Court on these claims.

■ I

To set out a proper framework for the case, we first recount the history of the litigation and recent districting in Texas. An appropriate starting point is not the reapportionment in 2000 but the one from the census in 1990. . . .

Faced with a Republican opposition that could be moving toward majority status, the state legislature drew a congressional redistricting plan designed to favor Democratic candidates. Using then-emerging computer technology to draw district lines with artful precision, the legislature enacted a plan later described as the "shrewdest gerrymander of the 1990s." Although the 1991 plan was enacted by the state legislature, Democratic Congressman Martin Frost was acknowledged as its architect. The 1991 plan "carefully constructs democratic districts 'with incredibly convoluted lines' and packs 'heavily Republican' suburban areas into just a few districts."

Voters who considered this unfair and unlawful treatment sought to invalidate the 1991 plan as an unconstitutional partisan gerrymander, but to no avail. The 1991 plan realized the hopes of Democrats and the fears of Republicans with respect to the composition of the Texas congressional delegation. The 1990's were years of continued growth for the Texas Republican Party, and by the end of the decade it was sweeping elections for statewide office. Nevertheless, despite carrying 59% of the vote in statewide elections in 2000, the Republicans only won 13 congressional seats to the Democrats' 17.

These events likely were not forgotten by either party when it came time to draw congressional districts in conformance with the 2000 census and to incorporate two additional seats for the Texas delegation. The Republican Party controlled the governorship and the State Senate; it did not yet control the State House of Representatives, however. As so constituted, the legislature was unable to pass a redistricting scheme, resulting in litigation and the necessity of a court-ordered plan to comply with the Constitution's one-person, one-vote requirement. The congressional districting map resulting from the Balderas litigation is known as Plan 1151C.

[T]wo members of the three-judge court that drew Plan 1151C later served on the three-judge court that issued the judgment now under review ... Under Plan 1151C, the 2002 congressional elections resulted in a 17-to-15 Democratic majority in the Texas delegation, compared to a 59% to 40% Republican majority in votes for statewide office in 2000.

The continuing influence of a court-drawn map that "perpetuated much of [the 1991] gerrymander" was not lost on Texas Republicans when, in 2003, they gained control of the State House of Representatives and, thus, both houses of the legislature. The Republicans in the legislature "set out to increase their representation in the congressional delegation." After a protracted partisan struggle, during which Democratic legislators left the State for a time to frustrate quorum requirements, the legislature enacted a new congressional districting map in October 2003. It is called Plan 1374C. The 2004 congressional elections did not disappoint the plan's drafters. Republicans won 21 seats to the Democrats' 11, while also obtaining 58% of the vote in statewide races against the Democrats' 41%. . . .

■ IIA

Based on two similar theories that address the mid-decade character of the 2003 redistricting, appellants now argue that Plan 1374C should be invalidated as an unconstitutional partisan gerrymander. In *Davis v. Bandemer*, 478 U.S. 109 (1986), the Court held that an equal protection challenge to a political gerrymander presents a justiciable case or controversy, but there was disagreement over what substantive standard to apply. That disagreement persists. A plurality of the Court in *Vieth v. Jubelirer* [541 U.S. 267 (2006)], would have held such challenges to be nonjusticiable political questions, but a majority declined to do so. We do not revisit the justiciability holding but do proceed to examine whether appellants' claims offer the Court a manageable, reliable measure of fairness for determining whether a partisan gerrymander violates the Constitution. . . .

■ IIC

Appellants claim that Plan 1374C, enacted by the Texas Legislature in 2003, is an unconstitutional political gerrymander. A decision, they claim, to effect mid-decennial redistricting, when solely motivated by partisan objectives, violates equal protection and the First Amendment because it serves no legitimate public purpose and burdens one group because of its political opinions and affiliation. The mid-decennial nature of the redistricting, appellants say, reveals the legislature's sole motivation. Unlike *Vieth*, where the legislature acted in the context of a required decennial redistricting, the Texas Legislature voluntarily replaced a plan that itself was designed to comply with new census data.

A rule, or perhaps a presumption, of invalidity when a mid-decade redistricting plan is adopted solely for partisan motivations is a salutary one, in appellants' view, for then courts need not inquire about, nor parties prove, the discriminatory effects of partisan gerrymandering—a matter that has proved elusive since *Bandemer*.

For a number of reasons, appellants' case for adopting their test is not convincing. To begin with, the state appellees dispute the assertion that partisan gain was the "sole" motivation for the decision to replace Plan 1151C. There is some merit to that criticism, for the pejorative label overlooks indications that partisan motives did not dictate the plan in its entirety....

Evaluating the legality of acts arising out of mixed motives can be complex, and affixing a single label to those acts can be hazardous, even when the actor is an individual performing a discrete act. When the actor is a legislature and the act is a composite of manifold choices, the task can be even more daunting. We are skeptical, however, of a claim that seeks to invalidate a statute based on a legislature's unlawful motive but does so without reference to the content of the legislation enacted.

Even setting this skepticism aside, a successful claim attempting to identify unconstitutional acts of partisan gerrymandering must do what appellants' sole-motivation theory explicitly disavows: show a burden, as measured by a reliable standard, on the complainants' representational rights. For this reason, a majority of the Court rejected a test proposed in *Vieth* that is markedly similar to the one appellants present today.

The sole-intent standard offered here is no more compelling when it is linked to the circumstance that Plan 1374C is mid-decennial legislation. The text and structure of the Constitution and our case law indicate there is nothing inherently suspect about a legislature's decision to replace mid-decade a court-ordered plan with one of its own. And even if there were, the fact of mid-decade redistricting alone is no sure indication of unlawful political gerrymanders....

D

Appellants' second political gerrymandering theory is that mid-decade redistricting for exclusively partisan purposes violates the one-person, one-vote requirement. They observe that population variances in legislative districts are tolerated only if they "are unavoidable despite a good-faith effort to achieve absolute equality, or for which justification is shown." *Karcher v. Daggett*, 462 U.S. 725 (1983). Working from this unchallenged premise, appellants contend that, because the population of Texas has shifted since the 2000 census, the 2003 redistricting, which relied on that census, created unlawful interdistrict population variances....

[W]e disagree with appellants' view that a legislature's decision to override a valid, court-drawn plan mid-decade is sufficiently suspect to give shape to a reliable standard for identifying unconstitutional political gerrymanders.

We conclude that appellants have established no legally impermissible use of political classifications. For this reason, they state no claim on which relief may be granted for their statewide challenge.

■ III

Plan 1374C made changes to district lines in south and west Texas that appellants challenge as violations of Section 2 of the Voting Rights Act and the Equal Protection Clause of the Fourteenth Amendment. The most significant changes occurred to District 23, which—both before and after the redistricting—covers a large land area in west Texas, and to District 25, which earlier included Houston but now includes a different area, a north-south strip from Austin to the Rio Grande Valley.

After the 2002 election, it became apparent that District 23 as then drawn had an increasingly powerful Latino population that threatened to oust the incumbent Republican, Henry Bonilla. Before the 2003 redistricting, the Latino share of the citizen voting-age population was 57.5%, and Bonilla's support among Latinos had dropped with each successive election since 1996. In 2002, Bonilla captured only 8% of the Latino vote, and 51.5% of the overall vote. Faced with this loss of voter support, the legislature acted to protect Bonilla's incumbency by changing the lines—and hence the population mix—of the district. To begin with, the new plan divided Webb County and the city of Laredo, on the Mexican border, that formed the county's population base. Webb County, which is 94% Latino, had previously rested entirely within District 23; under the new plan, nearly 100,000 people were shifted into neighboring District 28. The rest of the county, approximately 93,000 people, remained in District 23. To replace the numbers District 23 lost, the State added voters in counties comprising a largely Anglo, Republican area in central Texas. In the newly drawn district, the Latino share of the citizen voting-age population dropped to 46%, though the Latino share of the total voting-age population remained just over 50%....

The District Court summed up the purposes underlying the redistricting in south and west Texas: "The change to Congressional District 23 served the dual goal of increasing Republican seats in general and protecting Bonilla's incumbency in particular, with the additional political nuance that Bonilla would be reelected in a district that had a majority of Latino voting-age population—although clearly not a majority of citizen voting-age population and certainly not an effective voting majority." The goal in creating District 25 was just as clear: "[t]o avoid retrogression under Section 5" of the Voting Rights Act given the reduced Latino voting strength in District 23.

A

The question we address is whether Plan 1374C violates Section 2 of the Voting Rights Act. A State violates Section 2 "if, based on the totality of circumstances, it is shown that the political processes leading to nomination or election in the State or political subdivision are not equally open to participation by members of [a racial group] in that its members have less opportunity than other members of the electorate to participate in the political process and to elect representatives of their choice."

The Court has identified three threshold conditions for establishing a Section 2 violation: (1) the racial group is "sufficiently large and geographically compact to constitute a majority in a single-member district";

(2) the racial group is "politically cohesive"; and (3) the majority "vot[es] sufficiently as a bloc to enable it ... usually to defeat the minority's preferred candidate." *Johnson v. De Grandy*, 512 U.S. 997 (1994) (quoting *Thornburg v. Gingles*, 478 U.S. 30 (1986)). These are the so-called *Gingles* requirements.

If all three *Gingles* requirements are established, the statutory text directs us to consider the "totality of circumstances" to determine whether members of a racial group have less opportunity than do other members of the electorate. The general terms of the statutory standard "totality of circumstances" require judicial interpretation. For this purpose, the Court has referred to the Senate Report on the 1982 amendments to the Voting Rights Act, which identifies factors typically relevant to a Section 2 claim, including: "the history of voting-related discrimination in the State or political subdivision; the extent to which voting in the elections of the State or political subdivision is racially polarized; the extent to which the State or political subdivision has used voting practices or procedures that tend to enhance the opportunity for discrimination against the minority group ...; the extent to which minority group members bear the effects of past discrimination in areas such as education, employment, and health, which hinder their ability to participate effectively in the political process; the use of overt or subtle racial appeals in political campaigns; and the extent to which members of the minority group have been elected to public office in the jurisdiction. The Report notes also that evidence demonstrating that elected officials are unresponsive to the particularized needs of the members of the minority group and that the policy underlying the State's or the political subdivision's use of the contested practice or structure is tenuous may have probative value."

Another relevant consideration is whether the number of districts in which the minority group forms an effective majority is roughly proportional to its share of the population in the relevant area.

The District Court's determination whether the Section 2 requirements are satisfied must be upheld unless clearly erroneous. Where "the ultimate finding of dilution" is based on "a misreading of the governing law," however, there is reversible error.

B

Appellants argue that the changes to District 23 diluted the voting rights of Latinos who remain in the district. Specifically, the redrawing of lines in District 23 caused the Latino share of the citizen voting-age population to drop from 57.5% to 46%. The District Court recognized that "Latino voting strength in Congressional District 23 is, unquestionably, weakened under Plan 1374C." The question is whether this weakening amounts to vote dilution. . . .

[The] problem remains [that] the District Court failed to perform a comparable compactness inquiry for Plan 1374C as drawn. *De Grandy* requires a comparison between a challenger's proposal and the "existing number of reasonably compact districts." To be sure, Section 2 does not forbid the creation of a noncompact majority-minority district. The noncompact district cannot, however, remedy a violation elsewhere in the State. Simply put, the State's creation of an opportunity district for those without a Section 2 right offers no excuse for its failure to provide an opportunity district for those with a Section 2 right. And since there is no Section 2 right to a district that is not reasonably compact, the creation of a noncompact district does not compensate for the dismantling of a compact opportunity district.

THE CHIEF JUSTICE claims compactness should be only a factor in the analysis, but his approach comports neither with our precedents nor with the nature of the right established by Section 2. *De Grandy* expressly stated that the first *Gingles* prong looks only to the number of "reasonably compact districts." *Shaw II*, [*Shaw v. Hunt*, 527 U.S. 899 (1996)], moreover, refused to consider a noncompact district as a possible remedy for a Section 2 violation....

The District Court did evaluate compactness for the purpose of deciding whether race predominated in the drawing of district lines. The Latinos in the Rio Grande Valley and those in Central Texas, it found, are "disparate communities of interest," with "differences in socio-economic status, education, employment, health, and other characteristics." The court's conclusion that the relative smoothness of the district lines made the district compact, despite this combining of discrete communities of interest, is inapposite because the court analyzed the issue only for equal protection purposes. In the equal protection context, compactness focuses on the contours of district lines to determine whether race was the predominant factor in drawing those lines. See *Miller v. Johnson*, 515 U. S. 900 (1995). Under Section 2, by contrast, the injury is vote dilution, so the compactness inquiry embraces different considerations.

While no precise rule has emerged governing Section 2 compactness, the "inquiry should take into account 'traditional districting principles such as maintaining communities of interest and traditional boundaries.'" The recognition of nonracial communities of interest reflects the principle that a State may not "assum[e] from a group of voters' race that they 'think alike, share the same political interests, and will prefer the same candidates at the polls.'" *Miller* (quoting *Shaw v. Reno*, 509 U.S. 630 (1993)). In the absence of this prohibited assumption, there is no basis to believe a district that combines two far-flung segments of a racial group with disparate interests provides the opportunity that Section 2 requires or that the first *Gingles* condition contemplates. "The purpose of the Voting Rights Act is to prevent discrimination in the exercise of the electoral franchise and to foster our transformation to a society that is no longer fixated on race." *Georgia v. Ashcroft*, 539 U.S. 461 (2003). We do a disservice to these important goals by failing to account for the differences between people of the same race.

While the District Court recognized the relevant differences, by not performing the compactness inquiry it failed to account for the significance of these differences under Section 2. In these cases the District Court's findings regarding the different characteristics, needs, and interests of the Latino community near the Mexican border and the one in and around Austin are well supported and uncontested. Legitimate yet differing communities of interest should not be disregarded in the interest of race. The practical consequence of drawing a district to cover two distant, disparate communities is that one or both groups will be unable to achieve their political goals. Compactness is, therefore, about more than "style points," (opinion of Roberts, C. J.); it is critical to advancing the ultimate purposes of Section 2, ensuring minority groups equal "opportunity ... to participate in the political process and to elect representatives of their choice." ...

Since District 25 is not reasonably compact, Plan 1374C contains only five reasonably compact Latino opportunity districts. Plan 1151C, by contrast, created six such districts. The District Court did not find, and the State does not contend, that any of the Latino opportunity districts in Plan 1151C are noncompact. Contrary to THE CHIEF JUSTICE's suggestion, moreover, the Latino population in old District 23 is, for the most part, in closer geographic proximity than is the Latino population in new District 25. More importantly, there has been no contention that different pockets of the Latino population in old District 23 have divergent needs and interests, and it is clear that, as set out below, the Latino population of District 23 was split apart particularly because it was becoming so cohesive. The Latinos in District 23 had found an efficacious political identity, while this would be an entirely new and difficult undertaking for the Latinos in District 25, given their geographic and other differences.

Appellants have thus satisfied all three *Gingles* requirements as to District 23, and the creation of new District 25 does not remedy the problem.

C

We proceed now to the totality of the circumstances, and first to the proportionality inquiry, comparing the percentage of total districts that are Latino opportunity districts with the Latino share of the citizen voting-age population. As explained in *De Grandy*, proportionality is "a relevant fact in the totality of circumstances." It does not, however, act as a "safe harbor" for States in complying with Section 2....

We conclude the answer in these cases is to look at proportionality statewide. The State contends that the seven districts in south and west Texas correctly delimit the boundaries for proportionality because that is the only area of the State where reasonably compact Latino opportunity districts can be drawn. This argument, however, misunderstands the role of proportionality. We have already determined, under the first *Gingles* factor, that another reasonably compact Latino district can be drawn. The question now is whether the absence of that additional district constitutes impermissible vote dilution. This inquiry requires an "'intensely local appraisal'" of the challenged district. A local appraisal is necessary because the right to an undiluted vote does not belong to the "minority as a group," but rather to "its individual members." And a State may not trade off the rights of some members of a racial group against the rights of other members of that group. The question is therefore not "whether line-drawing in the challenged area as a whole dilutes minority voting strength," but whether line-drawing dilutes the voting strength of the Latinos in District 23.

The role of proportionality is not to displace this local appraisal or to allow the State to trade off the rights of some against the rights of others. Instead, it provides some evidence of whether "the political processes leading to nomination or election in the State or political subdivision are not equally open to participation." For this purpose, the State's seven-district area is arbitrary. It just as easily could have included six or eight districts. Appellants have alleged statewide vote dilution based on a statewide plan, so the electoral opportunities of Latinos across the State can bear on whether the lack of electoral opportunity for Latinos in District 23 is a consequence of Plan 1374C's redrawing of lines or simply a consequence of the inevitable 'win some, lose some' in a State with racial bloc voting. Indeed, several of the other factors in the totality of circumstances have been characterized with reference to the State as a whole. Particularly given the presence of racially polarized voting—and the possible submergence of minority votes—throughout Texas, it makes sense to use the entire State in assessing proportionality.

Looking statewide, there are 32 congressional districts. The five reasonably compact Latino opportunity districts amount to roughly 16% of the total, while Latinos make up 22% of Texas' citizen voting-age population. Latinos are, therefore, two districts shy of proportional representation. There is, of course, no "magic parameter," *De Grandy*, and "rough proportionality" must allow for some deviations. We need not decide whether the two-district deficit in these cases weighs in favor of a Section 2 violation. Even if Plan 1374C's disproportionality were deemed insubstantial, that consideration would not overcome the other evidence of vote dilution for Latinos in District 23....

The changes to District 23 undermined the progress of a racial group that has been subject to significant voting-related discrimination and that was becoming increasingly politically active and cohesive....

Furthermore, the reason for taking Latinos out of District 23, according to the District Court, was to protect Congressman Bonilla from a constituency that was increasingly voting against him. The Court has noted that incumbency protection can be a legitimate factor in districting, see *Karcher v. Daggett*, but experience teaches that incumbency protection can take various forms, not all of them in the interests of the constituents. If the justification for incumbency protection is to keep the constituency intact so the officeholder is accountable for promises made or broken, then the protection seems to accord with concern for the voters. If, on the other hand, incumbency protection means excluding some voters from the district simply because they are likely to vote against the officeholder, the change is to benefit the officeholder, not the voters. By purposely redrawing lines around those who opposed Bonilla, the state legislature took the latter course. This policy, whatever its validity in the realm of politics, cannot justify the effect on Latino voters. The policy becomes even more suspect when considered in light of evidence suggesting that the State intentionally drew District 23 to have a nominal Latino voting-age majority (without a citizen voting-age majority) for political reasons. This use of race to create the facade of a Latino district also weighs in favor of appellants' claim....

Based on the foregoing, the totality of the circumstances demonstrates a Section 2 violation. Even assuming Plan 1374C provides something close to proportional representation for Latinos, its troubling blend of politics and race—and the resulting vote dilution of a group that was beginning to achieve Section 2's goal of overcoming prior electoral discrimination—cannot be sustained.

D

Because we hold Plan 1374C violates Section 2 in its redrawing of District 23, we do not address appellants' claims that the use of race and politics in drawing that district violates the First Amendment and equal protection. We also need not confront appellants' claim of an equal protection violation in the drawing of District 25. The districts in south and west Texas will have to be redrawn to remedy the violation in District 23, and we have no cause to pass on the legitimacy of a district that must be changed. District 25, in particular, was formed to compensate for the loss of District 23 as a Latino opportunity district, and there is no reason to believe District 25 will remain in its current form once District 23 is brought into compliance with Section 2. We therefore vacate the District Court's judgment as to these claims.

IV

Appellants also challenge the changes to district lines in the Dallas area, alleging they dilute African-American voting strength in violation of Section 2 of the Voting Rights Act. Specifically, appellants contend that an African-American minority effectively controlled District 24 under Plan 1151C, and that Section 2 entitles them to this district. . . .

That African-Americans had influence in the district does not suffice to state a Section 2 claim in these cases. The opportunity "to elect representatives of their choice" requires more than the ability to influence the outcome between some candidates, none of whom is their candidate of choice. There is no doubt African-Americans preferred Martin Frost to the Republicans who opposed him. The fact that African-Americans preferred Frost to some others does not, however, make him their candidate of choice. Accordingly, the ability to aid in Frost's election does not make the old District 24 an African-American opportunity district for purposes of Section 2. If Section 2 were interpreted to protect this kind of influence, it would unnecessarily infuse race into virtually every redistricting, raising serious constitutional questions. . . .

We reject the statewide challenge to Texas' redistricting as an unconstitutional political gerrymander and the challenge to the redistricting in the Dallas area as a violation of Section 2 of the Voting Rights Act. We do hold that the redrawing of lines in District 23 violates Section 2 of the Voting Rights Act. The judgment of the District Court is affirmed in part, reversed in part, and vacated in part, and the cases are remanded for further proceedings.

☐ *Justice STEVENS, with whom Justice BREYER joins as to Parts I and II, concurring in part and dissenting in part.*

This is a suit in which it is perfectly clear that judicially manageable standards enable us to decide the merits of a statewide challenge to a political gerrymander. Applying such standards, I shall explain why the wholly unnecessary replacement of the neutral plan fashioned by the three-judge court in *Balderas v. Texas* (Plan 1151C or Balderas Plan) with Plan 1374C, which creates districts with less compact shapes, violates the Voting Rights Act, and fragments communities of interest—all for purely partisan purposes—violated the State's constitutional duty to govern impartially. Prior misconduct by the Texas Legislature neither excuses nor justifies that violation. Accordingly, while I join the Court's decision to invalidate District 23, I would hold that Plan 1374C is entirely invalid and direct the District Court to reinstate Plan 1151C. Moreover, as I shall explain, even if the remainder of the plan were valid, the cracking of Balderas District 24 would still be unconstitutional.

III

Relying solely on *Vieth*, Justice KENNEDY maintains that even if legislation is enacted based solely on a desire to harm a politically unpopular minority, this fact is insufficient to establish unconstitutional partisan gerrymandering absent proof that the legislation did in fact burden "the complainants' representative rights." This conclusion—which clearly goes to the merits, rather than the manageability, of a partisan gerrymandering claim—is not only inconsistent with the constitutional requirement that state action must be supported by a legitimate interest, but also provides an insufficient response to appellants' claim on the merits. . . .

In my judgment the record amply supports the conclusion that Plan 1374C not only burdens the minority party in District 23, but also imposes a severe statewide burden on the ability of Democratic voters and politicians to influence the political process. . . .

IV

[T]he record in this litigation makes clear that the predominant motive underlying the fragmentation of Balderas District 24 was to maximize Republicans' electoral opportunities and ensure that Congressman Frost was defeated.

Turning now to the effects test I have proposed, plaintiffs in new Districts 6, 24, 36, and 32 could easily meet the three parts of that test because: (1) under the Balderas plan, they lived in District 24 and their candidate of choice (Frost) was the winning candidate; (2) under Plan 1374C, they have been placed in districts that are safe seats for the Republican party (the Democratic share of the two-party vote in statewide elections from 1996 to 2002 was 40% or less in Districts 6, 24, 26, and 32); and (3) their new districts are less compact than Balderas District 24.

Justice KENNEDY rejects my proposed effects test, as applied in this case, because, in his view Balderas District 24 lacks "any special claim to fairness." But my analysis in no way depends on the proposition that Balderas District 24 was fair. The district was more compact than four of the districts that replaced it, and, as explained above, compactness serves important values in the districting process. This is why, in my view, a State that creates more compact districts should enjoy a safe harbor from partisan gerrymandering claims. However, the mere fact that a prior district was unfair should surely not provide a safe harbor for the creation of an even more unfair district. Conversely, a State may of course create less compact districts without violating the Constitution so long as its purpose is not to disadvantage a politically disfavored group. The reason I focus on Balderas District 24 is not because the district was fair, but because the prior district provides a clear benchmark in analyzing whether plaintiffs have been harmed.

In sum, applying the judicially manageable test set forth in this Part of my opinion reveals that the cracking of Balderas District 24 created several unconstitutional partisan gerrymanders. Even if I believed that Plan 1374C were not invalid in its entirety, I would reverse the judgment below with regard to Districts 6, 24, 26, and 32.

For the foregoing reasons, although I concur with the majority's decision to invalidate District 23 under Section 2 of the Voting Rights Act, I respectfully dissent from the Court's decision to affirm the judgment below with respect to plaintiffs' partisan gerrymandering claim. I would reverse with respect to the plan as a whole, and also, more specifically, with respect to Districts 6, 24, 26, and 32.

☐ *Justice SOUTER, with whom Justice GINSBURG joins, concurring in part and dissenting in part.*

I join Part II–D of the principal opinion, rejecting the one-person, one-vote challenge to Plan 1374C based simply on its mid-decade timing, and I also join Part II–A, in which the Court preserves the principle that partisan gerrymandering can be recognized as a violation of equal protection, see *Vieth v. Jubelirer.* I see nothing to be gained by working through these cases on the standard I would have applied in *Vieth*, because here as in *Vieth* we have no majority for any single criterion of impermissible gerrymander (and none for a conclusion that Plan 1374C is unconstitutional across the board). I therefore treat the broad issue of gerrymander much as the subject of an improvident grant of *certiorari*, and add only two thoughts for the future: that I do not share Justice KENNEDY's seemingly flat rejection of any test of gerrymander turning on the process followed in redistricting, nor do I rule out the utility of a criterion of symmetry as a test. Perhaps further attention could be devoted to the administrability of such a criterion at all levels of redistricting and its review.

I join Part III of the principal opinion, in which the Court holds that Plan 1374C's Districts 23 and 25 violate Section 2 of the Voting Rights Act of 1965 in diluting minority voting strength. But I respectfully dissent from Part IV, in which a plurality upholds the District Court's rejection of the claim that Plan 1374C violated Section 2 in cracking the black population in the prior District 24 and submerging its fragments in new Districts 6, 12, 24, 26, and 32. On the contrary, I would vacate the judgment and remand for further consideration. . . .

☐ *Justice BREYER, concurring in part and dissenting in part.*

I join Parts II–A and III of the Court's opinion. I also join Parts I and II of Justice STEVENS' opinion concurring in part and dissenting in part.

For one thing, the timing of the redistricting (between census periods), the radical departure from traditional boundary-drawing criteria, and the other evidence to which Justice STEVENS refers in Parts I and II of his opinion make clear that a "desire to maximize partisan advantage" was the "sole purpose behind the decision to promulgate Plan 1374C."

For another thing, the evidence to which Justice STEVENS refers in Part III of his opinion demonstrates that the plan's effort "to maximize partisan advantage," encompasses an effort not only to exaggerate the favored party's electoral majority but also to produce a majority of congressional representatives even if the favored party receives only a minority of popular votes.

Finally, because the plan entrenches the Republican Party, the State cannot successfully defend it as an effort simply to neutralize the Democratic Party's previous political gerrymander. Nor has the State tried to justify the plan on nonpartisan grounds, either as an effort to achieve legislative stability by avoiding legislative exaggeration of small shifts in party preferences.

In sum, "the risk of entrenchment is demonstrated," "partisan considerations [have] render[ed] the traditional district-drawing compromises irrelevant," and "no justification other than party advantage can be found." The record reveals a plan that overwhelmingly relies upon the unjustified use of purely partisan line-drawing considerations and which will likely have seriously harmful electoral consequences. For these reasons, I believe the plan in its entirety violates the Equal Protection Clause.

☐ *CHIEF JUSTICE ROBERTS, with whom Justice ALITO joins, concurring in part, concurring in the judgment in part, and dissenting in part.*

I join Parts I and IV of the plurality opinion. With regard to Part II, I agree with the determination that appellants have not provided "a reliable standard for identifying unconstitutional political gerrymanders." The question whether any such standard exists—that is, whether a challenge to a political gerrymander presents a justiciable case or controversy—has not been argued in these cases. I therefore take no position on that question, which has divided the Court, see *Vieth v. Jubelirer*, 541 U. S. 267 (2004), and I join the Court's disposition in Part II without specifying whether appellants have failed to state a claim on which relief can be granted, or have failed to present a justiciable controversy.

I must, however, dissent from Part III of the Court's opinion. According to the District Court's factual findings, the State's drawing of district lines in south and west Texas caused the area to move from five out of seven effective Latino opportunity congressional districts, with an additional district "moving" in that direction, to six out of seven effective Latino opportunity districts. The end result is that while Latinos make up 58% of the citizen voting-age population in the area, they control 85% (six of seven) of the districts under the State's plan.

In the face of these findings, the majority nonetheless concludes that the State's plan somehow dilutes the voting strength of Latinos in violation of Section 2 of the Voting Rights Act. The majority reaches its surprising result because it finds that Latino voters in one of the State's Latino opportunity districts—District 25—are insufficiently compact, in that they consist of two different groups, one from around the Rio Grande and another from around Austin. According to the majority, this may make it more difficult for certain Latino-preferred candidates to be elected from that district—even though Latino voters make up 55% of the citizen voting-age population in the district and vote as a bloc. The majority prefers old District 23, despite the District Court determination that new District 25 is "a more effective Latino opportunity district than Congressional District 23 had been." The District Court based that determination on a careful examination of regression analysis showing that "the Hispanic-preferred candidate [would win] every primary and general election examined in District 25," compared to the only partial success such candidates enjoyed in former District 23.

The majority dismisses the District Court's careful factfinding on the ground that the experienced judges did not properly consider whether District 25 was "compact" for purposes of Section 2. But the District Court opinion itself clearly demonstrates that the court carefully considered the compactness of the minority group in District 25, just as the majority says it should have. The District Court recognized the very features of District 25 highlighted by the majority and unambiguously concluded, under the totality of the circumstances, that the district was an effective Latino opportunity district, and that no violation of Section 2 in the area had been shown.

Unable to escape the District Court's factfinding, the majority is left in the awkward position of maintaining that its theory about compactness is more important under Section 2 than the actual prospects of electoral success for Latino-preferred candidates under a State's apportionment plan. And that theory is a novel one to boot. Never before has this or any other court struck down a State's redistricting plan under Section 2, on the ground that the plan achieves the maximum number of possible majority-minority districts, but loses on style points, in that the minority voters in one of those districts are not as "compact" as the minority voters would be in another district were the lines drawn differently. Such a basis for liability pushes voting rights litigation into a whole new area—an area far removed from the concern of the Voting Rights Act to ensure minority voters an equal opportunity "to elect representatives of their choice." . . .

☐ Justice SCALIA, with whom Justice THOMAS joins, and with whom THE CHIEF JUSTICE and Justice ALITO join as to Part III, concurring in the judgment in part and dissenting in part.

As I have previously expressed, claims of unconstitutional partisan gerrymandering do not present a justiciable case or controversy. See *Vieth v. Jubelirer* (2004). Justice KENNEDY's discussion of appellants' political gerrymandering claims ably demonstrates that, yet again, no party or judge has put forth a judicially discernable standard by which to evaluate them. Unfortunately, the opinion then concludes that the appellants have failed to state a claim as to political gerrymandering, without ever articulating what the elements of such a claim consist of. That is not an available disposition of this appeal. We must either conclude that the claim is nonjusticiable and dismiss it, or else set forth a standard and measure appellant's claim against it. Instead, we again dispose of this claim in a way that provides no guidance to lower-court judges and perpetuates a cause of action with no discernible content. We should simply dismiss appellants' claims as nonjusticiable.

I would dismiss appellants' vote-dilution claims premised on Section 2 of the Voting Rights Act of 1965 for failure to state a claim, for the reasons set forth in Justice THOMAS's opinion, which I joined, in *Holder v. Hall*, 512 U.S. 874 (1994). As THE CHIEF JUSTICE makes clear, the Court's Section 2 jurisprudence continues to drift ever further from the Act's purpose of ensuring minority voters equal electoral opportunities.

■ III

Because I find no merit in either of the claims addressed by the Court, I must consider appellants' race-based equal protection claims. The GI Forum appellants focus on the removal of 100,000 residents, most of whom are Latino, from District 23. They assert that this action constituted intentional vote dilution in violation of the Equal Protection Clause. The Jackson appellants contend that the intentional creation of District 25 as a majority-minority district was an impermissible racial gerrymander. The District Court rejected the equal protection challenges to both districts. . . .

In determining whether a redistricting decision was reasonably necessary, a court must bear in mind that a State is permitted great flexibility in deciding how to comply with Section 5's mandate. See *Georgia v. Ashcroft*, 539 U.S. 461 (2003). For instance, we have recognized that Section 5 does not constrain a State's choice between creating majority-minority districts or minority-influence districts. And we have emphasized that, in determining whether a State has impaired a minority's "effective exercise of the electoral franchise," a court should look to the totality of the circumstances statewide. These circumstances include the ability of a minority group "to elect a candidate of its choice" or "to participate in the political process," the positions of legislative leadership held by individuals representing minority districts, and support for the new plan by the representatives previously elected from these districts.

In light of these many factors bearing upon the question whether the State had a strong evidentiary basis for believing that the creation of District 25 was reasonably necessary to comply with Section 5, I would normally remand for the District Court to undertake that "fact-intensive" inquiry. Appellants concede, however, that the changes made to District 23 "necessitated creating an additional effective Latino district elsewhere, in an attempt to avoid Voting Rights Act liability." This is, of course, precisely the State's position. Nor do appellants charge that in creating District 25 the State did more than what was required by Section 5. In light of these concessions, I do not believe a remand is necessary, and I would affirm the judgment of the District Court.

C | *Campaigns and Elections*

In *Garcetti v. Ceballos* (2006) (excerpted below) the Court split five to four in holding that government employees do not receive First Amendment free speech protection against a supervisor's alleged retaliation for their speech. Writing for the majority, however, Justice Kennedy noted that employees still have First Amendment protection as citizens who voice their views publicly in, for example, letters to the editor or in op-ed articles in newspapers. Justices Souter, Stevens, Ginsburg, and Breyer dissented.

In addition, in a plurality opinion for the Court's decision, Justice Breyer, joined by Chief Justice Roberts and Justice Alito, struck down Vermont's 1997 law (Act 64) imposing restrictions on campaign spending and contributions, which ranged from $200 per election cycle for state house candidates to $400 for statewide candidates. Justice Breyer held that the $200 limitation was "way, way, way lower" than the $1,000 federal campaign contribution restriction upheld in *Buckley v. Valeo*, 424 U.S. 1 (1976) (excerpted in Vol. 1, Ch. 8), as well as refused to reconsider *Buckley*. Justice Breyer suggested that courts should consider, first, whether there are "danger signals" that restrictions would stifle electoral competition; and, second, more specifically, whether (a) contribution limits significantly restrict the money available to challengers, (b) limits impinge on political parties' freedom of association, (c) volunteer expenses are treated too harshly, (d) the limits are not adjusted for inflation, and (e) the record does not show past evidence of corruption.

In separate concurring opinions, Justices Alito, Thomas (joined by Justice Scalia), and Kennedy took the position that virtually all contribution limitations violate the First Amendment. By contrast, Justices Souter and Stevens, joined by Justice Ginsburg, filed dissenting opinions and would have upheld the state's restrictions.

Garcetti v. Ceballos
126 S.Ct. 1951 (2006)

Richard Ceballos, a Los Angeles deputy district attorney, was contacted by a defense counsel in a pending case who claimed that there were factual errors in the affidavit filed to secure a search warrant against his client. Ceballos reviewed the matter and agreed. He wrote his supervisor a memo recommending that the case be dismissed and later testified for the defense about the affidavit's misrepresentations. Subsequently, Ceballos was reassigned to another court and denied a promotion. He, then, filed a lawsuit claiming that his supervisor's retaliation violated his First Amendment freedom of speech. A federal district court ruled that he was not entitled to First Amendment protection because he wrote the memo "as part of his job" as a government employee. However, the U.S. Court of Appeals for the Ninth Circuit reversed, upon concluding that the memo touched on matters of public concern and was entitled to First Amendment protection.

The appellate court's decision was reversed by a five to four vote. Justice Kennedy delivered the opinion for the Court. Justices Souter, Stevens, and Breyer filed dissenting opinions; Justice Ginsburg joined Justice Souter's dissent.

☐ *Justice KENNEDY delivered the opinion of the Court.*

It is well settled that "a State cannot condition public employment on a basis that infringes the employee's constitutionally protected interest in freedom of expression." *Connick v. Myers*, 461 U.S. 138 (1983). The question presented by the instant case is whether the First Amendment protects a government employee from discipline based on speech made pursuant to the employee's official duties....

As the Court's decisions have noted, for many years "the unchallenged dogma was that a public employee had no right to object to conditions placed upon the terms of employment—including those which restricted the exercise of constitutional rights." *Connick*. That dogma has been qualified in important respects. The Court has made clear that public employees do not surrender all their First Amendment rights by reason of their employment. Rather, the First Amendment protects a public employee's right, in certain circumstances, to speak as a citizen addressing matters of public concern.

Pickering [*v. Board of Education*, 391 U.S. 563 (1968)], provides a useful starting point in explaining the Court's doctrine. There the relevant speech was a teacher's letter to a local newspaper addressing issues including the funding policies of his school board. "The problem in any case," the Court stated, "is to arrive at a balance between the interests of the teacher, as a citizen, in commenting upon matters of public concern and the interest of the State, as an employer, in promoting the efficiency of the public services it performs through its employees." The Court found the teacher's speech "neither [was] shown nor can be presumed to have in any way either impeded the teacher's proper performance of his daily duties in the classroom or to have interfered with the regular operation of the schools generally." Thus, the Court concluded that "the interest of the school administration in limiting teachers' opportunities to contribute to public debate is not significantly greater than its interest in limiting a similar contribution by any member of the general public."

Pickering and the cases decided in its wake identify two inquiries to guide interpretation of the constitutional protections accorded to public employee speech. The first requires determining whether the employee spoke as a citizen on a matter of public concern. If the answer is no, the employee has no First Amendment cause of action based on his or her employer's reaction to the speech. If the answer is yes, then the possibility of a First Amendment claim arises. The question becomes whether the relevant government entity had an adequate justification for treating the employee differently from any other member of the general public. This consideration reflects the importance of the relationship between the speaker's expressions and employment. A government entity has broader discretion to restrict speech when it acts in its role as employer, but the restrictions it imposes must be directed at speech that has some potential to affect the entity's operations....

When a citizen enters government service, the citizen by necessity must accept certain limitations on his or her freedom. Government employers, like private employers, need a significant degree of control over their employees' words and actions; without it, there would be little chance for the efficient provision of public services. Public employees, moreover, often occupy trusted positions in society. When they speak out, they can express views that contravene governmental policies or impair the proper performance of governmental functions.

At the same time, the Court has recognized that a citizen who works for the government is nonetheless a citizen. The First Amendment limits the ability of a public employer to leverage the employment relationship to restrict, incidentally or intentionally, the liberties employees enjoy in their capacities as private citizens. So long as employees are speaking as citizens about matters of public concern, they must face only those speech restrictions that are necessary for their employers to operate efficiently and effectively....

Underlying our cases has been the premise that while the First Amendment invests public employees with certain rights, it does not empower them to "constitutionalize the employee grievance."

With these principles in mind we turn to the instant case. Respondent Ceballos believed the affidavit used to obtain a search warrant contained serious misrepresentations.... That Ceballos expressed his views inside his office, rather than publicly, is not dispositive. Employees in some cases may receive First Amendment protection for expressions made at work. Many citizens do much of their talking inside their respective workplaces, and it would not serve the goal of treating public employees like "any member of the general public" to hold that all speech within the office is automatically exposed to restriction.

The memo concerned the subject matter of Ceballos' employment, but this, too, is nondispositive. The First Amendment protects some expressions related to the speaker's job. As the Court noted in *Pickering*: "Teachers are, as a class, the members of a community most likely to have informed and definite opinions as to how funds allotted to the operation of the schools should be spent. Accordingly, it is essential that they be able to speak out freely on such questions without fear of retaliatory dismissal." The same is true of many other categories of public employees.

The controlling factor in Ceballos' case is that his expressions were made pursuant to his duties as a calendar deputy. That consideration—the fact that Ceballos spoke as a prosecutor fulfilling a responsibility to advise his supervisor about how best to proceed with a pending case—distinguishes Ceballos' case from those in which the First Amendment provides protection against discipline. We hold that when public employees make statements pursuant to their official duties, the employees are not speaking as citizens for First Amendment purposes, and the Constitution does not insulate their communications from employer discipline.

Ceballos wrote his disposition memo because that is part of what he, as a calendar deputy, was employed to do.... The significant point is that the memo was written pursuant to Ceballos' official duties....

Ceballos did not act as a citizen when he went about conducting his daily professional activities, such as supervising attorneys, investigating charges, and preparing filings. In the same way he did not speak as a citizen by writing a memo that addressed the proper disposition of a pending criminal case. When he went to work and performed the tasks he was paid to perform, Ceballos acted as a government employee. The fact that his duties sometimes required him to speak or write does not mean his supervisors were prohibited from evaluating his performance....

Two final points warrant mentioning. First, as indicated above, the parties in this case do not dispute that Ceballos wrote his disposition memo pursuant to his employment duties. We thus have no occasion to articulate a comprehensive framework for defining the scope of an employee's duties in cases where there is room for serious debate. We reject, however, the suggestion that employers can restrict employees' rights by creating excessively broad job descriptions. The proper inquiry is a practical one. Formal job descriptions often bear little resemblance to the duties an employee actually is expected to perform, and the listing of a given task in an employee's written job description is neither necessary nor sufficient to demonstrate that conducting the task is within the scope of the employee's professional duties for First Amendment purposes.

Second, Justice SOUTER suggests today's decision may have important ramifications for academic freedom, at least as a constitutional value. There is some argument that expression related to academic scholarship or classroom instruction implicates additional constitutional interests that are not fully accounted for by this Court's customary employee-speech jurisprudence. We need not, and for that reason do not, decide whether the analysis we conduct today would apply in the same manner to a case involving speech related to scholarship or teaching....

☐ *Justice SOUTER, with whom Justice STEVENS and Justice GINSBURG join, dissenting.*

I would hold that private and public interests in addressing official wrongdoing and threats to health and safety can outweigh the government's stake in the efficient implementation of policy, and when they do public employees who speak on these matters in the course of their duties should be eligible to claim First Amendment protection.

Open speech by a private citizen on a matter of public importance lies at the heart of expression subject to protection by the First Amendment. At the other extreme, a statement by a government employee complaining about nothing beyond treatment under personnel rules raises no greater claim to constitutional protection against retaliatory response than the remarks of a private employee. In between these points lies a public employee's speech unwelcome to the government but on a significant public issue. Such an employee speaking as a citizen, that is, with a citizen's interest, is protected from reprisal unless the statements are too damaging to the government's capacity to conduct public business to be justified by any individual or public benefit thought to flow from the statements. *Pickering v. Board of Ed. of Township High School Dist. 205, Will Cty.*, 391 U.S. 563 (1968). Entitlement to protection is thus not absolute.

This significant, albeit qualified, protection of public employees who irritate the government is understood to flow from the First Amendment, in part, because a government paycheck does nothing to eliminate the value to an individual of speaking on public matters, and there is no good reason for categorically discounting a speaker's interest in commenting on a matter of public concern just because the government employs him. Still, the First Amendment safeguard rests on something more, being the value to the public of receiving the opinions and information that a public employee may disclose.

The reason that protection of employee speech is qualified is that it can distract co-workers and supervisors from their tasks at hand and thwart the implementation of legitimate policy, the risks of which grow greater the closer the employee's speech gets to commenting on his own workplace and responsibilities. It is one thing for an office clerk to say there is waste in government and quite another to charge that his own department pays full-time salaries to part-time workers. Even so, we have regarded eligibility for protection by *Pickering* balancing as the proper approach when an employee speaks critically about the administration of his own government employer.

As all agree, the qualified speech protection embodied in *Pickering* balancing resolves the tension between individual and public interests in the speech, on the one hand, and the government's interest in operating efficiently without distraction or embarrassment by talkative or headline-grabbing employees. The need for a balance hardly disappears when an employee speaks on matters his job requires him to address; rather, it seems obvious that the individual and public value of such speech is no less, and may well be greater, when the employee speaks pursuant to his duties in addressing a subject he knows intimately for the very reason that it falls within his duties. . . .

Indeed, the very idea of categorically separating the citizen's interest from the employee's interest ignores the fact that the ranks of public service include those who share the poet's "object . . . to unite [m]y avocation and my vocation;" these citizen servants are the ones whose civic interest rises highest when they speak pursuant to their duties, and these are exactly the ones government employers most want to attract. There is no question that public employees speaking on matters they are obliged to address would generally place a high value on a right to speak, as any responsible citizen would. . . .

Nothing accountable on the individual and public side of the *Pickering* balance changes when an employee speaks "pursuant" to public duties. On the side of the government employer, however, something is different, and to this extent, I agree with the majority of the Court. The majority is rightly concerned that the employee who speaks out on matters subject to comment in doing his own work has the greater leverage to create office uproars and fracture the government's authority to set policy to be carried out coherently through the ranks. "Official communications have official consequences, creating a need for substantive consistency and clarity. Supervisors must ensure that their employees' official communications are accurate, demonstrate sound judgment, and promote the employer's mission." Up to a point, then, the majority makes good points: government needs civility in the workplace, consistency in policy, and honesty and competence in public service.

But why do the majority's concerns, which we all share, require categorical exclusion of First Amendment protection against any official retaliation for things said on the job? Is it not possible to respect the unchallenged individual and public interests in the speech through a *Pickering* balance ...? This is, to be sure, a matter of judgment, but the judgment has to account for the undoubted value of speech to those, and by those, whose specific public job responsibilities bring them face to face with wrongdoing and incompetence in government, who refuse to avert their eyes and shut their mouths. And it has to account for the need actually to disrupt government if its officials are corrupt or dangerously incompetent. It is thus no adequate justification for the suppression of potentially valuable information simply to recognize that the government has a huge interest in managing its employees and preventing the occasionally irresponsible one from turning his job into a bully pulpit. Even there, the lesson of *Pickering* (and the object of most constitutional adjudication) is still to the point: when constitutionally significant interests clash, resist the demand for winner-take-all; try to make adjustments that serve all of the values at stake....

☐ *Justice BREYER, dissenting.*

While I agree with much of Justice SOUTER's analysis, I believe that the constitutional standard he enunciates fails to give sufficient weight to the serious managerial and administrative concerns that the majority describes. The standard would instruct courts to apply *Pickering* balancing in all cases, but says that the government should prevail unless the employee (1) "speaks on a matter of unusual importance," and (2) "satisfies high standards of responsibility in the way he does it." Justice SOUTER adds that "only comment on official dishonesty, deliberately unconstitutional action, other serious wrongdoing, or threats to health and safety can weigh out in an employee's favor."

There are, however, far too many issues of public concern, even if defined as "matters of unusual importance," for the screen to screen out very much. Government administration typically involves matters of public concern. Why else would government be involved? And "public issues," indeed, matters of "unusual importance," are often daily bread-and-butter concerns for the police, the intelligence agencies, the military, and many whose jobs involve protecting the public's health, safety, and the environment. This aspect of Justice SOUTER's "adjustment" of "the basic *Pickering* balancing scheme" is similar to the Court's present insistence that speech be of "legitimate news interest", when the employee speaks only as a private citizen. It gives no extra weight to the government's augmented need to direct speech that is an ordinary part of the employee's job-related duties....

The underlying problem with this breadth of coverage is that the standard (despite predictions that the government is likely to prevail in the balance unless the speech concerns "official dishonesty, deliberately unconstitutional action, other serious wrongdoing, or threats to health and safety") does not avoid the judicial need to undertake the balance in the first place. And this form of judicial activity ... may interfere unreasonably with both the managerial function (the ability of the employer to control the way in which an employee performs his basic job) and with the use of other grievance-resolution mechanisms, such as arbitration, civil service review boards, and whistle-blower remedies, for which employees and employers may have bargained or which legislatures may have enacted....

I conclude that the First Amendment sometimes does authorize judicial actions based upon a government employee's speech that both (1) involves a matter of public concern and also (2) takes place in the course of ordinary job-related duties. But it does so only in the presence of augmented need for constitutional protection and diminished risk of undue judicial interference with governmental management of the public's affairs. In my view, these conditions are met in this case and *Pickering* balancing is consequently appropriate.

☐ *Justice STEVENS, dissenting.*

The proper answer to the question "whether the First Amendment protects a government employee from discipline based on speech made pursuant to the employee's official duties" is "Sometimes," not "Never." Of course a supervisor may take corrective action when such speech is "inflammatory or misguided." But what if it is just unwelcome speech because it reveals facts that the supervisor would rather not have anyone else discover?

As Justice SOUTER explains, public employees are still citizens while they are in the office. The notion that there is a categorical difference between speaking as a citizen and speaking in the course of one's employment is quite wrong. [I]t seems perverse to fashion a new rule that provides employees with an incentive to voice their concerns publicly before talking frankly to their superiors.

Randall v. Sorrell
126 S.Ct. 2479 (2006)

In 1997, Vermont's legislature passed and then-governor Howard Dean signed into law one of the country's most restrictive campaign finance laws (Act 64). Under the law, expenditure limits, for a two-year general election cycle, were imposed on races for governor ($300,000), lieutenant governor ($100,000), other statewide offices ($45,000), and state representatives ($2,000). The law also restricted individuals' campaign contributions to statewide office candidates to $400, state senators to $300, and state representatives to $200. Political committees were also subject to the restrictions and they were immediately challenged as a violation of the First Amendment. A federal district court held that the restrictions violate the First Amendment and ran afoul of the ruling in *Buckley v. Valeo*, 424 U.S. 1 (1976), but the U.S. Court of Appeals for the Second Circuit reversed and upheld all of the limitations.

By a six to three vote the Court reversed the appellate court's decision. Justice Breyer delivered a plurality opinion for the Court's decision. Justices Alito, Kennedy, and Thomas filed concurring opinions. Justices

Souter and Stevens filed dissenting opinion; Justice Ginsburg joined Justice Souter's dissent.

☐ *Justice BREYER announced the judgment of the Court, and delivered an opinion in which THE CHIEF JUSTICE joins, and in which Justice ALITO joins except as to Parts II–B–1 and II–B–2.*

We here consider the constitutionality of a Vermont campaign finance statute that limits both (1) the amounts that candidates for state office may spend on their campaigns (expenditure limitations) and (2) the amounts that individuals, organizations, and political parties may contribute to those campaigns. We hold that both sets of limitations are inconsistent with the First Amendment. Well-established precedent makes clear that the expenditure limits violate the First Amendment. *Buckley v. Valeo*, 424 U.S. 1 (1976) (*per curiam*). The contribution limits are unconstitutional because in their specific details (involving low maximum levels and other restrictions) they fail to satisfy the First Amendment's requirement of careful tailoring. That is to say, they impose burdens upon First Amendment interests that (when viewed in light of the statute's legitimate objectives) are disproportionately severe....

We turn first to the Act's expenditure limits. Do those limits violate the First Amendment's free speech guarantees?

In *Buckley v. Valeo*, the Court considered the constitutionality of the Federal Election Campaign Act of 1971 (FECA), a statute that, much like the Act before us, imposed both expenditure and contribution limitations on campaigns for public office. The Court, while upholding FECA's contribution limitations as constitutional, held that the statute's expenditure limitations violated the First Amendment.

Buckley stated that both kinds of limitations "implicate fundamental First Amendment interests." It noted that the Government had sought to justify the statute's infringement on those interests in terms of the need to prevent "corruption and the appearance of corruption." In the Court's view, this rationale provided sufficient justification for the statute's contribution limitations, but it did not provide sufficient justification for the expenditure limitations.

The Court explained that the basic reason for this difference between the two kinds of limitations is that expenditure limitations "impose significantly more severe restrictions on protected freedoms of political expression and association than" do contribution limitations. Contribution limitations, though a "marginal restriction upon the contributor's ability to engage in free communication," nevertheless leave the contributor "fre[e] to discuss candidates and issues." Expenditure limitations, by contrast, impose "[a] restriction on the amount of money a person or group can spend on political communication during a campaign." They thereby necessarily "reduc[e] the quantity of expression by restricting the number of issues discussed, the depth of their exploration, and the size of the audience reached." Indeed, the freedom "to engage in unlimited political expression subject to a ceiling on expenditures is like being free to drive an automobile as far and as often as one desires on a single tank of gasoline."

The Court concluded that "[n]o governmental interest that has been suggested is sufficient to justify the restriction on the quantity of political expression imposed by" the statute's expenditure limitations.

Over the last 30 years, in considering the constitutionality of a host of different campaign finance statutes, this Court has repeatedly adhered to *Buckley*'s constraints, including those on expenditure limits.

■ II B 1

The respondents recognize that, in respect to expenditure limits, *Buckley* appears to be a controlling—and unfavorable—precedent. They seek to overcome that precedent in two ways. First, they ask us in effect to overrule *Buckley*. Post-*Buckley* experience, they believe, has shown that contribution limits (and disclosure requirements) alone cannot effectively deter corruption or its appearance; hence experience has undermined an assumption underlying that case. Indeed, the respondents have devoted several pages of their briefs to attacking *Buckley*'s holding on expenditure limits.

Second, in the alternative, they ask us to limit the scope of *Buckley* significantly by distinguishing *Buckley* from the present case. They advance as a ground for distinction a justification for expenditure limitations that, they say, *Buckley* did not consider, namely that such limits help to protect candidates from spending too much time raising money rather than devoting that time to campaigning among ordinary voters. We find neither argument persuasive.

■ II B 2

The Court has often recognized the "fundamental importance" of *stare decisis*, the basic legal principle that commands judicial respect for a court's earlier decisions and the rules of law they embody. The Court has pointed out that *stare decisis* "'promotes the evenhanded, predictable, and consistent development of legal principles, fosters reliance on judicial decisions, and contributes to the actual and perceived integrity of the judicial process.'" *United States v. International Business Machines Corp.*, 517 U.S. 843 (1996). *Stare decisis* thereby avoids the instability and unfairness that accompany disruption of settled legal expectations. For this reason, the rule of law demands that adhering to our prior case law be the norm. Departure from precedent is exceptional, and requires "special justification." *Arizona v. Rumsey*, 467 U.S. 203 (1984). This is especially true where, as here, the principle has become settled through iteration and reiteration over a long period of time.

We can find here no such special justification that would require us to overrule *Buckley*. Subsequent case law has not made *Buckley* a legal anomaly or otherwise undermined its basic legal principles. . . .

For all these reasons, we find this a case that fits the *stare decisis* norm. And we do not perceive the strong justification that would be necessary to warrant overruling so well established a precedent. We consequently decline the respondents' invitation to reconsider *Buckley*.

■ II B 3

The respondents also ask us to distinguish these cases from *Buckley*. But we can find no significant basis for that distinction. Act 64's expenditure limits are not substantially different from those at issue in *Buckley*. In both instances the limits consist of a dollar cap imposed upon a candidate's expenditures. Nor is Vermont's primary justification for imposing its expenditure limits significantly different from Congress' rationale for the *Buckley* limits: preventing corruption and its appearance....

■ III

We turn now to a more complex question, namely the constitutionality of Act 64's contribution limits. The parties, while accepting *Buckley*'s approach, dispute whether, despite *Buckley*'s general approval of statutes that limit campaign contributions, Act 64's contribution limits are so severe that in the circumstances its particular limits violate the First Amendment.

As with the Act's expenditure limits, we begin with *Buckley*. In that case, the Court upheld the $1,000 contribution limit before it. *Buckley* recognized that contribution limits, like expenditure limits, "implicate fundamental First Amendment interests," namely, the freedoms of "political expression" and "political association." But, unlike expenditure limits (which "necessarily reduc[e] the quantity of expression by restricting the number of issues discussed, the depth of their exploration, and the size of the audience reached"), contribution limits "involv[e] little direct restraint on" the contributor's speech. They do restrict "one aspect of the contributor's freedom of political association," namely, the contributor's ability to support a favored candidate, but they nonetheless "permi[t] the symbolic expression of support evidenced by a contribution," and they do "not in any way infringe the contributor's freedom to discuss candidates and issues."

Consequently, the Court wrote, contribution limitations are permissible as long as the Government demonstrates that the limits are "closely drawn" to match a "sufficiently important interest." It found that the interest advanced in the case, "prevent[ing] corruption" and its "appearance," was "sufficiently important" to justify the statute's contribution limits.

The Court also found that the contribution limits before it were "closely drawn." It recognized that, in determining whether a particular contribution limit was "closely drawn," the amount, or level, of that limit could make a difference....

Since *Buckley*, the Court has consistently upheld contribution limits in other statutes. The Court has recognized, however, that contribution limits might sometimes work more harm to protected First Amendment interests than their anticorruption objectives could justify. And individual Members of the Court have expressed concern lest too low a limit magnify the "reputation-related or media-related advantages of incumbency and thereby insulat[e] legislators from effective electoral challenge." In the cases before us, the petitioners challenge Act 64's contribution limits on that basis.

Following *Buckley*, we must determine whether Act 64's contribution limits prevent candidates from "amassing the resources necessary for effective [campaign] advocacy;" whether they magnify the advantages of incumbency to the point where they put challengers to a significant disadvantage; in a word, whether they are too low and too strict to survive First Amendment scrutiny. In answering these questions, we recognize, as *Buckley* stated, that we have "no scalpel to probe" each possible contribution level. We cannot determine with any degree of exactitude the precise restriction necessary to carry out the statute's legitimate objectives. In practice, the legislature is better equipped to make such empirical judgments, as legislators have "particular expertise" in matters related to the costs and nature of running for office. Thus ordinarily we have deferred to the legislature's determination of such matters.

Nonetheless, as *Buckley* acknowledged, we must recognize the existence of some lower bound. At some point the constitutional risks to the democratic electoral process become too great. After all, the interests underlying contribution limits, preventing corruption and the appearance of corruption, "directly implicate the integrity of our electoral process." Yet that rationale does not simply mean "the lower the limit, the better." That is because contribution limits that are too low can also harm the electoral process by preventing challengers from mounting effective campaigns against incumbent officeholders, thereby reducing democratic accountability. Were we to ignore that fact, a statute that seeks to regulate campaign contributions could itself prove an obstacle to the very electoral fairness it seeks to promote. Thus, we see no alternative to the exercise of independent judicial judgment as a statute reaches those outer limits. And, where there is strong indication in a particular case, i.e., danger signs, that such risks exist (both present in kind and likely serious in degree), courts, including appellate courts, must review the record independently and carefully with an eye toward assessing the statute's "tailoring," that is, toward assessing the proportionality of the restrictions.

We find those danger signs present here. As compared with the contribution limits upheld by the Court in the past, and with those in force in other States, Act 64's limits are sufficiently low as to generate suspicion that they are not closely drawn. The Act sets its limits per election cycle, which includes both a primary and a general election. Thus, in a gubernatorial race with both primary and final election contests, the Act's contribution limit amounts to $200 per election per candidate (with significantly lower limits for contributions to candidates for State Senate and House of Representatives). These limits apply both to contributions from individuals and to contributions from political parties, whether made in cash or in expenditures coordinated (or presumed to be coordinated) with the candidate. These limits are well below the limits this Court upheld in *Buckley*. Indeed, in terms of real dollars (i.e., adjusting for inflation), the Act's $200 per election limit on individual contributions to a campaign for governor is slightly more than one-twentieth of the limit on contributions to campaigns for federal office before the Court in *Buckley*. Adjusted to reflect its value in 1976 (the year *Buckley* was decided), Vermont's contribution limit on campaigns for statewide office (including governor) amounts to $113.91 per 2-year election cycle, or roughly $57 per election, as compared to the $1,000 per election limit on individual contributions at issue in *Buckley*.

Moreover, considered as a whole, Vermont's contribution limits are the lowest in the Nation. Act 64 limits contributions to candidates for statewide office (including governor) to $200 per candidate per election. We have found no State that imposes a lower per election limit. Indeed, we have found only seven States that impose limits on contributions to candidates for statewide office at or below $500 per election, more than twice Act 64's limit.

Finally, Vermont's limit is well below the lowest limit this Court has previously upheld, the limit of $1,075 per election (adjusted for inflation every two years).

But this does not necessarily mean that Vermont's limits are less objectionable than the limit upheld in *Shrink*. A campaign for state auditor is likely to be less costly than a campaign for governor; campaign costs do not automatically increase or decrease in precise proportion to the size of an electoral district.

The factors we have mentioned offset any neutralizing force of population differences. At the very least, they make it difficult to treat [*Nixon v. Shrink Missouri Government PAC*, 528 U.S. 431 (2000)] (then) $1,075 limit as providing affirmative support for the lawfulness of Vermont's far lower levels. And even were that not so, Vermont's failure to index for inflation means that Vermont's levels would soon be far lower than Missouri's regardless of the method of comparison.

In sum, Act 64's contribution limits are substantially lower than both the limits we have previously upheld and comparable limits in other States. These are danger signs that Act 64's contribution limits may fall outside tolerable First Amendment limits. We consequently must examine the record independently and carefully to determine whether Act 64's contribution limits are "closely drawn" to match the State's interests.

Our examination of the record convinces us that, from a constitutional perspective, Act 64's contribution limits are too restrictive. We reach this conclusion based not merely on the low dollar amounts of the limits themselves, but also on the statute's effect on political parties and on volunteer activity in Vermont elections. Taken together, Act 64's substantial restrictions on the ability of candidates to raise the funds necessary to run a competitive election, on the ability of political parties to help their candidates get elected, and on the ability of individual citizens to volunteer their time to campaigns show that the Act is not closely drawn to meet its objectives. In particular, five factors together lead us to this decision.

First, the record suggests, though it does not conclusively prove, that Act 64's contribution limits will significantly restrict the amount of funding available for challengers to run competitive campaigns. . . .

Second, Act 64's insistence that political parties abide by exactly the same low contribution limits that apply to other contributors threatens harm to a particularly important political right, the right to associate in a political party.

The Act applies its $200 to $400 limits—precisely the same limits it applies to an individual—to virtually all affiliates of a political party taken together as if they were a single contributor. That means, for example, that the Vermont Democratic Party, taken together with all its local affiliates, can make one contribution of at most $400 to the Democratic gubernatorial candidate, one contribution of at most $300 to a Democratic candidate for State Senate, and one contribution of at most $200 to a Democratic candidate for the State House of Representatives. The Act includes within these limits not only direct monetary contributions but also expenditures in kind: stamps, stationery, coffee, doughnuts, gasoline, campaign buttons, and so forth. Indeed, it includes all party expenditures "intended to promote the election of a specific candidate or group of candidates" as long as the candidate's campaign "facilitate[s]," "solicit[s]," or "approve[s]" them. And a party expenditure that "primarily benefits six or fewer candidates who are associated with the" party is "presumed" to count against the party's contribution limits. . . .

We recognize that we have previously upheld limits on contributions from political parties to candidates, in particular the federal limits on coordinated party spending. And we also recognize that any such limit will negatively affect to some extent the fund-allocating party function just described. But the contribution limits at issue in Colorado II were far less problematic, for they were significantly higher than Act 64's limits. And they were much higher than the federal limits on contributions from individuals to candidates, thereby reflecting an effort by Congress to balance (1) the need to allow individuals to participate in the political process by contributing to political parties that help elect candidates with (2) the need to prevent the use of political parties "to circumvent contribution limits that apply to individuals." Act 64, by placing identical limits upon contributions to candidates, whether made by an individual or by a political party, gives to the former consideration no weight at all. . . .

Third, the Act's treatment of volunteer services aggravates the problem. Like its federal statutory counterpart, the Act excludes from its definition of "contribution" all "services provided without compensation by individuals volunteering their time on behalf of a candidate." But the Act does not exclude the expenses those volunteers incur, such as travel expenses, in the course of campaign activities. The Act's broad definitions would seem to count those expenses against the volunteer's contribution limit, at least where the spending was facilitated or approved by campaign officials.

Fourth, unlike the contribution limits we upheld in *Shrink*, Act 64's contribution limits are not adjusted for inflation. . . .

Fifth, we have found nowhere in the record any special justification that might warrant a contribution limit so low or so restrictive as to bring about the serious associational and expressive problems that we have described. Rather, the basic justifications the State has advanced in support of such limits are those present in *Buckley*. The record contains no indication that, for example, corruption (or its appearance) in Vermont is significantly more serious a matter than elsewhere. . . .

These five sets of considerations, taken together, lead us to conclude that Act 64's contribution limits are not narrowly tailored. Rather, the Act burdens First Amendment interests by threatening to inhibit effective advocacy by those who seek election, particularly challengers; its contribution limits mute the voice of political parties; they hamper participation in campaigns through volunteer activities; and they are not indexed for inflation. . . .

We conclude that Act 64's expenditure limits violate the First Amendment as interpreted in *Buckley v. Valeo*. We also conclude that the specific details of Act 64's contribution limits require us to hold that those limits violate the First Amendment, for they burden First Amendment interests in a manner that is disproportionate to the public purposes they were enacted to advance. Given our holding, we need not, and do not, examine the constitutionality of the statute's presumption that certain party expenditures are coordinated with a candidate. Accordingly, the judgment of the Court of Appeals is reversed, and the cases are remanded for further proceedings.

☐ *Justice ALITO, concurring in part and concurring in the judgment.*

I concur in the judgment and join in Justice BREYER's opinion except for Parts II–B–1 and II–B–2. Contrary to the suggestion of those sections, respondents' primary defense of Vermont's expenditure limits is that those limits are consistent with *Buckley v. Valeo*. Only as a backup argument, an afterthought almost, do respondents make a naked plea for us to "revisit *Buckley*." This is fairly incongruous, given that respondents' defense of Vermont's contribution limits rests squarely on *Buckley* and later decisions that built on *Buckley*, and yet respondents fail to explain why it would be appropriate to reexamine only one part of the holding in *Buckley*. More to the point, respondents fail to discuss the doctrine of *stare decisis* or the Court's cases elaborating on the circumstances in which it is appropriate to reconsider a prior constitutional decision.

Whether or not a case can be made for reexamining *Buckley* in whole or in part, what matters is that respondents do not do so here, and so I think it unnecessary to reach the issue.

☐ *Justice KENNEDY, concurring in the judgment.*

The universe of campaign finance regulation is one this Court has in part created and in part permitted by its course of decisions. That new order may cause more problems than it solves. On a routine, operational level the present system requires us to explain why $200 is too restrictive a limit while $1,500 is not. Our own experience gives us little basis to make these judgments, and certainly no traditional or well-established body of law exists to offer guidance. On a broader, systemic level political parties have been denied basic First Amendment rights. Entering to fill the void have been new entities such as political action committees, which are as much the creatures of law as of traditional forces of speech and association. Those entities can manipulate the system and attract their own elite power brokers, who operate in ways obscure to the ordinary citizen.

Viewed within the legal universe we have ratified and helped create, the result the plurality reaches is correct; given my own skepticism regarding that system and its operation, however, it seems to me appropriate to concur only in the judgment.

☐ *Justice THOMAS, with whom Justice SCALIA joins, concurring in the judgment.*

Although I agree with the plurality that Act 64 is unconstitutional, I disagree with its rationale for striking down that statute. Invoking *stare decisis*, the plurality rejects the invitation to overrule *Buckley v. Valeo*. It then applies *Buckley* to invalidate the expenditure limitations and, less persuasively, the contribution limitations. I continue to believe that *Buckley* provides insufficient protection to political speech, the core of the First Amendment. The illegitimacy of *Buckley* is further underscored by the continuing inability of the Court to apply *Buckley* in a coherent and principled fashion. As a result, *stare decisis* should pose no bar to overruling *Buckley* and replacing it with a standard faithful to the First Amendment. Accordingly, I concur only in the judgment. . . .

☐ *Justice SOUTER, with whom Justice GINSBURG joins, and with whom Justice STEVENS joins as to Parts II and III, dissenting.*

In 1997, the Legislature of Vermont passed Act 64 after a series of public hearings persuaded legislators that rehabilitating the State's political process required campaign finance reform. A majority of the Court today decides that the expenditure and contribution limits enacted are irreconcilable with the Constitution's guarantee of free speech. I would adhere to the Court of Appeals's decision to remand for further enquiry bearing on the limitations on candidates' expenditures, and I think the contribution limits satisfy controlling precedent. I respectfully dissent.

Rejecting Act 64's expenditure limits as directly contravening *Buckley v. Valeo* is at least premature. We said in *Buckley* that "expenditure limitations impose far greater restraints on the freedom of speech and association than do ... contribution limitations," but the Buckley Court did not categorically foreclose the possibility that some spending limit might comport with the First Amendment. . . .

The legislature's findings are surely significant enough to justify the Court of Appeals's remand to the District Court to decide whether Vermont's spending limits are the least restrictive means of accomplishing what the court unexceptionably found to be worthy objectives. . . .

Although I would defer judgment on the merits of the expenditure limitations, I believe the Court of Appeals correctly rejected the challenge to the contribution limits. Low though they are, one cannot say that "the contribution limitation[s are] so radical in effect as to render political association ineffective, drive the sound of a candidate's voice below the level of notice, and render contributions pointless." *Nixon v. Shrink Missouri Government PAC*, 528 U.S. 377 (2000). . . .

Four issues of detail call for some attention, the first being the requirement that a volunteer's expenses count against the person's contribution limit. The plurality certainly makes out the case that accounting for these expenses will be a colossal nuisance, but there is no case here that the nuisance will noticeably limit volunteering, or that volunteers whose expenses reach the limit cannot continue with their efforts subject to charging their candidates for the excess. Granted, if the provisions for contribution limits were teetering on the edge of unconstitutionality, Act 64's treatment of volunteers' expenses might be the finger-flick that gives the fatal push, but it has no greater significance than that.

Second, the failure of the Vermont law to index its limits for inflation is even less important. This challenge is to the law as it is, not to a law that may have a different impact after future inflation if the state legislature fails to bring it up to economic date.

Third, subjecting political parties to the same contribution limits as individuals does not condemn the Vermont scheme. What we said in *Federal Election Comm'n v. Colorado Republican Federal Campaign Comm.*, 533 U.S. 431 (2001), dealing with regulation of coordinated expenditures, goes here, too. The capacity and desire of parties to make large contributions to competitive candidates with uphill fights are shared by rich individuals, and the risk that large party contributions would be channels to evade individual limits cannot be eliminated. Nor are these reasons to support the party limits undercut by claims that the restrictions render parties impotent, for the parties are not precluded from uncoordinated spending to benefit their candidates. That said, I acknowledge the suggestions in the petitioners' briefs that such restrictions in synergy with other influences weakening party power would justify a wholesale reexamination of the situation of party organization today. But whether such a comprehensive reexamination belongs in courts or only in legislatures is not an issue presented by these cases.

Finally, there is the issue of Act 64's presumption of coordinated expenditures on the part of political parties. The plurality has no occasion to reach it; I do reach it, but find it insignificant. . . .

Because I would not pass upon the constitutionality of Vermont's expenditure limits prior to further enquiry into their fit with the problem of fundraising demands on candidates, and because I do not see the contribution limits as depressed to the level of political inaudibility, I respectfully dissent.

□ *Justice STEVENS, dissenting.*

Justice BREYER and Justice SOUTER debate whether the *per curiam* decision in *Buckley v. Valeo* forecloses any constitutional limitations on candidate expenditures. This is plainly an issue on which reasonable minds can disagree. The *Buckley* Court never explicitly addressed whether the pernicious effects of endless fundraising can serve as a compelling state interest that justifies expenditure limits, yet its silence, in light of the record before it, suggests that it implicitly treated this proposed interest insufficient. Assuming this to be true, however, I am convinced that *Buckley*'s holding on expenditure limits is wrong, and that the time has come to overrule it. . . .

■ THE DEVELOPMENT OF LAW

Other Rulings on Campaigns and Elections

CASE	VOTE	RULING
Clingman v. Beaver, 544 U.S. 581 (2005)	6:3	Writing for the Court, Justice Thomas upheld Oklahoma's semiclosed primary law, under which political parties may permit only their own registered members and voters registered as independents to vote in a primary. The Libertarian Party had wanted to open its primary to members of other parties and challenged the law for infringing on its First Amendment freedom of association. But Justice Thomas held that the law imposed only minor burdens and advanced the state's compelling interests in preserving political parties "as viable and identifiable interest groups." Justices Stevens, O'Connor, and Souter dissented.

9

ECONOMIC RIGHTS AND AMERICAN CAPITALISM

C | The "Takings Clause" and Just Compensation

In a major ruling with wide-ranging ramifications for urban planners and homeowners, by a five to four vote the Court upheld the use of the government's power of eminent domain and to condemn and take, with just compensation, private property for the purpose of advancing the economic development of the community. Writing for the Court in *Kelo v. City of New London* (excerpted below), Justice Stevens held that "public use" was not limited to the use of public domain to build a road or a bridge; or to develop a blighted neighborhood, as in *Berman v. Parker*, 348 U.S. 26 (1954); or to redistribute land ownership, as in *Hawaii Housing Authority v. Midkiff*, 467 U.S. 229 (1984) (excerpted in Vol. 1, Ch. 9, and in Vol. 2, Ch. 3); but includes "promoting economic development," even if the property was taken and sold for development by private developers. Justice Stevens emphasized that courts should be deferential to the decisions of state and local authorities. Justice Kennedy cast the pivotal fifth vote and filed a concurring opinion, underscoring that courts should still exercise review in such cases in order to ensure that governments do not use their power of eminent domain to simply reward or advance the interests of businesses and powerful private interests. Justice O'Connor filed a dissenting opinion, which was joined by Chief Justice Rehnquist, and Justices Scalia and Thomas dissented. Justice Thomas also filed a dissenting opinion, criticizing the majority for departing from the "original intent" of the Fifth Amendment and warning that the decision would have an adverse impact on the poor and minorities living in inner cities, whose property could be condemned by the government and then sold to private developers.

Kelo v. City of New London, Connecticut
125 S.Ct. 2655 (2005)

The city of New London is at the junction of the Thames River and Long Island Sound in southeastern Connecticut. Decades of economic decline led the state in 1990 to designate the city a "distressed municipality." In 1996, the federal government closed the Naval Undersea Warfare Center, which had been located in the Fort Trumbull area of the city and had employed over 1,500 people. In 1998, the city's unemployment rate was nearly double that of the state, and its population of just under 24,000 residents was at its lowest since 1920. These conditions prompted state and local officials to target New London, and particularly its Fort Trumbull area, for economic revitalization. The New London Development Corporation (NLDC), a private nonprofit entity, was authorized to assist the city in planning economic development. In January 1998, Connecticut approved a $5.35 million bond issue to support the NLDC's planning activities and a $10 million bond issue for the creation of a Fort Trumbull State Park. In February, the pharmaceutical company Pfizer announced that it would build a $300 million research facility in the Fort Trumbull area, and the NLDC hoped that that would draw new business to the area. The Fort Trumbull area is on a peninsula that juts into the Thames River and includes approximately 115 privately owned properties, as well as the 32 acres of land formerly occupied by the naval facility. The NLDC's development plan called for the creation of a waterfront conference hotel at the center of a "small urban village," including restaurants and stores, as well as a pedestrian "riverwalk" that would continue down the coast, along with a new U.S. Coast Guard Museum, a renovated marina, and research and development office space. The NLDC's development plan aimed to capitalize on the arrival of the Pfizer facility and the new commerce it would attract. In addition to creating jobs and generating tax revenue, the plan sought to create recreational opportunities on the waterfront and in the park. The city council approved the plan in January 2000, and designated the NLDC its development agent. The city council also authorized the NLDC to purchase property or to acquire property by exercising eminent domain in the city's name. The NLDC successfully negotiated the purchase of most of the real estate in the 90-acre area, but its negotiations with some homeowners failed and the NLDC initiated the condemnation proceedings against them.

Susette Kelo lived in the Fort Trumbull area and had made extensive improvements to her well-maintained house, which overlooks the Thames River. In December 2000, Kelo and a few other homeowners of condemned property sued New London, claiming that the taking of their properties, even with just compensation, violated the "public use" restriction in the Fifth Amendment, because their properties would not be used for a public purpose, like building a road, but instead sold to private parties for development—development that the city claimed would economically benefit the community. A trial court granted a restraining order prohibiting New London's taking of some of the properties, but on appeal the state supreme court ruled that the city could take all of the properties. Kelo appealed that decision and the Supreme Court granted review.

The state supreme court's decision was affirmed by a five to four vote. Justice Stevens delivered the opinion of the Court. Justice Kennedy filed a concurring opinion. Justice O'Connor, joined by Chief Justice Rehnquist and Justices Scalia and Thomas, dissented. Justice Thomas also filed a dissenting opinion.

□ *Justice STEVENS delivered the opinion of the Court.*

We granted *certiorari* to determine whether a city's decision to take property for the purpose of economic development satisfies the "public use" requirement of the Fifth Amendment. Two polar propositions are perfectly clear. On the one hand, it has long been accepted that the sovereign may not take the property of A for the sole purpose of transferring it to another private party B, even though A is paid just compensation. On the other hand, it is equally clear that a State may transfer property from one private party to another if future "use by the public" is the purpose of the taking; the condemnation of land for a railroad with common-carrier duties is a familiar example. Neither of these propositions, however, determines the disposition of this case.

As for the first proposition, the City would no doubt be forbidden from taking petitioners' land for the purpose of conferring a private benefit on a particular private party. See [*Hawaii Housing Authority v.*] *Midkiff*, 467 U.S. [229 (1984)] ("A purely private taking could not withstand the scrutiny of the public use requirement; it would serve no legitimate purpose of government and would thus be void"). Nor would the City be allowed to take property under the mere pretext of a public purpose, when its actual purpose was to bestow a private benefit. The takings before us, however, would be executed pursuant to a "carefully considered" development plan. The trial judge and all the members of the Supreme Court of Connecticut agreed that there was no evidence of an illegitimate purpose in this case. Therefore, as was true of the statute challenged in *Midkiff*, the City's development plan was not adopted "to benefit a particular class of identifiable individuals."

On the other hand, this is not a case in which the City is planning to open the condemned land—at least not in its entirety—to use by the general public. Nor will the private lessees of the land in any sense be required to operate like common carriers, making their services available to all comers. But although such a projected use would be sufficient to satisfy the public use requirement, this "Court long ago rejected any literal requirement that condemned property be put into use for the general public." Indeed, while many state courts in the mid-19th century endorsed "use by the public" as the proper definition of public use, that narrow view steadily eroded over time. Not only was the "use by the public" test difficult to administer (e.g., what proportion of the public need have access to the property? at what price?), but it proved to be impractical given the diverse and always evolving needs of society. Accordingly, when this Court began applying the Fifth Amendment to the States at the close of the 19th century, it embraced the broader and more natural interpretation of public use as "public purpose." Thus, in a case upholding a mining company's use of an aerial bucket line to transport ore over property it did not own, Justice HOLMES' opinion for the Court stressed "the inadequacy of use by the general public as a universal test." *Strickley v. Highland Boy Gold Mining Co.*, 200 U.S. 527 (1906). We have repeatedly and consistently rejected that narrow test ever since.

The disposition of this case therefore turns on the question whether the City's development plan serves a "public purpose." Without exception, our cases have defined that concept broadly, reflecting our longstanding policy of deference to legislative judgments in this field.

In *Berman v. Parker*, 348 U.S. 26 (1954), this Court upheld a redevelopment plan targeting a blighted area of Washington, D.C., in which most of the housing for the area's 5,000 inhabitants was beyond repair. Under the plan, the area would be condemned and part of it utilized for the construction of streets, schools, and other public facilities. The remainder of the land would be leased or sold to private parties for the purpose of redevelopment, including the construction of low-cost housing.

The owner of a department store located in the area challenged the condemnation, pointing out that his store was not itself blighted and arguing that the creation of a "better balanced, more attractive community" was not a valid public use. Writing for a unanimous Court, Justice DOUGLAS refused to evaluate this claim in isolation, deferring instead to the legislative and agency judgment that the area "must be planned as a whole" for the plan to be successful. The Court explained that "community redevelopment programs need not, by force of the Constitution, be on a piecemeal basis—lot by lot, building by building." The public use underlying the taking was unequivocally affirmed: "We do not sit to determine whether a particular housing project is or is not desirable. The concept of the public welfare is broad and inclusive. . . . The values it represents are spiritual as well as physical, aesthetic as well as monetary. It is within the power of the legislature to determine that the community should be beautiful as well as healthy, spacious as well as clean, well-balanced as well as carefully patrolled. In the present case, the Congress and its authorized agencies have made determinations that take into account a wide variety of values. It is not for us to reappraise them. If those who govern the District of Columbia decide that the Nation's Capital should be beautiful as well as sanitary, there is nothing in the Fifth Amendment that stands in the way."

In *Hawaii Housing Authority v. Midkiff*, the Court considered a Hawaii statute whereby fee title was taken from lessors and transferred to lessees (for just compensation) in order to reduce the concentration of land ownership. We unanimously upheld the statute and rejected the Ninth Circuit's view that it was "a naked attempt on the part of the state of Hawaii to take the property of A and transfer it to B solely for B's private use and benefit." Reaffirming *Berman's* deferential approach to legislative judgments in this field, we concluded that the State's purpose of eliminating the "social and economic evils of a land oligopoly" qualified as a valid public use. Our opinion also rejected the contention that the mere fact that the State immediately transferred the properties to private individuals upon condemnation somehow diminished the public character of the taking. . . .

Those who govern the City were not confronted with the need to remove blight in the Fort Trumbull area, but their determination that the area was sufficiently distressed to justify a program of economic rejuvenation is entitled to our deference. The City has carefully formulated an economic development plan that it believes will provide appreciable benefits to the community, including—but by no means limited to—new jobs and increased tax revenue. As with other exercises in urban planning and development, the City is endeavoring to coordinate a variety of commercial, residential, and recreational uses of land, with the hope that they will form a whole greater than the sum of its parts. To effectuate this plan, the City has invoked a state statute that specifically authorizes the use of eminent domain to promote economic development. . . . Because that plan unquestionably serves a public purpose, the takings challenged here satisfy the public use requirement of the Fifth Amendment.

To avoid this result, petitioners urge us to adopt a new bright-line rule that economic development does not qualify as a public use. Putting aside the unpersuasive suggestion that the City's plan will provide only purely economic benefits, neither precedent nor logic supports petitioners' proposal. Promoting economic development is a traditional and long accepted function of government. There is, moreover, no principled way of distinguishing economic development from the other public purposes that we have recognized. . . .

Petitioners contend that using eminent domain for economic development impermissibly blurs the boundary between public and private takings. Again, our cases foreclose this objection. Quite simply, the government's pursuit of a public purpose will often benefit individual private parties. For example, in *Midkiff*, the forced transfer of property conferred a direct and significant benefit on those lessees who were previously unable to purchase their homes. . . .

It is further argued that without a bright-line rule nothing would stop a city from transferring citizen A's property to citizen B for the sole reason that citizen B will put the property to a more productive use and thus pay more taxes. Such a one-to-one transfer of property, executed outside the confines of an integrated development plan, is not presented in this case. While such an unusual exercise of government power would certainly raise a suspicion that a private purpose was afoot, the hypothetical cases posited by petitioners can be confronted if and when they arise. They do not warrant the crafting of an artificial restriction on the concept of public use.

Alternatively, petitioners maintain that for takings of this kind we should require a "reasonable certainty" that the expected public benefits will actually accrue. Such a rule, however, would represent an even greater departure from our precedent. "When the legislature's purpose is legitimate and its means are not irrational, our cases make clear that empirical debates over the wisdom of takings—no less than debates over the wisdom of other kinds of socioeconomic legislation—are not to be carried out in the federal courts." *Midkiff*. . . .

Just as we decline to second-guess the City's considered judgments about the efficacy of its development plan, we also decline to second-guess the City's determinations as to what lands it needs to acquire in order to effectuate the project. "It is not for the courts to oversee the choice of the boundary line nor to sit in review on the size of a particular project area. Once the question of the public purpose has been decided, the amount and character of land to be taken for the project and the need for a particular tract to complete the integrated plan rests in the discretion of the legislative branch."

In affirming the City's authority to take petitioners' properties, we do not minimize the hardship that condemnations may entail, notwithstanding the payment of just compensation. We emphasize that nothing in our opinion precludes any State from placing further restrictions on its exercise of the takings power. Indeed, many States already impose "public use" requirements that are stricter than the federal baseline. Some of these requirements have been established as a matter of state constitutional law, while others are expressed in state eminent domain statutes that carefully limit the grounds upon which takings may be exercised....

The judgment of the Supreme Court of Connecticut is affirmed.

☐ *Justice KENNEDY, concurring.*

I join the opinion for the Court and add these further observations. This Court has declared that a taking should be upheld as consistent with the Public Use Clause, U.S. Const., Amdt. 5., as long as it is "rationally related to a conceivable public purpose." *Hawaii Housing Authority v. Midkiff*; see also *Berman v. Parker*, 348 U.S. 26 (1954). This deferential standard of review echoes the rational-basis test used to review economic regulation under the Due Process and Equal Protection Clauses. The determination that a rational-basis standard of review is appropriate does not, however, alter the fact that transfers intended to confer benefits on particular, favored private entities, and with only incidental or pretextual public benefits, are forbidden by the Public Use Clause.

A court applying rational-basis review under the Public Use Clause should strike down a taking that, by a clear showing, is intended to favor a particular private party, with only incidental or pretextual public benefits, just as a court applying rational-basis review under the Equal Protection Clause must strike down a government classification that is clearly intended to injure a particular class of private parties, with only incidental or pretextual public justifications. See *Cleburne v. Cleburne Living Center, Inc.*, 473 U.S. 432 (1985). As the trial court in this case was correct to observe, "Where the purpose [of a taking] is economic development and that development is to be carried out by private parties or private parties will be benefited, the court must decide if the stated public purpose—economic advantage to a city sorely in need of it—is only incidental to the benefits that will be confined on private parties of a development plan."

A court confronted with a plausible accusation of impermissible favoritism to private parties should treat the objection as a serious one and review the record to see if it has merit, though with the presumption that the government's actions were reasonable and intended to serve a public purpose. Here, the trial court conducted a careful and extensive inquiry into "whether, in fact, the development plan is of primary benefit to ... the developer, and private businesses which may eventually locate in the plan area, and in that regard, only of incidental benefit to the city." The trial court considered testimony from government officials and corporate officers; documentary evidence of communications between these parties; respondents' awareness of New London's depressed economic condition and evidence corroborating the validity of this concern; the substantial commitment of public funds by the State to the development project before most of the private beneficiaries were known; evidence that respondents reviewed a variety of development plans and chose a private developer from a group of applicants rather than picking out a particular transferee beforehand; and the fact that the other private beneficiaries of the project are still unknown because the office space proposed to be built has not yet been rented. The trial court concluded, based on these findings, that benefiting Pfizer was not "the primary motivation or effect of this development plan"; instead, "the primary motivation for [respondents] was to take advantage of Pfizer's presence." Likewise, the trial court concluded that "[t]here is nothing in the record to indicate that . . . [respondents] were motivated by a desire to aid [other] particular private entities." . . .

My agreement with the Court that a presumption of invalidity is not warranted for economic development takings in general, or for the particular takings at issue in this case, does not foreclose the possibility that a more stringent standard of review than that announced in *Berman* and *Midkiff* might be appropriate for a more narrowly drawn category of takings. There may be private transfers in which the risk of undetected impermissible favoritism of private parties is so acute that a presumption (rebuttable or otherwise) of invalidity is warranted under the Public Use Clause. This demanding level of scrutiny, however, is not required simply because the purpose of the taking is economic development.

This is not the occasion for conjecture as to what sort of cases might justify a more demanding standard, but it is appropriate to underscore aspects of the instant case that convince me no departure from *Berman* and *Midkiff* is appropriate here. This taking occurred in the context of a comprehensive development plan meant to address a serious city-wide depression, and the projected economic benefits of the project cannot be characterized as *de minimus*. The identity of most of the private beneficiaries were unknown at the time the city formulated its plans. The city complied with elaborate procedural requirements that facilitate review of the record and inquiry into the city's purposes. In sum, while there may be categories of cases in which the transfers are so suspicious, or the procedures employed so prone to abuse, or the purported benefits are so trivial or implausible, that courts should presume an impermissible private purpose, no such circumstances are present in this case.

☐ *Justice O'CONNOR, with whom THE CHIEF JUSTICE, Justice SCALIA, and Justice THOMAS join, dissenting.*

Over two centuries ago, just after the Bill of Rights was ratified, Justice CHASE wrote: "An act of the Legislature (for I cannot call it a law) contrary to the great first principles of the social compact, cannot be considered a rightful exercise of legislative authority . . . . A few instances will suffice to explain what I mean . . . . [A] law that takes property from A. and gives it to B: It is against all reason and justice, for a people to entrust a Legislature with such powers; and, therefore, it cannot be presumed that they have done it." *Calder v. Bull*, 3 Dall. 386 (1798). Today the Court abandons this long-held, basic limitation on government power. Under the banner of economic development, all private property is now vulnerable to being taken and transferred to another private owner, so long as it might be upgraded—i.e., given to an owner who will use it in a way that the legislature deems more beneficial to the public—in the process. To reason, as the Court does, that the incidental public benefits resulting from the subsequent ordinary use of private property render economic development takings "for public use" is to wash out any distinction between private and public use of property—and thereby effectively to delete the words "for public use" from the Takings Clause of the Fifth Amendment. Accordingly I respectfully dissent. . . .

[W]e have read the Fifth Amendment's language to impose two distinct conditions on the exercise of eminent domain: "the taking must be for a 'public use' and 'just compensation' must be paid to the owner." *Brown v. Legal Foundation of Wash.*, 538 U.S. 216 (2003). These two limitations serve to protect "the security of Property," which Alexander Hamilton described to the Philadelphia Convention as one of the "great obj[ects] of Gov[ernment]." Together they ensure stable property ownership by providing safeguards against excessive, unpredictable, or unfair use of the government's eminent domain power—particularly against those owners who, for whatever reasons, may be unable to protect themselves in the political process against the majority's will.

While the Takings Clause presupposes that government can take private property without the owner's consent, the just compensation requirement spreads the cost of condemnations and thus "prevents the public from loading upon one individual more than his just share of the burdens of government." *Monongahela Nav. Co. v. United States*, 148 U.S. 312 (1893). The public use requirement, in turn, imposes a more basic limitation, circumscribing the very scope of the eminent domain power: Government may compel an individual to forfeit her property for the public's use, but not for the benefit of another private person. This requirement promotes fairness as well as security.

Where is the line between "public" and "private" property use? We give considerable deference to legislatures' determinations about what governmental activities will advantage the public. But were the political branches the sole arbiters of the public-private distinction, the Public Use Clause would amount to little more than hortatory fluff. An external, judicial check on how the public use requirement is interpreted, however limited, is necessary if this constraint on government power is to retain any meaning.

Our cases have generally identified three categories of takings that comply with the public use requirement, though it is in the nature of things that the boundaries between these categories are not always firm. Two are relatively straightforward and uncontroversial. First, the sovereign may transfer private property to public ownership—such as for a road, a hospital, or a military base. Second, the sovereign may transfer private property to private parties, often common carriers, who make the property available for the public's use—such as with a railroad, a public utility, or a stadium. But "public ownership" and "use-by-the-public" are sometimes too constricting and impractical ways to define the scope of the Public Use Clause. Thus we have allowed that, in certain circumstances and to meet certain exigencies, takings that serve a public purpose also satisfy the Constitution even if the property is destined for subsequent private use.

This case returns us for the first time in over 20 years to the hard question of when a purportedly "public purpose" taking meets the public use requirement. It presents an issue of first impression: Are economic development takings constitutional? I would hold that they are not. We are guided by two precedents about the taking of real property by eminent domain. In

Berman, we upheld takings within a blighted neighborhood of Washington, D.C. The neighborhood had so deteriorated that, for example, 64.3% of its dwellings were beyond repair....

In *Midkiff*, we upheld a land condemnation scheme in Hawaii whereby title in real property was taken from lessors and transferred to lessees. At that time, the State and Federal Governments owned nearly 49% of the State's land, and another 47% was in the hands of only 72 private landowners. Concentration of land ownership was so dramatic that on the State's most urbanized island, Oahu, 22 landowners owned 72.5% of the fee simple titles. The Hawaii Legislature had concluded that the oligopoly in land ownership was "skewing the State's residential fee simple market, inflating land prices, and injuring the public tranquility and welfare," and therefore enacted a condemnation scheme for redistributing title.

In those decisions, we emphasized the importance of deferring to legislative judgments about public purpose. Because courts are ill-equipped to evaluate the efficacy of proposed legislative initiatives, we rejected as unworkable the idea of courts'"'deciding on what is and is not a governmental function and ... invalidating legislation on the basis of their view on that question at the moment of decision, a practice which has proved impracticable in other fields.'" Likewise, we recognized our inability to evaluate whether, in a given case, eminent domain is a necessary means by which to pursue the legislature's ends.

Yet for all the emphasis on deference, *Berman* and *Midkiff* hewed to a bedrock principle without which our public use jurisprudence would collapse: "A purely private taking could not withstand the scrutiny of the public use requirement; it would serve no legitimate purpose of government and would thus be void." *Midkiff*. To protect that principle, those decisions reserved "a role for courts to play in reviewing a legislature's judgment of what constitutes a public use ... [though] the Court in *Berman* made clear that it is 'an extremely narrow' one."

The Court's holdings in *Berman* and *Midkiff* were true to the principle underlying the Public Use Clause. In both those cases, the extraordinary, precondemnation use of the targeted property inflicted affirmative harm on society—in *Berman* through blight resulting from extreme poverty and in *Midkiff* through oligopoly resulting from extreme wealth. And in both cases, the relevant legislative body had found that eliminating the existing property use was necessary to remedy the harm. Thus a public purpose was realized when the harmful use was eliminated. Because each taking directly achieved a public benefit, it did not matter that the property was turned over to private use. Here, in contrast, New London does not claim that Susette Kelo's ... well-maintained [home is] the source of any social harm. Indeed, it could not so claim without adopting the absurd argument that any single-family home that might be razed to make way for an apartment building, or any church that might be replaced with a retail store, or any small business that might be more lucrative if it were instead part of a national franchise, is inherently harmful to society and thus within the government's power to condemn.

In moving away from our decisions sanctioning the condemnation of harmful property use, the Court today significantly expands the meaning of public use. It holds that the sovereign may take private property currently put to ordinary private use, and give it over for new, ordinary private use, so long as the new use is predicted to generate some secondary benefit for the public— such as increased tax revenue, more jobs, maybe even aesthetic pleasure. But nearly any lawful use of real private property can be said to generate some incidental benefit to the public. Thus, if predicted (or even guaranteed) positive side-effects are enough to render transfer from one private party to another constitutional, then the words "for public use" do not realistically exclude any takings, and thus do not exert any constraint on the eminent domain power....

It was possible after *Berman* and *Midkiff* to imagine unconstitutional transfers from A to B. Those decisions endorsed government intervention when private property use had veered to such an extreme that the public was suffering as a consequence. Today nearly all real property is susceptible to condemnation on the Court's theory. Any property may now be taken for the benefit of another private party, but the fallout from this decision will not be random. The beneficiaries are likely to be those citizens with disproportionate influence and power in the political process, including large corporations and development firms. As for the victims, the government now has license to transfer property from those with fewer resources to those with more....

☐ *Justice THOMAS, dissenting.*

Long ago, William Blackstone wrote that "the law of the land ... postpone[s] even public necessity to the sacred and inviolable rights of private property." *Commentaries on the Laws of England* (1765). The Framers embodied that principle in the Constitution, allowing the government to take property not for "public necessity," but instead for "public use." Amdt. 5. Defying this understanding, the Court replaces the Public Use Clause with a "'[P]ublic [P]urpose'" Clause, a restriction that is satisfied, the Court instructs, so long as the purpose is "legitimate" and the means "not irrational." This deferential shift in phraseology enables the Court to hold, against all common sense, that a costly urban-renewal project whose stated purpose is a vague promise of new jobs and increased tax revenue, but which is also suspiciously agreeable to the Pfizer Corporation, is for a "public use."

I cannot agree. If such "economic development" takings are for a "public use," any taking is, and the Court has erased the Public Use Clause from our Constitution, as Justice O'CONNOR powerfully argues in dissent. I do not believe that this Court can eliminate liberties expressly enumerated in the Constitution and therefore join her dissenting opinion. Regrettably, however, the Court's error runs deeper than this. Today's decision is simply the latest in a string of our cases construing the Public Use Clause to be a virtual nullity, without the slightest nod to its original meaning. In my view, the Public Use Clause, originally understood, is a meaningful limit on the government's eminent domain power. Our cases have strayed from the Clause's original meaning, and I would reconsider them....

The consequences of today's decision are not difficult to predict, and promise to be harmful. So-called "urban renewal" programs provide some compensation for the properties they take, but no compensation is possible for the subjective value of these lands to the individuals displaced and the indignity inflicted by uprooting them from their homes. Allowing the government to take property solely for public purposes is bad enough, but extending the concept of public purpose to encompass any economically beneficial goal guarantees that these losses will fall disproportionately on poor communities. Those communities are not only systematically less likely to put their lands to the highest and best social use, but are also the least politically powerful. If ever there were justification for intrusive judicial review of constitutional provisions that protect "discrete and insular minorities," *United States v. Carolene Products Co.*, 304 U.S. 144 (1938), surely that principle would apply with great force to the powerless groups and individuals the Public Use Clause protects. The deferential standard this Court has adopted for the Public Use Clause is therefore deeply perverse. It encourages "those citizens with disproportionate influence and power in the political process, including large corporations and development firms" to victimize the weak.

Those incentives have made the legacy of this Court's "public purpose" test an unhappy one. In the 1950's, no doubt emboldened in part by the expansive understanding of "public use" this Court adopted in *Berman*, cities "rushed to draw plans" for downtown development. "Of all the families displaced by urban renewal from 1949 through 1963, 63 percent of those whose race was known were nonwhite, and of these families, 56 percent of nonwhites and 38 percent of whites had incomes low enough to qualify for public housing, which, however, was seldom available to them." Public works projects in the 1950's and 1960's destroyed predominantly minority communities in St. Paul, Minnesota, and Baltimore, Maryland. In 1981, urban planners in Detroit, Michigan, uprooted the largely "lower-income and elderly" Poletown neighborhood for the benefit of the General Motors Corporation. Urban renewal projects have long been associated with the displacement of blacks; "[i]n cities across the country, urban renewal came to be known as 'Negro removal.'" Over 97 percent of the individuals forcibly removed from their homes by the "slum-clearance" project upheld by this Court in *Berman* were black. Regrettably, the predictable consequence of the Court's decision will be to exacerbate these effects....

■ THE DEVELOPMENT OF LAW

Other Important Rulings on the Takings Clause

CASE	VOTE	RULING
Lingle v. Chevron, 544 U.S. 528 (2005)	9:0	Writing for a unanimous Court, Justice O'Connor upheld Hawaii's law capping the rent paid by gasoline dealers and ruled that it was not an unconstitutional takings. The appellate court had applied a test, suggested in *Agins v. City of Tiburon*, 447 U.S. 255 (1980), that "[t]he application of a general zoning law to particular property effects a takings if the ordinance does not substantially advance state interests." But Justice O'Connor ruled that the "substantially advance state interests" test was *dictum* and inappropriate for determining when a takings of private property occurs. Instead, as other precedents established, in particular *Penn Central Transportation Co. v. New York*, 438 U.S. 104 (1978), a multi-factored and more deferential test should apply because taxes and fees, like that at issue here, are not per se takings.

Supreme Court Watch 2006
Volume Two

4

THE NATIONALIZATION OF THE BILL OF RIGHTS

B | *The Rise and (Partial) Retreat of the "Due Process Revolution"*

In its 2006–2007 term, the Court will once again revisit the complicated issue of when large punitive damage awards violate the due process clause. In *BMW v. Gore* (1996) (excerpted in Vol. 2, Ch. 4), the Court held that excessive damage awards run afoul of due process. More recently, *State Farm Mutual Automobile Insurance v. Campbell*, 538 U.S. 408 (2003), held that damage awards exceeding a nine to one ratio are constitutionally suspect. In *Phillip Morris USA v. Williams* (No. 05-1256) the Court will consider whether a $79.5 million award to the family of a smoker who died against Phillip Morris was excessive. The Oregon state supreme court had ruled that the award did not violate the Fourteenth Amendment's guarantee of due process.

■ The Development of Law
Other Recent Rulings on Substantive and Procedural Due Process

CASE	VOTE	RULING
Deck v. Mississippi, 544 U.S. 622 (2005)	7:2	Writing for the Court, Justice Breyer held that the shackling of a defendant during the sentencing phase of a capital trial is inherently prejudicial and runs afoul of the Fifth and Fourteenth Amendments, unless the use of visible shackles is justified by an "essential state interest." Justices Scalia and Thomas dissented.
Town of Castle Rock v. Gonzales, 125 S.Ct. 2796 (2005)	7:2	Writing for the Court, Justice Scalia ruled that Due Process Clauses do not protect everything deemed to be a government "benefit." Jessica Gonzales filed a suit for damages because the town's police failed to enforce a court-ordered restraining order against her estranged husband, who took her three children in violation of the order and murdered them. Under Colorado law, police are required to enforce restraining orders and thus Gonzales argued that that was an entitlement and government benefit. In rejecting that claim, Justice Scalia observed: "The procedural component of the Due Process Clause does not protect everything that might be described as a 'benefit,'" and reaffirmed the holding in *Board of Regents of State Colleges v. Roth,* 408 U.S. (1972) that "To have a property interest in a benefit, a person clearly must have more than an abstract need or desire" and "more than a unilateral expectation of it. He must, instead, have a legitimate claim of entitlement to it." Justice Souter concurred and Justices Stevens and Ginsburg dissented.
Jones v. Flowers, 126 S.Ct. 1708 (2006)	5:3	Writing for the Court, Chief Justice Roberts held that Arkansas violated the Fourteenth Amendment due process clause in selling private property after a notice to the property owner was returned unclaimed and then took no further steps to notify the owner of the forfeiture. Justice Thomas dissented and was joined by Justices Scalia and Kennedy.

5

FREEDOM OF EXPRESSION AND ASSOCIATION

In 2006 the Court ruled on the constitutionality of the so-called Solomon Amendment, a federal law requiring the cutoff of federal funding to colleges and universities that refuse to permit the military access to recruit their students, because of the Amerian Law Schools' policy of nondiscrimination against sexual orientation, in *Rumsfeld v. Forum for Academic and Institutional Rights* (excerpted beow).

Rumsfeld v. Forum for Academic and Institutional Rights
126 S.Ct. 327 (2006)

Since 1991 the Association of American Law Schools required adherence to a policy of nondiscrimination on sexual orientation as a condition if membership in accredited law schools. As a result, law schools denied the military to recruit students due to its "don't ask, don't tell" policy. In response, in 2004 the so-called Solomon Amendment to an appropriations bill required access for military recruiters "that is at least equal in quality and scope" to other employers, and if not the forfeiture of federal funding from eight agencies including the Departments of Defense, Education, and Health and Human Services. A group of law schools, the Forum for Academic and Institutional Rights (FAIR), in turn challenged the constitutionality of the requirement. A federal district court rejected FAIR's challenge, but the U.S. Court of Appeals for the Third Circuit reversed and held that the requirement was unconstitutional. That decision was appealed to the Supreme Court, which granted review.

The appellate court's decision was reversed by a unanimous vote, with Justice Alito not participating. Chief Justice Roberts delivered the opinion of the Court.

☐ *CHIEF JUSTICE ROBERTS delivered the opinion of the Court.*

FAIR members have adopted policies expressing their opposition to discrimination based on, among other factors, sexual orientation. They would like to restrict military recruiting on their campuses because they object to the policy Congress has adopted with respect to homosexuals in the military. The Solomon Amendment, however, forces institutions to choose between enforcing their nondiscrimination policy against military recruiters in this way and continuing to receive specified federal funding.

In 2003, FAIR sought a preliminary injunction against enforcement of the Solomon Amendment, which at that time—it has since been amended—prevented the Department of Defense (DOD) from providing specified federal funds to any institution of higher education "that either prohibits, or in effect prevents" military recruiters "from gaining entry to campuses." FAIR considered the DOD's interpretation of this provision particularly objectionable. Although the statute required only "entry to campuses," the Government—after the terrorist attacks on September 11, 2001—adopted an informal policy of "'requir[ing] universities to provide military recruiters access to students equal in quality and scope to that provided to other recruiters.'" Prior to the adoption of this policy, some law schools sought to promote their nondiscrimination policies while still complying with the Solomon Amendment by having military recruiters interview on the undergraduate campus. But under the equal access policy, military recruiters had to be permitted to interview at the law schools, if other recruiters did so.

FAIR argued that this forced inclusion and equal treatment of military recruiters violated the law schools' First Amendment freedoms of speech and association. According to FAIR, the Solomon Amendment was unconstitutional because it forced law schools to choose between exercising their First Amendment right to decide whether to disseminate or accommodate a military recruiter's message, and ensuring the availability of federal funding for their universities....

We think it appropriate in the present case to consider whether institutions can comply with the Solomon Amendment by applying a general nondiscrimination policy to exclude military recruiters.

We conclude that they cannot and that the Government and FAIR correctly interpret the Solomon Amendment. The statute requires the Secretary of Defense to compare the military's "access to campuses" and "access to students" to "the access to campuses and to students that is provided to any other employer." The statute does not call for an inquiry into why or how the "other employer" secured its access.... We do not think that the military recruiter has received equal "access" in this situation—regardless of whether the disparate treatment is attributable to the military's failure to comply with the school's nondiscrimination policy.

The Solomon Amendment does not focus on the content of a school's recruiting policy.... Instead, it looks to the result achieved by the policy and compares the "access ... provided" military recruiters to that provided other recruiters. Applying the same policy to all recruiters is therefore insufficient to comply with the statute if it results in a greater level of access for other recruiters than for the military. Law schools must ensure that their recruiting policy operates in such a way that military recruiters are given access to students at least equal to that "provided to any other employer."

We therefore read the Solomon Amendment the way both the Government and FAIR interpret it. It is insufficient for a law school to treat the military as it treats all other employers who violate its nondiscrimination policy. Under the statute, military recruiters must be given the same access as recruiters who comply with the policy.

The Constitution grants Congress the power to "provide for the common Defense," "[t]o raise and support Armies," and "[t]o provide and maintain a Navy." Art. I, Sec. 8, cls. 1, 12–13. Congress' power in this area "is broad and sweeping," and there is no dispute in this case that it includes the authority to require campus access for military recruiters. That is, of course, unless Congress exceeds constitutional limitations on its power in enacting such legislation.

Although Congress has broad authority to legislate on matters of military recruiting, it nonetheless chose to secure campus access for military recruiters indirectly, through its Spending Clause power. The Solomon Amendment gives universities a choice: Either allow military recruiters the same access to students afforded any other recruiter or forgo certain federal funds. Congress' decision to proceed indirectly does not reduce the deference given to Congress in the area of military affairs. Congress' choice to promote its goal by creating a funding condition deserves at least as deferential treatment as if Congress had imposed a mandate on universities.

Congress' power to regulate military recruiting under the Solomon Amendment is arguably greater because universities are free to decline the federal funds....

The Solomon Amendment neither limits what law schools may say nor requires them to say anything. Law schools remain free under the statute to express whatever views they may have on the military's congressionally mandated employment policy, all the while retaining eligibility for federal funds. As a general matter, the Solomon Amendment regulates conduct, not speech. It affects what law schools must do—afford equal access to military recruiters—not what they may or may not say....

Some of this Court's leading First Amendment precedents have established the principle that freedom of speech prohibits the government from telling people what they must say. In *West Virginia Bd. of Ed. v. Barnette*, 319 U.S. 624 (1943), we held unconstitutional a state law requiring schoolchildren to recite the Pledge of Allegiance and to salute the flag. And in *Wooley v. Maynard*, 430 U.S. 705 (1977), we held unconstitutional another that required New Hampshire motorists to display the state motto—"Live Free or Die"—on their license plates.

The Solomon Amendment does not require any similar expression by law schools. Nonetheless, recruiting assistance provided by the schools often includes elements of speech. For example, schools may send e-mails or post notices on bulletin boards on an employer's behalf. Law schools offering such services to other recruiters must also send e-mails and post notices on behalf of the military to comply with the Solomon Amendment. As FAIR points out, these compelled statements of fact, like compelled statements of opinion, are subject to First Amendment scrutiny.

This sort of recruiting assistance, however, is a far cry from the compelled speech in *Barnette* and *Wooley*. The Solomon Amendment, unlike the laws at issue in those cases, does not dictate the content of the speech at all, which is only "compelled" if, and to the extent, the school provides such speech for other recruiters. There is nothing in this case approaching a Government-mandated pledge or motto that the school must endorse.

The compelled speech to which the law schools point is plainly incidental to the Solomon Amendment's regulation of conduct, and "it has never been deemed an abridgment of freedom of speech or press to make a course of conduct illegal merely because the conduct was in part initiated, evidenced, or carried out by means of language, either spoken, written, or printed." Congress, for example, can prohibit employers from discriminating in hiring on the basis of race. The fact that this will require an employer to take down a sign reading "White Applicants Only" hardly means that the law should be analyzed as one regulating the employer's speech rather than conduct. See *R. A. V. v. St. Paul*, 505 U.S. 377 (1992). Compelling a law school that sends scheduling e-mails for other recruiters to send one for a military recruiter is simply not the same as forcing a student to pledge allegiance, or forcing a Jehovah's Witness to display the motto "Live Free or Die," and it trivializes the freedom protected in *Barnette* and *Wooley* to suggest that it is.

Our compelled-speech cases are not limited to the situation in which an individual must personally speak the government's message. We have also in a number of instances limited the government's ability to force one speaker to host or accommodate another speaker's message. See *Hurley v. Irish-American Gay, Lesbian and Bisexual Group of Boston, Inc.*, 515 U.S. 557 (1995). . . .

The compelled-speech violation in each of our prior cases, however, resulted from the fact that the complaining speaker's own message was affected by the speech it was forced to accommodate. The expressive nature of a parade was central to our holding in *Hurley*. We concluded that because "every participating unit affects the message conveyed by the [parade's] private organizers," a law dictating that a particular group must be included in the parade "alter[s] the expressive content of th[e] parade." As a result, we held that the State's public accommodation law, as applied to a private parade, "violates the fundamental rule of protection under the First Amendment, that a speaker has the autonomy to choose the content of his own message." . . .

In this case, accommodating the military's message does not affect the law schools' speech, because the schools are not speaking when they host interviews and recruiting receptions. Unlike a parade organizer's choice of parade contingents, a law school's decision to allow recruiters on campus is not inherently expressive. Law schools facilitate recruiting to assist their students in obtaining jobs. A law school's recruiting services lack the expressive quality of a parade, a newsletter, or the editorial page of a newspaper; its accommodation of a military recruiter's message is not compelled speech because the accommodation does not sufficiently interfere with any message of the school.

The schools respond that if they treat military and nonmilitary recruiters alike in order to comply with the Solomon Amendment, they could be viewed as sending the message that they see nothing wrong with the military's policies, when they do. We rejected a similar argument in *PruneYard Shopping Center v. Robins*, 447 U.S. 74 (1980). In that case, we upheld a state law requiring a shopping center owner to allow certain expressive activities by others on its property. We explained that there was little likelihood that the views of those engaging in the expressive activities would be identified with the owner, who remained free to disassociate himself from those views and who was "not . . . being compelled to affirm [a] belief in any governmentally prescribed position or view."

The same is true here. Nothing about recruiting suggests that law schools agree with any speech by recruiters, and nothing in the Solomon Amendment restricts what the law schools may say about the military's policies. We have held that high school students can appreciate the difference between speech a school sponsors and speech the school permits because legally required to do so, pursuant to an equal access policy. *Board of Ed. of Westside Community Schools (Dist. 66) v. Mergens*, 496 U.S. 226 (1990). Surely students have not lost that ability by the time they get to law school.

Having rejected the view that the Solomon Amendment impermissibly regulates speech, we must still consider whether the expressive nature of the conduct regulated by the statute brings that conduct within the First Amendment's protection. . . .

Unlike flag burning, the conduct regulated by the Solomon Amendment is not inherently expressive. Prior to the adoption of the Solomon Amendment's equal-access requirement, law schools "expressed" their disagreement with the military by treating military recruiters differently from other recruiters. But these actions were expressive only because the law schools accompanied their conduct with speech explaining it. For example, the point of requiring military interviews to be conducted on the undergraduate campus is not "overwhelmingly apparent." An observer who sees military recruiters interviewing away from the law school has no way of knowing whether the law school is expressing its disapproval of the military, all the law school's interview rooms are full, or the military recruiters decided for reasons of their own that they would rather interview someplace else.

The expressive component of a law school's actions is not created by the conduct itself but by the speech that accompanies it. The fact that such explanatory speech is necessary is strong evidence that the conduct at issue here is not so inherently expressive that it warrants protection. . . .

The Solomon Amendment does not violate law schools' freedom of speech, but the First Amendment's protection extends beyond the right to speak. We have recognized a First Amendment right to associate for the purpose of speaking, which we have termed a "right of expressive association." See *Boy Scouts of America v. Dale*, 530 U.S. 640 (2000). The reason we have extended First Amendment protection in this way is clear: The right to speak is often exercised most effectively by combining one's voice with the voices of others. If the government were free to restrict individuals' ability to join together and speak, it could essentially silence views that the First Amendment is intended to protect.

FAIR argues that the Solomon Amendment violates law schools' freedom of expressive association. According to FAIR, law schools' ability to express their message that discrimination on the basis of sexual orientation is wrong is significantly affected by the presence of military recruiters on campus and the schools' obligation to assist them.

In *Dale*, we held that the Boy Scouts' freedom of expressive association was violated by New Jersey's public accommodations law, which required the organization to accept a homosexual as a scoutmaster. After determining that the Boy Scouts was an expressive association, that "the forced inclusion of *Dale* would significantly affect its expression," and that the State's interests did not justify this intrusion, we concluded that the Boy Scout's First Amendment rights were violated.

The Solomon Amendment, however, does not similarly affect a law school's associational rights. To comply with the statute, law schools must allow military recruiters on campus and assist them in whatever way the school chooses to assist other employers. Law schools therefore "associate" with military recruiters in the sense that they interact with them. But recruiters are not part of the law school. Recruiters are, by definition, outsiders who come onto campus for the limited purpose of trying to hire students—not to become members of the school's expressive association. This distinction is critical. Unlike the public accommodations law in *Dale*, the Solomon Amendment does not force a law school "'to accept members it does not desire.'" The law schools say that allowing military recruiters equal access impairs their own expression by requiring them to associate with the recruiters, but just as saying conduct is undertaken for expressive purposes cannot make it symbolic speech, so too a speaker cannot "erect a shield" against laws requiring access "simply by asserting" that mere association "would impair its message." . . .

Because Congress could require law schools to provide equal access to military recruiters without violating the schools' freedoms of speech or association, the Court of Appeals erred in holding that the Solomon Amendment likely violates the First Amendment. We therefore reverse the judgment of the Third Circuit and remand the case for further proceedings consistent with this opinion. It is so ordered.

C | *Libel*

■ IN COMPARATIVE PERSPECTIVE
Blasphemy and Other Hate Speech

A major controversy erupted in 2005–2006 when the Danish newspaper *Jyllands-Posten* published twelve cartoons depicting the Islamic Prophet Muhammad, including one with a bomb under his turban. As the cartoons were reprinted in other European newspapers and circulated on the Internet, the controversy grew, particularly in Muslim countries. Riots broke out in Pakistan and the Danish and Norwegian embassies in Syria were burned, as well as the Danish General Consulate in Beirut, Lebanon.

In Denmark, blasphemy—the defamation of the name of God—remains a crime, but has been unenforced since 1938. By contrast, Pakistan has one of the harshest blasphemy laws, punishing "defiling the Holy Qu'ran" with life imprisonment. Other countries with blasphemy laws, though infrequently enforced, include Austria, Finland, Germany, Ireland, Italy, the Netherlands, Spain, Switzerland, and the United Kingdom. In 2006, for instance, a German court convicted Manfred von H. (whose full name was not released) for sending to mosques and the media rolls of toilet paper on which had stamped "Qu'ran, the Holy Qu'ran." He was sentenced to one year in prison but placed on probation.

In some countries, blasphemy has been expanded to include nonreligious hate speech. A number of European and other countries, for example, criminalize the denial of the Holocaust. Austria, Australia, Belgium, Canada, the Czech Republic, France, Germany, Israel, Lithuania, New Zealand, Poland, Romania, Slovakia, and Switzerland have such laws. In 2006, English historian and author of *Hitler's War*, David Irving, was sentenced to three years imprisonment by an Austrian court for speeches previously made in the country that asserted that only 74,000 Jews died of natural causes and millions were sent to Palestine during World War II.

In the United States, the Supreme Court struck down New York's blasphemy law as an unconstitutional prior restraint in *Joseph Burstyn v. Wilson*, 343 U.S. 495 (1952). New York had banned Roberto Rossellini's film *The Miracle*, about a peasant woman who believed she was the Virgin Mary. The Catholic Church denounced the film as sacrilegious, but the Supreme Court struck down the state's law, observing: "It is not the business of government in our nation to suppress real or imagined attacks upon a particular religious doctrine."

For further reading, see Leonard Levy, *Blasphemy: Verbal Offense Against the Sacred from Moses to Salman Rushdie* (New York: Knopf, 1993).

D | *Commercial Speech*

■ THE DEVELOPMENT OF LAW

Other Recent Rulings on Commercial Speech and the First Amendment

CASE	VOTE	RULING
Johanns v. Livestock Marketing Association, 544 U.S. 550 (2005)	6:3	Writing for the Court, Justice Scalia upheld the beef promotion and Research Act of 1985, which requires cattle producers to pay $1 for each head of cattle in order to finance a marketing campaign, "Beef: It's What's for Dinner." Although the Court invalidated a similar program for the marketing of mushrooms, in *United States v. United Foods*, 533 U.S. 405 (2001), it did not address the question of whether such programs are "government speech." Some independent cattle producers objected to the program,

contending that it constituted unconstitutionally "compelled speech." Justice Scalia, however, ruled that "government speech" is not subject to ordinary First Amendment analysis. In his words: "Compelled funding of government speech does not alone raise First Amendment concerns. . . . Citizens may challenge compelled support of private speech, but have no First Amendment right not to fund government speech." Justices Stevens, Kennedy, and Souter dissented.

E | *Freedom of the Press*

(2) *Indirect Prior Restraints*

Extending prior rulings (see the section on indirect prior restraints in Vol. 2, Ch. 5) that the First Amendment does not convey a right to receive information, in *Beard v. Banks*, 126 S.Ct. 2572 (2006), the Court upheld a prison policy of conditioning access to nonreligious periodicals upon inmates' good behavior. Writing for the Court, Justice Breyer held that prisons may impose reasonable restrictions on the constitutional rights of inmates. Justices Stevens and Ginsburg dissented.

6

FREEDOM FROM AND OF RELIGION

A | *The (Dis)Establishment Clause*

In a continuation of a dialogue between Congress and the Court over congressional power, religious freedom, and the tensions between the First Amendment's (Dis)Establishment and Free Exercise clauses, the Court handed down *Cutter v. Wilkinson* (excerpted below), upholding the Religious Land Use and Institutionalized Persons Act (RLUIPA) of 2000.

In two other widely watched cases, the Court also revisited the controversy over the public display of the Ten Commandments and other religious symbols, addressed in *Stone v. Graham*, 449 U.S. 39 (1980), which held unconstitutional a Kentucky statute requiring the posting of the Ten Commandments in every public school room; and in *County of Allegheny v. American Civil Liberties Union, Greater Pittsburgh Chapter*, 492 U.S. 573 (1989) (see the "constitutional history" box in Vol. 2, Ch. 6). In both cases, the Court split five to four. In *Van Orden v. Perry* (excerpted below), writing for a plurality Chief Justice Rehnquist held that the erection of a six-foot granite monument on which the Ten Commandments were chiseled did not violate the First Amendment (Dis)Establishment Clause. Justices Stevens, O'Connor, Souter, and Ginsburg dissented. However, in *McCreary v. American Civil Liberties Union of Kentucky* (excerpted below), Justice Souter ruled that two Kentucky counties violated the First Amendment by prominently displaying the Ten Commandments in their courthouses. Chief Rehnquist and Justices Scalia, Kennedy, and Thomas dissented. In both cases, Justice Breyer cast the pivotal vote and formed bare majorities. He did so on pragmatic grounds, reasoning that the Texas monument had stood unchallenged for over 40 years, whereas the Kentucky displays immediately sparked controversy and appeared to clearly aim at endorsing religion. The rulings are certain to invite some confusion and further litigation. As the Court is currently constituted, a bare majority appears willing to uphold the display of religious symbols, surrounded by other symbols or monuments, but to rule against more recently installed public displays of religious symbols if they have solely a religious purpose.

Cutter v. Wilkinson
544 U.S. 709, 125 S.Ct. 2113 (2005)

In response to the invalidation of the Religious Freedom Restoration Act (RFRA) of 1993 in *City of Boerne v. Flores*, 521 U.S. 507 (1997) (excerpted in Vol. 2, Ch. 6), Congress enacted the Religious Land Use and Institutionalized Persons Act (RLUIPA) of 2000. The RFRA had aimed to reestablish the test for determining religious freedom under the Free Exercise clause that was discarded in *Employment Division, Department of Human Resources of Oregon v. Smith*, 494 U.S. 872 (1990) (excerpted in Vol. 2, Ch. 6). But *City of Boerne* held that Congress lacked the authority to enact the law under its power in Section 5 of the Fourteenth Amendment, because that power is only remedial and may not be relied on to define the scope of constitutional rights. In turn, Congress passed the narrower RLUIPA based on its powers under the Spending and Commerce clauses. The RLUIPA specifies that state and local governments that receive federal funding for services may not "impose a substantial burden on the religious exercise of a person residing in or confined to an institution," unless the burden is necessary to achieving a "compelling" governmental purpose.

When inmates in Ohio prisons were denied special services for their observance of rituals associated with Wicca, Satanism, Asatru, and the Church of Jesus Christ Christian, a clinical legal program at the Ohio State University Moritz College of Law took up their representation and sued the state for violating the RLUIPA. The state countered that the RLUIPA violated the (Dis)Establishment clause, would compromise prison security, and prove costly. A federal district court refused to dismiss the suit, but the Court of Appeals for the Sixth Circuit ruled that the RLUIPA violated the (Dis)Establishment clause "by giving greater protection to religious rights than to other constitutionally protected rights." That decision was appealed and the Court granted review.

The appellate court's decision was reversed by a unanimous Court. Justice Ginsburg delivered the opinion of the Court and Justice Thomas filed a concurring opinion.

☐ *Justice* GINSBURG *delivered the opinion of the Court.*

Section 3 of the Religious Land Use and Institutionalized Persons Act of 2000 (RLUIPA) provides in part: "No government shall impose a substantial burden on the religious exercise of a person residing in or confined to an institution," unless the burden furthers "a compelling governmental interest," and does so by "the least restrictive means." . . .

"This Court has long recognized that the government may . . . accommodate religious practices . . . without violating the Establishment Clause." *Hobbie v. Unemployment Appeals Comm'n of Fla.*, 480 U.S. 136 (1987). Just last Term, in *Locke v. Davey*, 540 U.S. 712 (2004), the Court reaffirmed that "there is room for play in the joints between" the Free Exercise and Establishment Clauses, allowing the government to accommodate religion beyond free exercise requirements, without offense to the Establishment Clause. But Section 3 of RLUIPA, we hold, does not, on its face, exceed the limits of permissible government accommodation of religious practices.

RLUIPA is the latest of long-running congressional efforts to accord religious exercise heightened protection from government-imposed burdens, consistent with this Court's precedents. Ten years before RLUIPA's enactment, the Court held, in *Employment Div., Dept. of Human Resources of Ore. v. Smith*, 494 U.S. 872 (1990), that the First Amendment's Free Exercise Clause does not inhibit enforcement of otherwise valid laws of general application that incidentally burden religious conduct. In particular, we ruled that the Free Exercise Clause did not bar Oregon from enforcing its blanket ban on peyote possession with no allowance for sacramental use of the drug. Accordingly, the State could deny unemployment benefits to persons dismissed from their jobs because of their religiously inspired peyote use. The Court recognized, however, that the political branches could shield religious exercise through legislative accommodation, for example, by making an exception to proscriptive drug laws for sacramental peyote use.

Responding to *Smith*, Congress enacted the Religious Freedom Restoration Act of 1993 (RFRA). RFRA "prohibits '[g]overnment' from 'substantially burden[ing]' a person's exercise of religion even if the burden results from a rule of general applicability unless the government can demonstrate the burden '(1) is in furtherance of a compelling governmental interest; and (2) is the least restrictive means of furthering that compelling governmental interest.'" *City of Boerne v. Flores*, 521 U.S. 507 (1997). "[U]niversal" in its coverage, RFRA "applie[d] to all Federal and State law," but notably lacked a Commerce Clause underpinning or a Spending Clause limitation to recipients of federal funds. In *City of Boerne*, this Court invalidated RFRA as applied to States and their subdivisions, holding that the Act exceeded Congress's remedial powers under the Fourteenth Amendment.

Congress again responded, this time by enacting RLUIPA. Less sweeping than RFRA, and invoking federal authority under the Spending and Commerce Clauses, RLUIPA targets two areas: Section 2 of the Act concerns land-use regulation; Section 3 relates to religious exercise by institutionalized persons. Section 3, at issue here, provides that "[n]o [state or local] government shall impose a substantial burden on the religious exercise of a person residing in or confined to an institution," unless the government shows that the burden furthers "a compelling governmental interest" and does so by "the least restrictive means." The Act defines "religious exercise" to include "any exercise of religion, whether or not compelled by, or central to, a system of religious belief." Section 3 applies when "the substantial burden [on religious exercise] is imposed in a program or activity that receives Federal financial assistance," or "the substantial burden affects, or removal of that substantial burden would affect, commerce with foreign nations, among the several States, or with Indian tribes."

The Religion Clauses of the First Amendment provide: "Congress shall make no law respecting an establishment of religion, or prohibiting the free exercise thereof." The first of the two Clauses, commonly called the Establishment Clause, commands a separation of church and state. The second, the Free Exercise Clause, requires government respect for, and noninterference with, the religious beliefs and practices of our Nation's people. While the two Clauses express complementary values, they often exert conflicting pressures.

Our decisions recognize that "there is room for play in the joints" between the Clauses, some space for legislative action neither compelled by the Free Exercise Clause nor prohibited by the Establishment Clause. In accord with the majority of Courts of Appeals that have ruled on the question, we hold that Section 3 of RLUIPA fits within the corridor between the Relgion Clauses: On its face, the Act qualifies as a permissible legislative accommodation of religion that is not barred by the Establishment Clause.

Foremost, we find RLUIPA's institutionalized-persons provision compatible with the Establishment Clause because it alleviates exceptional government-created burdens on private religious exercise. Furthermore, the Act on its face does not founder on shoals our prior decisions have identified: Properly applying RLUIPA, courts must take adequate account of the burdens a requested accommodation may impose on nonbeneficiaries; and they must be satisfied that the Act's prescriptions are and will be administered neutrally among different faiths. . . .

RLUIPA thus protects institutionalized persons who are unable freely to attend to their religious needs and are therefore dependent on the government's permission and accommodation for exercise of their religion. . . . We do not read RLUIPA to elevate accommodation of religious observances over an institution's need to maintain order and safety. Our decisions indicate that an accommodation must be measured so that it does not override other significant interests.

We have no cause to believe that RLUIPA would not be applied in an appropriately balanced way, with particular sensitivity to security concerns. While the Act adopts a "compelling governmental interest" standard, "[c]ontext matters" in the application of that standard. Lawmakers supporting RLUIPA were mindful of the urgency of discipline, order, safety, and security in penal institutions. . . .

For the reasons stated, the judgment of the United States Court of Appeals for the Sixth Circuit is reversed, and the case is remanded for further proceedings consistent with this opinion.

☐ *Justice THOMAS, concurring.*

I write to explain why a proper historical understanding of the Clause as a federalism provision leads to the same conclusion.

The Establishment Clause provides that "Congress shall make no law respecting an establishment of religion." As I have explained, an important function of the Clause was to "ma[ke] clear that Congress could not interfere with state establishments." *Elk Grove Unified School Dist. v. Newdow*, 542 U.S. 1 (2004) (opinion concurring in judgment). The Clause, then, "is best understood as a federalism provision" that "protects state establishments from federal interference." Ohio contends that this federalism understanding of the Clause prevents federal oversight of state choices within the "'play in the joints'" between the Free Exercise and Establishment Clauses. *Locke v. Davey*, 540 U.S. 712 (2004). In other words, Ohio asserts that the Clause protects the States from federal interference with otherwise constitutionally permissible choices regarding religious policy. In Ohio's view, RLUIPA intrudes on such state policy choices and hence violates the Clause.

Ohio's vision of the range of protected state authority overreads the Clause.... To proscribe Congress from making laws "respecting an establishment of religion"... was to forbid legislation respecting coercive state establishments, not to preclude Congress from legislating on religion generally....

In short, the view that the Establishment Clause precludes Congress from legislating respecting religion lacks historical provenance, at least based on the history of which I am aware. Even when enacting laws that bind the States pursuant to valid exercises of its enumerated powers, Congress need not observe strict separation between church and state, or steer clear of the subject of religion. It need only refrain from making laws "respecting an establishment of religion"; it must not interfere with a state establishment of religion. For example, Congress presumably could not require a State to establish a religion any more than it could preclude a State from establishing a religion.

On its face—the relevant inquiry, as this is a facial challenge—RLUIPA is not a law "respecting an establishment of religion." RLUIPA provides, as relevant: "No government shall impose a substantial burden on the religious exercise of a person residing in or confined to an institution, . . . even if the burden results from a rule of general applicability, unless the government demonstrates that imposition of the burden on that person," first, "further[s] a compelling governmental interest," and second, "is the least restrictive means of furthering that compelling governmental interest." This provision does not prohibit or interfere with state establishments, since no State has established (or constitutionally could establish, given an incorporated Clause) a religion. Nor does the provision require a State to establish a religion: It does not force a State to coerce religious observance or payment of taxes supporting clergy, or require a State to prefer one religious sect over another. It is a law respecting religion, but not one respecting an establishment of religion....

It also bears noting that Congress, pursuant to its Spending Clause authority, conditioned the States' receipt of federal funds on their compliance with RLUIPA. RLUIPA may well exceed the spending power. Nonetheless, while Congress's condition stands, the States subject themselves to that condition by voluntarily accepting federal funds. The States' voluntary acceptance of Congress's condition undercuts Ohio's argument that Congress is encroaching on its turf.

Van Orden v. Perry
125 S.Ct. 2854 (2005)

In the 1950s and 1960s, the Fraternal Order of Eagles, a national civic organization, erected hundreds of granite Ten Commandments monuments around the country. One of these was among 21 historical markers and 17 monuments in a 22-acre public park surrounding the Texas State Capitol in Austin. The Ten Commandments are inscribed on a six-foot high monolith which the Eagles erected and donated to the city in an effort to combat juvenile delinquency. Thomas Van Orden, a lawyer who is homeless and who frequently visits the Capitol, where he spends his days in the law library of the state supreme court building, filed a lawsuit in 2001, contending that the monument violated the First Amendment (Dis)Establishment Clause. A federal district court held that, amid the other monuments, the display of the Ten Commandments had a secular purpose. That decision was affirmed by the Court of Appeals for the Fifth Circuit, and Van Orden appealed.

The appellate court's decision was affirmed by a five to four vote. Chief Justice Rehnquist delivered a plurality opinion for the Court, which Justices Scalia, Kennedy, and Thomas joined. Justices Scalia, Thomas, and Breyer each filed concurring opinions. Justices Stevens, O'Connor, Souter, and Ginsburg dissented.

☐ THE CHIEF JUSTICE *announced the judgment of the Court and delivered an opinion, in which Justice SCALIA, Justice KENNEDY, and Justice THOMAS join.*

Our cases, Januslike, point in two directions in applying the Establishment Clause. One face looks toward the strong role played by religion and religious traditions throughout our Nation's history. As we observed in *School Dist. of Abington Township v. Schempp*, 374 U.S. 203 (1963): "It is true that religion has been closely identified with our history and government ... The fact that the Founding Fathers believed devotedly that there was a God and that the unalienable rights of man were rooted in Him is clearly evidenced in their writings, from the Mayflower Compact to the Constitution itself.... It can be truly said, therefore, that today, as in the beginning, our national life reflects a religious people who, in the words of Madison, are 'earnestly praying, as ... in duty bound, that the Supreme Lawgiver of the Universe ... guide them into every measure which may be worthy of his [blessing....]'" The other face looks toward the principle that governmental intervention in religious matters can itself endanger religious freedom.

This case, like all Establishment Clause challenges, presents us with the difficulty of respecting both faces. Our institutions presuppose a Supreme Being, yet these institutions must not press religious observances upon their citizens. One face looks to the past in acknowledgment of our Nation's heritage, while the other looks to the present in demanding a separation between church and state. Reconciling these two faces requires that we neither abdicate our responsibility to maintain a division between church and state nor evince a hostility to religion by disabling the government from in some ways recognizing our religious heritage....

These two faces are evident in representative cases both upholding and invalidating laws under the Establishment Clause. Over the last 25 years, we have sometimes pointed to *Lemon v. Kurtzman*, 403 U.S. 602 (1971), as providing the governing test in Establishment Clause challenges. Compare *Wallace v. Jaffree*, 472 U.S. 38 (1985) (applying *Lemon*), with *Marsh v. Chambers*, 463 U.S. 783 (1983) (not applying *Lemon*). Yet, just two years after *Lemon* was decided, we noted that the factors identified in *Lemon* serve as "no more than helpful signposts." *Hunt v. McNair*, 413 U.S. 734 (1973). Many of our recent cases simply have not applied the *Lemon* test. See, e.g., *Zelman v. Simmons-Harris*, 536 U.S. 639 (2002); *Good News Club v. Milford Central School*, 533 U.S. 98 (2001). Others have applied it only after concluding that the challenged practice was invalid under a different Establishment Clause test.

Whatever may be the fate of the *Lemon* test in the larger scheme of Establishment Clause jurisprudence, we think it not useful in dealing with the sort of passive monument that Texas has erected on its Capitol grounds. Instead, our analysis is driven both by the nature of the monument and by our Nation's history. As we explained in *Lynch v. Donnelly*, 465 U.S. 668 (1984): "There is an unbroken history of official acknowledgment by all three branches of government of the role of religion in American life from at least 1789." For example, both Houses passed resolutions in 1789 asking President George Washington to issue a Thanksgiving Day Proclamation to "recommend to the people of the United States a day of public thanksgiving and prayer, to be observed by acknowledging, with grateful hearts, the many and signal favors of Almighty God." President Washington's proclamation directly attributed to the Supreme Being the foundations and successes of our young Nation. . . .

Recognition of the role of God in our Nation's heritage has also been reflected in our decisions. We have acknowledged, for example, that "religion has been closely identified with our history and government," *School Dist. of Abington Township v. Schempp*, and that "[t]he history of man is inseparable from the history of religion," *Engel v. Vitale*, 370 U.S. 421 (1962). This recognition has led us to hold that the Establishment Clause permits a state legislature to open its daily sessions with a prayer by a chaplain paid by the State. *Marsh v. Chambers*. Such a practice, we thought, was "deeply embedded in the history and tradition of this country." With similar reasoning, we have upheld laws, which originated from one of the Ten Commandments, that prohibited the sale of merchandise on Sunday. *McGowan v. Maryland*, 366 U.S. 420 (1961).

In this case we are faced with a display of the Ten Commandments on government property outside the Texas State Capitol. Such acknowledgments of the role played by the Ten Commandments in our Nation's heritage are common throughout America. We need only look within our own Courtroom. Since 1935, Moses has stood, holding two tablets that reveal portions of the Ten Commandments written in Hebrew, among other lawgivers in the south frieze. Representations of the Ten Commandments adorn the metal gates lining the north and south sides of the Courtroom as well as the doors leading into the Courtroom. Moses also sits on the exterior east facade of the building holding the Ten Commandments tablets. . . .

Our opinions, like our building, have recognized the role the Decalogue plays in America's heritage. The Executive and Legislative Branches have also acknowledged the historical role of the Ten Commandments. These displays and recognitions of the Ten Commandments bespeak the rich American tradition of religious acknowledgments.

Of course, the Ten Commandments are religious—they were so viewed at their inception and so remain. The monument, therefore, has religious significance. According to Judeo-Christian belief, the Ten Commandments were given to Moses by God on Mt. Sinai. But Moses was a lawgiver as well as a religious leader. And the Ten Commandments have an undeniable historical meaning, as the foregoing examples demonstrate. Simply having religious content or promoting a message consistent with a religious doctrine does not run afoul of the Establishment Clause.

There are, of course, limits to the display of religious messages or symbols. For example, we held unconstitutional a Kentucky statute requiring the posting of the Ten Commandments in every public schoolroom. *Stone v. Graham*, 449 U.S. 39 (1980). In the classroom context, we found that the Kentucky statute had an improper and plainly religious purpose. As evidenced by *Stone*'s almost exclusive reliance upon two of our school prayer cases (citing *School Dist. of Abington Township v. Schempp*, 374 U.S. 203 (1963), and *Engel v. Vitale*, 370 U.S. 421 (1962)), it stands as an example of the fact that we have "been particularly vigilant in monitoring compliance with the Establishment Clause in elementary and secondary schools," *Edwards v. Aguillard*, 482 U.S. 578 (1987). Indeed, *Edwards v. Aguillard* recognized that *Stone*—along with *Schempp* and *Engel*—was a consequence of the "particular concerns that arise in the context of public elementary and secondary schools." Neither *Stone* itself nor subsequent opinions have indicated that *Stone*'s holding would extend to a legislative chamber or to capitol grounds.

The placement of the Ten Commandments monument on the Texas State Capitol grounds is a far more passive use of those texts than was the case in *Stone*, where the text confronted elementary school students every day. Indeed, Van Orden, the petitioner here, apparently walked by the monument for a number of years before bringing this lawsuit. The monument is therefore also quite different from the prayers involved in *Schempp* and *Lee v. Weisman* [505 U.S. 577 (1992)]. Texas has treated her Capitol grounds monuments as representing the several strands in the State's political and legal history. The inclusion of the Ten Commandments monument in this group has a dual significance, partaking of both religion and government. We cannot say that Texas's display of this monument violates the Establishment Clause of the First Amendment.

☐ *Justice BREYER, concurring in the judgment.*

In *School Dist. of Abington Township v. Schempp*, 374 U.S. 203 (1963), Justice GOLDBERG, joined by Justice HARLAN, wrote, in respect to the First Amendment's Religion Clauses, that there is "no simple and clear measure which by precise application can readily and invariably demark the permissible from the impermissible." One must refer instead to the basic purposes of those Clauses. They seek to "assure the fullest possible scope of religious liberty and tolerance for all." They seek to avoid that divisiveness based upon religion that promotes social conflict, sapping the strength of government and religion alike. They seek to maintain that "separation of church and state" that has long been critical to the "peaceful dominion that religion exercises in [this] country," where the "spirit of religion" and the "spirit of freedom" are productively "united," "reign[ing] together" but in separate spheres "on the same soil." A. de Tocqueville, *Democracy in America* (1835). They seek to further the basic principles set forth today by Justice O'CONNOR in her concurring opinion in *McCreary County v. American Civil Liberties Union of Ky.*

The Court has made clear, as Justices GOLDBERG and HARLAN noted, that the realization of these goals means that government must "neither engage in nor compel religious practices," that it must "effect no favoritism among sects or between religion and nonreligion," and that it must "work deterrence of no religious belief." The government must avoid excessive interference with, or promotion of, religion. But the Establishment Clause does not compel the government to purge from the public sphere all that in any way partakes of the religious. Such absolutism is not only inconsistent with our national traditions, but would also tend to promote the kind of social conflict the Establishment Clause seeks to avoid.

Thus, as Justices GOLDBERG and HARLAN pointed out, the Court has found no single mechanical formula that can accurately draw the constitutional line in every case. Where the Establishment Clause is at issue, tests designed to measure "neutrality" alone are insufficient, both because it is sometimes difficult to determine when a legal rule is "neutral," and because "untutored devotion to the concept of neutrality can lead to invocation or approval of results which partake not simply of that noninterference and noninvolvement with the religious which the Constitution commands, but of a brooding and pervasive devotion to the secular and a passive, or even active, hostility to the religious."

Neither can this Court's other tests readily explain the Establishment Clause's tolerance, for example, of the prayers that open legislative meetings; certain references to, and invocations of, the Deity in the public words of public officials; the public references to God on coins, decrees, and buildings; or the attention paid to the religious objectives of certain holidays, including Thanksgiving.

If the relation between government and religion is one of separation, but not of mutual hostility and suspicion, one will inevitably find difficult borderline cases. And in such cases, I see no test-related substitute for the exercise of legal judgment. That judgment is not a personal judgment. Rather, as in all constitutional cases, it must reflect and remain faithful to the underlying purposes of the Clauses, and it must take account of context and consequences measured in light of those purposes. While the Court's prior tests provide useful guideposts—and might well lead to the same result the Court reaches today—no exact formula can dictate a resolution to such fact-intensive cases.

The case before us is a borderline case. It concerns a large granite monument bearing the text of the Ten Commandments located on the grounds of the Texas State Capitol. On the one hand, the Commandments' text undeniably has a religious message, invoking, indeed emphasizing, the Deity. On the other hand, focusing on the text of the Commandments alone cannot conclusively resolve this case. Rather, to determine the message that the text here conveys, we must examine how the text is used. And that inquiry requires us to consider the context of the display.

In certain contexts, a display of the tablets of the Ten Commandments can convey not simply a religious message but also a secular moral message (about proper standards of social conduct). And in certain contexts, a display of the tablets can also convey a historical message (about a historic relation between those standards and the law)—a fact that helps to explain the display of those tablets in dozens of courthouses throughout the Nation, including the Supreme Court of the United States.

Here the tablets have been used as part of a display that communicates not simply a religious message, but a secular message as well. The circumstances surrounding the display's placement on the capitol grounds and its physical setting suggest that the State itself intended the latter, nonreligious aspects of the tablets' message to predominate. And the monument's 40-year history on the Texas state grounds indicates that that has been its effect.

The group that donated the monument, the Fraternal Order of Eagles, a private civic (and primarily secular) organization, while interested in the religious aspect of the Ten Commandments, sought to highlight the Commandments' role in shaping civic morality as part of that organization's efforts to combat juvenile delinquency. The Eagles' consultation with a committee composed of members of several faiths in order to find a nonsectarian text underscores the group's ethics-based motives. The tablets, as displayed on the monument, prominently acknowledge that the Eagles donated the display, a factor which, though not sufficient, thereby further distances the State itself from the religious aspect of the Commandments' message.

The physical setting of the monument, moreover, suggests little or nothing of the sacred. The monument sits in a large park containing 17 monuments and 21 historical markers, all designed to illustrate the "ideals" of those who settled in Texas and of those who have lived there since that time....

If these factors provide a strong, but not conclusive, indication that the Commandments' text on this monument conveys a predominantly secular message, a further factor is determinative here. As far as I can tell, 40 years passed in which the presence of this monument, legally speaking, went unchallenged (until the single legal objection raised by petitioner). And I am not aware of any evidence suggesting that this was due to a climate of intimidation. Hence, those 40 years suggest more strongly than can any set of formulaic tests that few individuals, whatever their system of beliefs, are likely to have understood the monument as amounting, in any significantly detrimental way, to a government effort to favor a particular religious sect, primarily to promote religion over nonreligion, to "engage in" any "religious practic[e]," to "compel" any "religious practic[e]," or to "work deterrence" of any "religious belief." *Schempp* (GOLDBERG, J., concurring). Those 40 years suggest that the public visiting the capitol grounds has considered the religious aspect of the tablets' message as part of what is a broader moral and historical message reflective of a cultural heritage.

This case, moreover, is distinguishable from instances where the Court has found Ten Commandments displays impermissible. The display is not on the grounds of a public school, where, given the impressionability of the young, government must exercise particular care in separating church and state. This case also differs from *McCreary County*, where the short (and stormy) history of the courthouse Commandments' displays demonstrates the substantially religious objectives of those who mounted them, and the effect of this readily apparent objective upon those who view them....

For these reasons, I believe that the Texas display—serving a mixed but primarily nonreligious purpose, not primarily "advanc[ing]" or "inhibit[ing] religion," and not creating an "excessive government entanglement with religion,"—might satisfy this Court's more formal Establishment Clause tests. *Lemon*. But, as I have said, in reaching the conclusion that the Texas display falls on the permissible side of the constitutional line, I rely less upon a literal application of any particular test than upon consideration of the basic purposes of the First Amendment's Religion Clauses themselves. This display has stood apparently uncontested for nearly two generations. That experience helps us understand that as a practical matter of degree this display is unlikely to prove divisive. And this matter of degree is, I believe, critical in a borderline case such as this one.

At the same time, to reach a contrary conclusion here based primarily upon the religious nature of the tablets' text would, I fear, lead the law to exhibit a hostility toward religion that has no place in our Establishment Clause traditions. Such a holding might well encourage disputes concerning the removal of longstanding depictions of the Ten Commandments from public buildings across the Nation. And it could thereby create the very kind of religiously based divisiveness that the Establishment Clause seeks to avoid.

In light of these considerations, I cannot agree with today's plurality's analysis. Nor can I agree with Justice SCALIA's dissent in *McCreary County*. I do agree with Justice O'CONNOR's statement of principles in *McCreary County*, though I disagree with her evaluation of the evidence as it bears on the application of those principles to this case.

☐ *Justice SCALIA, concurring.*

I join the opinion of THE CHIEF JUSTICE because I think it accurately reflects our current Establishment Clause jurisprudence—or at least the Establishment Clause jurisprudence we currently apply some of the time. I would prefer to reach the same result by adopting an Establishment Clause jurisprudence that is in accord with our Nation's past and present practices, and that can be consistently applied—the central relevant feature of which is that there is nothing unconstitutional in a State's favoring religion generally, honoring God through public prayer and acknowledgment, or, in a nonproselytizing manner, venerating the Ten Commandments.

☐ *Justice THOMAS, concurring.*

The Court holds that the Ten Commandments monument found on the Texas State Capitol grounds does not violate the Establishment Clause. Rather than trying to suggest meaninglessness where there is meaning, THE CHIEF JUSTICE rightly recognizes that the monument has "religious significance." He properly recognizes the role of religion in this Nation's history and the permissibility of government displays acknowledging that history. For those reasons, I join THE CHIEF JUSTICE's opinion in full.

This case would be easy if the Court were willing to abandon the inconsistent guideposts it has adopted for addressing Establishment Clause challenges, and return to the original meaning of the Clause. I have previously suggested that the Clause's text and history "resis[t] incorporation" against the States. See *Elk Grove Unified School Dist. v. Newdow*, 542 U.S. 1 (2004). If the Establishment Clause does not restrain the States, then it has no application here, where only state action is at issue.

Even if the Clause is incorporated, or if the Free Exercise Clause limits the power of States to establish religions, our task would be far simpler if we returned to the original meaning of the word "establishment" than it is under the various approaches this Court now uses. The Framers understood an establishment "necessarily [to] involve actual legal coercion." *Newdow* (THOMAS, J., concurring in judgment); *Lee v. Weisman*, 505 U.S. 577 (1992) (SCALIA, J., dissenting) ("The coercion that was a hallmark of historical establishments of religion was coercion of religious orthodoxy and of financial support by force of law and threat of penalty"). "In other words, establishment at the founding involved, for example, mandatory observance or mandatory payment of taxes supporting ministers." And "government practices that have nothing to do with creating or maintaining ... coercive state establishments" simply do not "implicate the possible liberty interest of being free from coercive state establishments." *Newdow* (THOMAS, J., concurring in judgment).

There is no question that, based on the original meaning of the Establishment Clause, the Ten Commandments display at issue here is constitutional. In no sense does Texas compel petitioner Van Orden to do anything.

The only injury to him is that he takes offense at seeing the monument as he passes it on his way to the Texas Supreme Court Library. He need not stop to read it or even to look at it, let alone to express support for it or adopt the Commandments as guides for his life. The mere presence of the monument along his path involves no coercion and thus does not violate the Establishment Clause.

Returning to the original meaning would do more than simplify our task. It also would avoid the pitfalls present in the Court's current approach to such challenges. This Court's precedent elevates the trivial to the proverbial "federal case," by making benign signs and postings subject to challenge. Yet even as it does so, the Court's precedent attempts to avoid declaring all religious symbols and words of longstanding tradition unconstitutional, by counterfactually declaring them of little religious significance. Even when the Court's cases recognize that such symbols have religious meaning, they adopt an unhappy compromise that fails fully to account for either the adherent's or the nonadherent's beliefs, and provides no principled way to choose between them. Even worse, the incoherence of the Court's decisions in this area renders the Establishment Clause impenetrable and incapable of consistent application. All told, this Court's jurisprudence leaves courts, governments, and believers and nonbelievers alike confused—an observation that is hardly new. . . .

While the Court correctly rejects the challenge to the Ten Commandments monument on the Texas Capitol grounds, a more fundamental rethinking of our Establishment Clause jurisprudence remains in order.

☐ *Justice SOUTER, with whom Justice STEVENS and Justice GINSBURG join, dissenting.*

Although the First Amendment's Religion Clauses have not been read to mandate absolute governmental neutrality toward religion, cf. *Sherbert v. Verner*, 374 U.S. 398 (1963), the Establishment Clause requires neutrality as a general rule, e.g., *Everson v. Board of Ed. of Ewing*, 330 U.S. 1 (1947), and thus expresses Madison's condemnation of "employ[ing] Religion as an engine of Civil policy," *Memorial and Remonstrance Against Religious Assessments*. A governmental display of an obviously religious text cannot be squared with neutrality, except in a setting that plausibly indicates that the statement is not placed in view with a predominant purpose on the part of government either to adopt the religious message or to urge its acceptance by others.

Until today, only one of our cases addressed the constitutionality of posting the Ten Commandments, *Stone v. Graham*, 449 U.S. 39 (1980). A Kentucky statute required posting the Commandments on the walls of public school classrooms, and the Court described the State's purpose (relevant under the tripartite test laid out in *Lemon v. Kurtzman*, 403 U.S. 602 (1971)) as being at odds with the obligation of religious neutrality. [T]he simple realities [are] that the Ten Commandments constitute a religious statement, that their message is inherently religious, and that the purpose of singling them out in a display is clearly the same.

Thus, a pedestrian happening upon the monument at issue here needs no training in religious doctrine to realize that the statement of the Commandments, quoting God himself, proclaims that the will of the divine being is the source of obligation to obey the rules, including the facially secular ones. In this case, moreover, the text is presented to give particular prominence to the Commandments' first sectarian reference, "I am the Lord thy God." That proclamation is centered on the stone and written in slightly larger letters than the subsequent recitation. To ensure that the religious nature of the monument is clear to even the most casual passerby, the word "Lord" appears in all capital letters (as does the word "am"), so that the most eye-catching segment of the quotation is the declaration "I AM the LORD thy God." What follows, of course, are the rules against other gods, graven images, vain swearing, and Sabbath breaking. And the full text of the fifth Commandment puts forward filial respect as a condition of long life in the and "which the Lord they God giveth thee." These "[w]ords . . . make [the] . . . religious meaning unmistakably clear." *County of Allegheny v. American Civil Liberties Union, Greater Pittsburgh Chapter*, 492 U.S. 573 (1989).

To drive the religious point home, and identify the message as religious to any viewer who failed to read the text, the engraved quotation is framed by religious symbols: two tablets with what appears to be ancient script on them, two Stars of David, and the superimposed Greek letters Chi and Rho as the familiar monogram of Christ. Nothing on the monument, in fact, detracts from its religious nature, and the plurality does not suggest otherwise. It would therefore be difficult to miss the point that the government of Texas is telling everyone who sees the monument to live up to a moral code because God requires it, with both code and conception of God being rightly understood as the inheritances specifically of Jews and Christians. And it is likewise unsurprising that the District Court expressly rejected Texas's argument that the State's purpose in placing the monument on the capitol grounds was related to the Commandments' role as "part of the foundation of modern secular law in Texas and elsewhere."

The monument's presentation of the Commandments with religious text emphasized and enhanced stands in contrast to any number of perfectly constitutional depictions of them, the frieze of our own Courtroom providing a good example, where the figure of Moses stands among history's great lawgivers.

While Moses holds the tablets of the Commandments showing some Hebrew text, no one looking at the lines of figures in marble relief is likely to see a religious purpose behind the assemblage or take away a religious message from it. Only one other depiction represents a religious leader, and the historical personages are mixed with symbols of moral and intellectual abstractions like Equity and Authority. Since Moses enjoys no especial prominence on the frieze, viewers can readily take him to be there as a lawgiver in the company of other lawgivers; and the viewers may just as naturally see the tablets of the Commandments (showing the later ones, forbidding things like killing and theft, but without the divine preface) as background from which the concept of law emerged, ultimately having a secular influence in the history of the Nation. Government may, of course, constitutionally call attention to this influence, and may post displays or erect monuments recounting this aspect of our history no less than any other, so long as there is a context and that context is historical. Hence, a display of the Commandments accompanied by an exposition of how they have influenced modern law would most likely be constitutionally unobjectionable. And the Decalogue could, as *Stone* suggested, be integrated constitutionally into a course of study in public schools.

Texas seeks to take advantage of the recognition that visual symbol and written text can manifest a secular purpose in secular company, when it argues that its monument (like Moses in the frieze) is not alone and ought to be viewed as only 1 among 17 placed on the 22 acres surrounding the state capitol. Texas, indeed, says that the Capitol grounds are like a museum for a collection of exhibits, the kind of setting that several Members of the Court have said can render the exhibition of religious artifacts permissible, even though in other circumstances their display would be seen as meant to convey a religious message forbidden to the State. So, for example, the Government of the United States does not violate the Establishment Clause by hanging Giotto's Madonna on the wall of the National Gallery.

But 17 monuments with no common appearance, history, or aesthetic role scattered over 22 acres is not a museum, and anyone strolling around the lawn would surely take each memorial on its own terms without any dawning sense that some purpose held the miscellany together more coherently than fortuity and the edge of the grass. One monument expresses admiration for pioneer women. One pays respect to the fighters of World War II. And one quotes the God of Abraham whose command is the sanction for moral law. The themes are individual grit, patriotic courage, and God as the source of Jewish and Christian morality; there is no common denominator.

If the State's museum argument does nothing to blunt the religious message and manifestly religious purpose behind it, neither does the plurality's reliance on generalities culled from cases factually different from this one. In fact, it is not until the end of its opinion that the plurality turns to the relevant precedent of *Stone*, a case actually dealing with a display of the Decalogue.

When the plurality finally does confront *Stone*, it tries to avoid the case's obvious applicability by limiting its holding to the classroom setting. . . . I would reverse the judgment of the Court of Appeals.

☐ *Justice STEVENS, with whom Justice GINSBURG joins, dissenting.*

The sole function of the monument on the grounds of Texas's State Capitol is to display the full text of one version of the Ten Commandments. The monument is not a work of art and does not refer to any event in the history of the State. It is significant because, and only because, it communicates the following message:

> "I AM the LORD thy God.
> "Thou shalt have no other gods before me.
> "Thou shalt not make to thyself any graven images.
> "Thou shalt not take the Name of the Lord thy God in vain.
> "Remember the Sabbath day, to keep it holy.
> "Honor thy father and thy mother, that thy days may be long upon the land which the Lord thy God giveth thee.
> "Thou shalt not kill.
> "Thou shalt not commit adultery.
> "Thou shalt not steal.
> "Thou shalt not bear false witness against thy neighbor.
> "Thou shalt not covet thy neighbor's house.
> "Thou shalt not covet thy neighbor's wife, nor his manservant, nor his maidservant, nor his cattle, nor anything that is thy neighbor's."

Viewed on its face, Texas's display has no purported connection to God's role in the formation of Texas or the founding of our Nation; nor does it provide the reasonable observer with any basis to guess that it was erected to honor any individual or organization. The message transmitted by Texas's chosen display is quite plain: This State endorses the divine code of the "Judeo-Christian" God.

For those of us who learned to recite the King James version of the text long before we understood the meaning of some of its words, God's Commandments may seem like wise counsel. The question before this Court, however, is whether it is counsel that the State of Texas may proclaim without violating the Establishment Clause of the Constitution. If any fragment of Jefferson's metaphorical "wall of separation between church and State" is to be preserved—if there remains any meaning to the "wholesome 'neutrality' of which this Court's [Establishment Clause] cases speak," *School Dist. of Abington Township v. Schempp*, 374 U.S. 203 (1963)—a negative answer to that question is mandatory.

In my judgment, at the very least, the Establishment Clause has created a strong presumption against the display of religious symbols on public property. The adornment of our public spaces with displays of religious symbols and messages undoubtedly provides comfort, even inspiration, to many individuals who subscribe to particular faiths. Unfortunately, the practice also runs the risk of "offend[ing] nonmembers of the faith being advertised as well as adherents who consider the particular advertisement disrespectful."

Government's obligation to avoid divisiveness and exclusion in the religious sphere is compelled by the Establishment and Free Exercise Clauses, which together erect a wall of separation between church and state. This metaphorical wall protects principles long recognized and often recited in this Court's cases. The first and most fundamental of these principles, one that a majority of this Court today affirms, is that the Establishment Clause demands religious neutrality—government may not exercise a preference for one religious faith over another. This essential command, however, is not merely a prohibition against the government's differentiation among religious sects. We have repeatedly reaffirmed that neither a State nor the Federal Government "can constitutionally pass laws or impose requirements which aid all religions as against non-believers, and neither can aid those religions based on a belief in the existence of God as against those religions founded on different beliefs." *Torcaso v. Watkins*, 367 U.S. 488 (1961). This principle is based on the straightforward notion that governmental promotion of orthodoxy is not saved by the aggregation of several orthodoxies under the State's banner. . . .

The monolith displayed on Texas Capitol grounds cannot be discounted as a passive acknowledgment of religion, nor can the State's refusal to remove it upon objection be explained as a simple desire to preserve a historic relic. This Nation's resolute commitment to neutrality with respect to religion is flatly inconsistent with the plurality's wholehearted validation of an official state endorsement of the message that there is one, and only one, God.

When the Ten Commandments monument was donated to the State of Texas in 1961, it was not for the purpose of commemorating a noteworthy event in Texas history, signifying the Commandments' influence on the development of secular law, or even denoting the religious beliefs of Texans at that time. To the contrary, the donation was only one of over a hundred largely identical monoliths, and of over a thousand paper replicas, distributed to state and local governments throughout the Nation over the course of several decades. This ambitious project was the work of the Fraternal Order of Eagles, a well-respected benevolent organization whose good works have earned the praise of several Presidents.

As the story goes, the program was initiated by the late Judge E. J. Ruegemer, a Minnesota juvenile court judge and then-Chairman of the Eagles National Commission on Youth Guidance. Inspired by a juvenile offender who had never heard of the Ten Commandments, the judge approached the Minnesota Eagles with the idea of distributing paper copies of the Commandments to be posted in courthouses nationwide. The State's Aerie undertook this project and its popularity spread. When Cecil B. DeMille, who at that time was filming the movie *The Ten Commandments*, heard of the judge's endeavor, he teamed up with the Eagles to produce the type of granite monolith now displayed in front of the Texas Capitol and at courthouse squares, city halls, and public parks throughout the Nation. Granite was reportedly chosen over DeMille's original suggestion of bronze plaques to better replicate the original Ten Commandments.

The donors were motivated by a desire to "inspire the youth" and curb juvenile delinquency by providing children with a "code of conduct or standards by which to govern their actions." It is the Eagles' belief that disseminating the message conveyed by the Ten Commandments will help to persuade young men and women to observe civilized standards of behavior, and will lead to more productive lives. Significantly, although the Eagles' organization is nonsectarian, eligibility for membership is premised on a belief in the existence of a "Supreme Being."

The desire to combat juvenile delinquency by providing guidance to youths is both admirable and unquestionably secular. But achieving that goal through biblical teachings injects a religious purpose into an otherwise secular endeavor. By spreading the word of God and converting heathens to Christianity, missionaries expect to enlighten their converts, enhance their satisfaction with life, and improve their behavior. Similarly, by disseminating the "law of God"—directing fidelity to God and proscribing murder, theft, and adultery—the Eagles hope that this divine guidance will help wayward youths conform their behavior and improve their lives. In my judgment, the significant secular byproducts that are intended consequences of religious instruction—indeed, of the establishment of most religions—are not the type of "secular" purposes that justify government promulgation of sacred religious messages....

The judgment of the Court in this case stands for the proposition that the Constitution permits governmental displays of sacred religious texts. This makes a mockery of the constitutional ideal that government must remain neutral between religion and irreligion. If a State may endorse a particular deity's command to "have no other gods before me," it is difficult to conceive of any textual display that would run afoul of the Establishment Clause....
I respectfully dissent.

McCreary County v. American Civil Liberties Union of Kentucky
125 S.Ct. 2722 (2005)

Two Kentucky counties, McCreary and Pulaski, in 1999 had installed in their courthouses large copies of the King James version of the Ten Commandments. The constitutionality of those public displays was immediately challenged by the American Civil Liberties Union (ACLU) chapter in the state. Subsequently, the counties passed resolutions declaring the Ten Commandments a "precedent legal code" for Kentucky's laws, and directing the addition of other historical documents, such as President Abraham Lincoln's declaration of a national prayer in 1863. After a federal district court found that display to run afoul of the First Amendment in 2000, the counties added several other secular documents, including the Magna Carta and the lyrics of "The Star Spangled Banner." That third display of the Ten Commandments, surrounded by other historical documents, was again challenged by the ACLU. In 2000, a district court ordered the removal of the displays. The counties appealed, arguing that the displays had a secular and educational purpose, but the Court of Appeals for the Sixth Circuit disagreed and affirmed the trial court. Whereupon, McCreary county appealed and the Supreme Court granted review.

The appellate court's decision was affirmed on a five to four vote. Justice Souter delivered the opinion for the Court. Justice O'Connor filed a concurring opinion. Justice Scalia filed a dissenting opinion, which Chief Justice Rehnquist and Justices Kennedy and Thomas joined.

☐ *Justice SOUTER delivered the opinion of the Court.*

Twenty-five years ago in a case prompted by posting the Ten Commandments in Kentucky's public schools, this Court recognized that the Commandments "are undeniably a sacred text in the Jewish and Christian faiths" and held that their display in public classrooms violated the First Amendment's bar against establishment of religion. *Stone* [*v. Graham*] 449 U.S. [39 (1980)]. *Stone* found a predominantly religious purpose in the government's posting of the Commandments, given their prominence as "'an instrument of religion'" (quoting *School Dist. of Abington Township v. Schempp*, 374 U.S. 203 (1963)). The Counties ask for a different approach here by arguing that official purpose is unknowable and the search for it inherently vain. In the alternative, the Counties would avoid the District Court's conclusion by having us limit the scope of the purpose enquiry so severely that any trivial rationalization would suffice, under a standard oblivious to the history of religious government action like the progression of exhibits in this case.

Ever since *Lemon v. Kurtzman* [403 U.S. 602 (1971)] summarized the three familiar considerations for evaluating Establishment Clause claims, looking to whether government action has "a secular legislative purpose" has been a common, albeit seldom dispositive, element of our cases. Though we have found government action motivated by an illegitimate purpose only four times since *Lemon*, and "the secular purpose requirement alone may rarely be determinative . . . , it nevertheless serves an important function." *Wallace v. Jaffree*, 472 U.S. 38 (1985) (O'CONNOR, J., concurring in judgment).

The touchstone for our analysis is the principle that the "First Amendment mandates governmental neutrality between religion and religion, and between religion and nonreligion." *Epperson v. Arkansas*, 393 U.S. 97 (1968); *Everson v. Board of Ed. of Ewing*, 330 U.S. 1 (1947); *Wallace v. Jaffree*. When the government acts with the ostensible and predominant purpose of advancing religion, it violates that central Establishment Clause value of official religious neutrality, there being no neutrality when the government's ostensible object is to take sides.

Indeed, the purpose apparent from government action can have an impact more significant than the result expressly decreed: when the government maintains Sunday closing laws, it advances religion only minimally because many working people would take the day as one of rest regardless, but if the government justified its decision with a stated desire for all Americans to honor Christ, the divisive thrust of the official action would be inescapable. This is the teaching of *McGowan v. Maryland*, 366 U.S. 420 (1961), which upheld Sunday closing statutes on practical, secular grounds after finding that the government had forsaken the religious purposes behind centuries-old predecessor laws.

Despite the intuitive importance of official purpose to the realization of Establishment Clause values, the Counties ask us to abandon *Lemon*'s purpose test, or at least to truncate any enquiry into purpose here. Their first argument is that the very consideration of purpose is deceptive: according to them, true "purpose" is unknowable, and its search merely an excuse for courts to act selectively and unpredictably in picking out evidence of subjective intent. The assertions are as seismic as they are unconvincing.

Examination of purpose is a staple of statutory interpretation that makes up the daily fare of every appellate court in the country, and governmental purpose is a key element of a good deal of constitutional doctrine, *Church of Lukumi Babalu Aye, Inc. v. Hialeah*, 508 U.S. 520 (1993) (discriminatory purpose raises level of scrutiny required by free exercise claim). With enquiries into purpose this common, if they were nothing but hunts for mares' nests deflecting attention from bare judicial will, the whole notion of purpose in law would have dropped into disrepute long ago.

But scrutinizing purpose does make practical sense, as in Establishment Clause analysis, where an understanding of official objective emerges from readily discoverable fact, without any judicial psychoanalysis of a drafter's heart of hearts. The eyes that look to purpose belong to an "'objective observer,'" one who takes account of the traditional external signs that show up in the "'text, legislative history, and implementation of the statute,'" or comparable official act. There is, then, nothing hinting at an unpredictable or disingenuous exercise when a court enquires into purpose after a claim is raised under the Establishment Clause.

The cases with findings of a predominantly religious purpose point to the straightforward nature of the test. In *Wallace*, for example, we inferred purpose from a change of wording from an earlier statute to a later one, each dealing with prayer in schools. . . .

After declining the invitation to abandon concern with purpose wholesale, we also have to avoid the Counties' alternative tack of trivializing the enquiry into it. The Counties would read the cases as if the purpose enquiry were so naive that any transparent claim to secularity would satisfy it, and they would cut context out of the enquiry, to the point of ignoring history, no matter what bearing it actually had on the significance of current circumstances. There is no precedent for the Counties' arguments, or reason supporting them.

Lemon said that government action must have "a secular . . . purpose," and after a host of cases it is fair to add that although a legislature's stated reasons will generally get deference, the secular purpose required has to be genuine, not a sham, and not merely secondary to a religious objective. . . .

We take *Stone* as the initial legal benchmark, our only case dealing with the constitutionality of displaying the Commandments. *Stone* recognized that the Commandments are an "instrument of religion" and that, at least on the facts before it, the display of their text could presumptively be understood as meant to advance religion: although state law specifically required their posting in public school classrooms, their isolated exhibition did not leave room even for an argument that secular education explained their being there. But *Stone* did not purport to decide the constitutionality of every possible way the Commandments might be set out by the government, and under the Establishment Clause detail is key. *County of Allegheny v. American Civil Liberties Union, Greater Pittsburgh Chapter*, 492 U.S. 573 (1989) (opinion of BLACKMUN, J.) ("[T]he question is what viewers may fairly understand to be the purpose of the display. That inquiry, of necessity, turns upon the context in which the contested object appears"). Hence, we look to the record of evidence showing the progression leading up to the third display of the Commandments.

The display rejected in *Stone* had two obvious similarities to the first one in the sequence here: both set out a text of the Commandments as distinct from any traditionally symbolic representation, and each stood alone, not part of an arguably secular display. *Stone* stressed the significance of integrating the Commandments into a secular scheme to forestall the broadcast of an otherwise clearly religious message, and for good reason, the Commandments being a central point of reference in the religious and moral history of Jews and Christians. They proclaim the existence of a monotheistic god (no other gods).... The reasonable observer could only think that the Counties meant to emphasize and celebrate the Commandments' religious message.

This is not to deny that the Commandments have had influence on civil or secular law; a major text of a majority religion is bound to be felt. The point is simply that the original text viewed in its entirety is an unmistakably religious statement dealing with religious obligations and with morality subject to religious sanction. When the government initiates an effort to place this statement alone in public view, a religious object is unmistakable.

Once the Counties were sued, they modified the exhibits and invited additional insight into their purpose in a display that hung for about six months. This new one was the product of forthright and nearly identical Pulaski and McCreary County resolutions listing a series of American historical documents with theistic and Christian references, which were to be posted in order to furnish a setting for displaying the Ten Commandments and any "other Kentucky and American historical documen[t]" without raising concern about "any Christian or religious references" in them. As mentioned, the resolutions expressed support for an Alabama judge who posted the Commandments in his courtroom, and cited the fact the Kentucky Legislature once adjourned a session in honor of "Jesus Christ, Prince of Ethics."

In this second display, unlike the first, the Commandments were not hung in isolation, merely leaving the Counties' purpose to emerge from the pervasively religious text of the Commandments themselves. Instead, the second version was required to include the statement of the government's purpose expressly set out in the county resolutions, and underscored it by juxtaposing the Commandments to other documents with highlighted references to God as their sole common element. The display's unstinting focus was on religious passages, showing that the Counties were posting the Commandments precisely because of their sectarian content. That demonstration of the government's objective was enhanced by serial religious references and the accompanying resolution's claim about the embodiment of ethics in Christ. Together, the display and resolution presented an indisputable, and undisputed, showing of an impermissible purpose.

Today, the Counties make no attempt to defend their undeniable objective, but instead hopefully describe version two as "dead and buried." Their refusal to defend the second display is understandable, but the reasonable observer could not forget it. After the Counties changed lawyers, they mounted a third display, without a new resolution or repeal of the old one. The result was the "Foundations of American Law and Government" exhibit, which placed the Commandments in the company of other documents the Counties thought especially significant in the historical foundation of American government. In trying to persuade the District Court to lift the preliminary injunction, the Counties cited several new purposes for the third version, including a desire "to educate the citizens of the county regarding some of the documents that played a significant role in the foundation of our system of law and government." The Counties' claims did not, however, persuade the court, intimately familiar with the details of this litigation, or the Court of Appeals, neither of which found a legitimizing secular purpose in this third version of the display. The conclusions of the two courts preceding us in this case are well warranted.

These new statements of purpose were presented only as a litigating position, there being no further authorizing action by the Counties' governing boards. And although repeal of the earlier county authorizations would not have erased them from the record of evidence bearing on current purpose, the extraordinary resolutions for the second display passed just months earlier were not repealed or otherwise repudiated. Indeed, the sectarian spirit of the common resolution found enhanced expression in the third display, which quoted more of the purely religious language of the Commandments than the first two displays had done ("I the LORD thy God am a jealous God") (text of Second Commandment in third display); ("the LORD will not hold him guiltless that taketh his name in vain") (from text of Third Commandment); and ("that thy days may be long upon the land which the LORD thy God giveth thee") (text of Fifth Commandment). No reasonable observer could swallow the claim that the Counties had cast off the objective so unmistakable in the earlier displays.

Nor did the selection of posted material suggest a clear theme that might prevail over evidence of the continuing religious object. In a collection of documents said to be "foundational" to American government, it is at least odd to include a patriotic anthem, but to omit the Fourteenth Amendment, the most significant structural provision adopted since the original Framing....

In holding the preliminary injunction adequately supported by evidence that the Counties' purpose had not changed at the third stage, we do not decide that the Counties' past actions forever taint any effort on their part to deal with the subject matter. We hold only that purpose needs to be taken seriously under the Establishment Clause and needs to be understood in light of context; an implausible claim that governmental purpose has changed should not carry the day in a court of law any more than in a head with common sense....

Nor do we have occasion here to hold that a sacred text can never be integrated constitutionally into a governmental display on the subject of law, or American history. We do not forget, and in this litigation have frequently been reminded, that our own courtroom frieze was deliberately designed in the exercise of governmental authority so as to include the figure of Moses holding tablets exhibiting a portion of the Hebrew text of the later, secularly phrased Commandments; in the company of 17 other lawgivers, most of them secular figures, there is no risk that Moses would strike an observer as evidence that the National Government was violating neutrality in religion.

The importance of neutrality as an interpretive guide is no less true now than it was when the Court broached the principle in *Everson v. Board of Ed. of Ewing*, 330 U.S. 1 (1947), and a word needs to be said about the different view taken in today's dissent. We all agree, of course, on the need for some interpretative help. The First Amendment contains no textual definition of "establishment," and the term is certainly not self-defining. No one contends that the prohibition of establishment stops at a designation of a national (or with Fourteenth Amendment incorporation, *Cantwell v. Connecticut*, 310 U.S. 296 (1940), a state) church, but nothing in the text says just how much more it covers. There is no simple answer, for more than one reason.

The prohibition on establishment covers a variety of issues from prayer in widely varying government settings, to financial aid for religious individuals and institutions, to comment on religious questions. In these varied settings, issues of about interpreting inexact Establishment Clause language, like difficult interpretative issues generally, arise from the tension of competing values, each constitutionally respectable, but none open to realization to the logical limit. . . .

Given the variety of interpretative problems, the principle of neutrality has provided a good sense of direction: the government may not favor one religion over another, or religion over irreligion, religious choice being the prerogative of individuals under the Free Exercise Clause. The principle has been helpful simply because it responds to one of the major concerns that prompted adoption of the Religion Clauses. The Framers and the citizens of their time intended not only to protect the integrity of individual conscience in religious matters, *Wallace v. Jaffree*, but to guard against the civic divisiveness that follows when the Government weighs in on one side of religious debate; nothing does a better job of roiling society, a point that needed no explanation to the descendants of English Puritans and Cavaliers (or Massachusetts Puritans and Baptists). A sense of the past thus points to governmental neutrality as an objective of the Establishment Clause, and a sensible standard for applying it. To be sure, given its generality as a principle, an appeal to neutrality alone cannot possibly lay every issue to rest, or tell us what issues on the margins are substantial enough for constitutional significance, a point that has been clear from the Founding era to modern times. But invoking neutrality is a prudent way of keeping sight of something the Framers of the First Amendment thought important. . . .

[W]e affirm the Sixth Circuit in upholding the preliminary injunction.

☐ *Justice SCALIA, with whom THE CHIEF JUSTICE and Justice THOMAS join, and with whom Justice KENNEDY joins [in part], dissenting.*

[O]ne model of the relationship between church and state—a model spread across Europe by the armies of Napoleon, and reflected in the Constitution of France, which begins "France is [a] . . . secular . . . Republic." Religion is to be strictly excluded from the public forum. This is not, and never was, the model adopted by America. George Washington added to the form of Presidential oath prescribed by Art. II, Sec. 1, cl. 8, of the Constitution, the concluding words "so help me God." The Supreme Court under JOHN MARSHALL opened its sessions with the prayer, "God save the United States and this Honorable Court." The First Congress instituted the practice of beginning its legislative sessions with a prayer. *Marsh v. Chambers*, 463 U.S. 783 (1983). The same week that Congress submitted the Establishment Clause as part of the Bill of Rights for ratification by the States, it enacted legislation providing for paid chaplains in the House and Senate. The day after the First Amendment was proposed, the same Congress that had proposed it requested the President to proclaim "a day of public thanksgiving and prayer, to be observed, by acknowledging, with grateful hearts, the many and signal favours of Almighty God." President Washington offered the first Thanksgiving Proclamation shortly thereafter, devoting November 26, 1789, on behalf of the American people "'to the service of that great and glorious Being who is the beneficent author of all the good that is, that was, or that will be,'" thus beginning a tradition of offering gratitude to God that continues today. The same Congress also reenacted the Northwest Territory Ordinance of 1787, 1 Stat. 50, Article III of which provided: "Religion, morality, and knowledge, being necessary to good government and the happiness of mankind, schools and the means of education shall forever be encouraged." And of course the First Amendment itself accords religion (and no other manner of belief) special constitutional protection.

These actions of our First President and Congress and the MARSHALL Court were not idiosyncratic; they reflected the beliefs of the period. Those who wrote the Constitution believed that morality was essential to the well-being of society and that encouragement of religion was the best way to foster morality....

Nor have the views of our people on this matter significantly changed. Presidents continue to conclude the Presidential oath with the words "so help me God." Our legislatures, state and national, continue to open their sessions with prayer led by official chaplains. The sessions of this Court continue to open with the prayer "God save the United States and this Honorable Court." Invocation of the Almighty by our public figures, at all levels of government, remains commonplace. Our coinage bears the motto "IN GOD WE TRUST." And our Pledge of Allegiance contains the acknowledgment that we are a Nation "under God." As one of our Supreme Court opinions rightly observed, "We are a religious people whose institutions presuppose a Supreme Being." *Zorach v. Clauson*, 343 U.S. 306 (1952), repeated with approval in *Lynch v. Donnelly*, 465 U.S. 668 (1984).

With all of this reality (and much more) staring it in the face, how can the Court possibly assert that "'the First Amendment mandates governmental neutrality between ... religion and nonreligion,'" and that "[m]anifesting a purpose to favor ... adherence to religion generally," is unconstitutional? Who says so? Surely not the words of the Constitution. Surely not the history and traditions that reflect our society's constant understanding of those words. Surely not even the current sense of our society.... Nothing stands behind the Court's assertion that governmental affirmation of the society's belief in God is unconstitutional except the Court's own say-so, citing as support only the unsubstantiated say-so of earlier Courts going back no farther than the mid-20th century....

What distinguishes the rule of law from the dictatorship of a shifting Supreme Court majority is the absolutely indispensable requirement that judicial opinions be grounded in consistently applied principle. That is what prevents judges from ruling now this way, now that—thumbs up or thumbs down—as their personal preferences dictate. Today's opinion forthrightly (or actually, somewhat less than forthrightly) admits that it does not rest upon consistently applied principle. In a revealing footnote, the Court acknowledges that the "Establishment Clause doctrine" it purports to be applying "lacks the comfort of categorical absolutes." What the Court means by this lovely euphemism is that sometimes the Court chooses to decide cases on the principle that government cannot favor religion, and sometimes it does not. The footnote goes on to say that "[i]n special instances we have found good reason" to dispense with the principle, but "[n]o such reasons present themselves here." It does not identify all of those "special instances," much less identify the "good reason" for their existence. . . .

Besides appealing to the demonstrably false principle that the government cannot favor religion over irreligion, today's opinion suggests that the posting of the Ten Commandments violates the principle that the government cannot favor one religion over another. That is indeed a valid principle where public aid or assistance to religion is concerned, see *Zelman v. Simmons-Harris*, 536 U.S. 639 (2002), or where the free exercise of religion is at issue, *Church of Lukumi Babalu Aye, Inc. v. Hialeah*, 508 U.S. 520 (1993), but it necessarily applies in a more limited sense to public acknowledgment of the Creator. If religion in the public forum had to be entirely nondenominational, there could be no religion in the public forum at all. One cannot say the word "God," or "the Almighty," one cannot offer public supplication or thanksgiving, without contradicting the beliefs of some people that there are many gods, or that God or the gods pay no attention to human affairs. With respect to public acknowledgment of religious belief, it is entirely clear from our Nation's historical practices that the Establishment Clause permits this disregard of polytheists and believers in unconcerned deities, just as it permits the disregard of devout atheists. The Thanksgiving Proclamation issued by George Washington at the instance of the First Congress was scrupulously nondenominational—but it was monotheistic. In *Marsh v. Chambers*, we said that the fact the particular prayers offered in the Nebraska Legislature were "in the Judeo-Christian tradition," posed no additional problem, because "there is no indication that the prayer opportunity has been exploited to proselytize or advance any one, or to disparage any other, faith or belief."

Historical practices thus demonstrate that there is a distance between the acknowledgment of a single Creator and the establishment of a religion. The former is, as *Marsh v. Chambers* put it, "a tolerable acknowledgment of beliefs widely held among the people of this country." The three most popular religions in the United States, Christianity, Judaism, and Islam—which combined account for 97.7% of all believers—are monotheistic. All of them, moreover (Islam included), believe that the Ten Commandments were given by God to Moses, and are divine prescriptions for a virtuous life. Publicly honoring the Ten Commandments is thus indistinguishable, insofar as discriminating against other religions is concerned, from publicly honoring God. . . .

To any person who happened to walk down the hallway of the McCreary or Pulaski County Courthouse during the roughly nine months when the Foundations Displays were exhibited, the displays must have seemed unremarkable—if indeed they were noticed at all. The walls of both courthouses were already lined with historical documents and other assorted portraits; each Foundations Display was exhibited in the same format as these other displays and nothing in the record suggests that either County took steps to give it greater prominence.

Entitled "The Foundations of American Law and Government Display," each display consisted of nine equally sized documents: the original version of the Magna Carta, the Declaration of Independence, the Bill of Rights, the

Star Spangled Banner, the Mayflower Compact of 1620, a picture of Lady Justice, the National Motto of the United States ("In God We Trust"), the Preamble to the Kentucky Constitution, and the Ten Commandments. The displays did not emphasize any of the nine documents in any way: The frame holding the Ten Commandments was of the same size and had the same appearance as that which held each of the other documents.

Posted with the documents was a plaque, identifying the display, and explaining that it "contains documents that played a significant role in the foundation of our system of law and government." [T]he Foundations Displays manifested the purely secular purpose that the Counties asserted before the District Court: "to display documents that played a significant role in the foundation of our system of law and government." That the Displays included the Ten Commandments did not transform their apparent secular purpose into one of impermissible advocacy for Judeo-Christian beliefs....

Acknowledgment of the contribution that religion has made to our Nation's legal and governmental heritage partakes of a centuries-old tradition....

Perhaps in recognition of the centrality of the Ten Commandments as a widely recognized symbol of religion in public life, the Court is at pains to dispel the impression that its decision will require governments across the country to sandblast the Ten Commandments from the public square. The constitutional problem, the Court says, is with the Counties' purpose in erecting the Foundations Displays, not the displays themselves. The Court adds in a footnote: "One consequence of taking account of the purpose underlying past actions is that the same government action may be constitutional if taken in the first instance and unconstitutional if it has a sectarian heritage."

This inconsistency may be explicable in theory, but I suspect that the "objective observer" with whom the Court is so concerned will recognize its absurdity in practice. By virtue of details familiar only to the parties to litigation and their lawyers, McCreary and Pulaski Counties, Kentucky, and Rutherford County, Tennessee, have been ordered to remove the same display that appears in courthouses from Mercer County, Kentucky to Elkhart County, Indiana. Displays erected in silence (and under the direction of good legal advice) are permissible, while those hung after discussion and debate are deemed unconstitutional. Reduction of the Establishment Clause to such minutiae trivializes the Clause's protection against religious establishment; indeed, it may inflame religious passions by making the passing comments of every government official the subject of endless litigation....

In sum: The first displays did not necessarily evidence an intent to further religious practice; nor did the second displays, or the resolutions authorizing them; and there is in any event no basis for attributing whatever intent motivated the first and second displays to the third. Given the presumption of regularity that always accompanies our review of official action, the Court has identified no evidence of a purpose to advance religion in a way that is inconsistent with our cases. The Court may well be correct in identifying the third displays as the fruit of a desire to display the Ten Commandments, ante, at 24, but neither our cases nor our history support its assertion that such a desire renders the fruit poisonous.

For the foregoing reasons, I would reverse the judgment of the Court of Appeals.

B | *Free Exercise of Religion*

Although in *City of Boerne v. Flores*, 521 U.S. 507 (1997) (excerpted in Vol. 1, Ch. 6, and Vol. 2, Ch. 6), the Court ruled that the Religious Freedom Restoration Act (RFRA)'s application to state laws exceeded Congress's power, in *Gonzales v. O Centro Espirita Beneficente Uniao do Vegetal*, 126 S.Ct. 1211 (2006), the Court unanimously held that the RFRA permitted federal courts to make exceptions for religious minorities on a case-by-case basis from generally applicable federal laws on the use of drugs, if used in a "sincere exercise of religion." Writing for the Court, Chief Justice Roberts noted that peyote, a hallucinogen, had been made an exception to the Controlled Substances Act (CSA) for use by Native Americans for 35 years. In permitting the importation of *hoasca* (pronounced "wass-ca") for use by a small sect originating in the Amazon rainforest, he observed that: "If such use is permitted . . . for hundreds of thousands of Native Americans practicing their faith, it is difficult to see how those same findings alone can preclude any consideration of a similar exception for the 130 or so American members of the [O Centro Espirita Beneficente Uniao] who want to practice theirs." In so holding, Chief Justice Roberts rejected the Bush administration's arguments that it had compelling governmental interests in forbidding the importation of *hoasca* based on (1) protecting the health of users, (2) preventing the diversion of the drug to recreational users, and (3) complying with the 1971 U.N. Convention on Psychotropic Substances.

7

THE FOURTH AMENDMENT GUARANTEE AGAINST UNREASONABLE SEARCHES AND SEIZURES

A | *Requirements for a Warrant and Reasonable Searches and Seizures*

In *Muehler v. Mena*, 544 U.S. 93 (2005), the Court held unanimously that when executing a search warrant police may handcuff and detain the occupants in order to minimize the risk of harm to the officers. Writing for the Court, Chief Justice Rehnquist reaffirmed the holding in *Michigan v. Summers*, 452 U.S. 692 (1981), that police executing a warrant for contraband may "detain the occupants of the premises while a proper search is conducted."

In its 2005-2006 term, *United States v. Grubbs*, 126 S.Ct. 1492 (2006), held that judges may issue "anticipatory" search warrants based on probable cause that a crime is about to be committed. The case involved a warrant for a parcel containing a videotape of child pornography that would not be executed until the parcel arrived and was taken into possession. An undercover postal agent had alerted police that Grubbs had ordered the videotape. Justice Scalia upheld such "anticipatory" search warrants based on the traditional standard of probable cause when "there is a fair probability that contraband or evidence of crime" will be found, even though the warrant is issued in advance of the particular item deemed evidence of a crime. In short, the triggering event is not necessary for a warrant because the Fourth Amendment requires only that a warrant specifies the "place to be searched" and "the persons or things to be seized."

The Court also held, in *Georgia v. Randolph* (excerpted below), that police may not search a home without a warrant based on the consent of one spouse and over the objections of the other. The Court affirmed the Georgia state supreme court's holding that when both spouses are present they both must consent to a warrantless search of their premises, over the objections of dissenting Chief Justice Roberts and Justices Scalia and Thomas.

Georgia v. Randolph
126 S.Ct. 1515 (2006)

Scott Randolph and his wife were separated but she returned to their house and subsequently complained to police about a domestic dispute. When the police arrived, she told them that her husband was a cocaine addict and gave them permission to search the house. Scott Randolph repeatedly denied permission for a search of the house. Nonetheless, the police conducted a search and found evidence of cocaine use, which after his arrest was introduced at trial. Randolph's attorney moved to exclude the evidence because the search was conducted without Randolph's consent. The trial court denied the motion, but on appeal a state appellate court reversed that decision and was affirmed by the state supreme court on the ground that "the consent to conduct a warrantless search of a residence given by one occupant is not valid in the face of the refusal of another occupant who is physically present at the scene to permit a warrantless search." The state appealed and the Supreme Court granted review.

The state supreme court's decision was affirmed by a five to three vote, with Justice Alito not participating. Justice Souter delivered the opinion of the Court, and Justices Stevens and Breyer filed concurring opinions, while Chief Justice Roberts and Justices Scalia and Thomas filed dissenting opinions.

☐ *Justice SOUTER delivered the opinion of the Court.*

The Fourth Amendment recognizes a valid warrantless entry and search of premises when police obtain the voluntary consent of an occupant who shares, or is reasonably believed to share, authority over the area in common with a co-occupant who later objects to the use of evidence so obtained. *Illinois v. Rodriguez*, 497 U.S. 177 (1990); *United States v. Matlock*, 415 U.S. 164 (1974). The question here is whether such an when evidentiary seizure is likewise lawful with the permission of one occupant when the other, who later seeks to suppress the evidence, is present at the scene and expressly refuses to consent. We hold that, in the circumstances here at issue, a physically present co-occupant's stated refusal to permit entry prevails, rendering the warrantless search unreasonable and invalid as to him....

The constant element in assessing Fourth Amendment reasonableness in the consent cases, then, is the great significance given to widely shared social expectations, which are naturally enough influenced by the law of property, but not controlled by its rules. *Matlock* accordingly not only holds that a solitary co-inhabitant may sometimes consent to a search of shared premises, but stands for the proposition that the reasonableness of such a search is in significant part a function of commonly held understanding about the authority that co-inhabitants may exercise in ways that affect each other's interests....

As *Matlock* put it, shared tenancy is understood to include an "assumption of risk," on which police officers are entitled to rely, and although some group living together might make an exceptional arrangement that no one could admit a guest without the agreement of all, the chance of such an eccentric scheme is too remote to expect visitors to investigate a particular household's rules before accepting an invitation to come in. So, *Matlock* relied on what was usual and placed no burden on the police to eliminate the possibility of atypical arrangements, in the absence of reason to doubt that the regular scheme was in place....

Although we have not dealt directly with the reasonableness of police entry in reliance on consent by one occupant subject to immediate challenge by another, we took a step toward the issue in an earlier case dealing with the Fourth Amendment rights of a social guest arrested at premises the police entered without a warrant or the benefit of any exception to the warrant requirement. *Minnesota v. Olson*, 495 U.S. 91 (1990), held that overnight houseguests have a legitimate expectation of privacy in their temporary quarters because "it is unlikely that [the host] will admit someone who wants to see or meet with the guest over the objection of the guest." If that customary expectation of courtesy or deference is a foundation of Fourth Amendment rights of a houseguest, it presumably should follow that an inhabitant of shared premises may claim at least as much, and it turns out that the co-inhabitant naturally has an even stronger claim.

To begin with, it is fair to say that a caller standing at the door of shared premises would have no confidence that one occupant's invitation was a sufficiently good reason to enter when a fellow tenant stood there saying, "stay out." Without some very good reason, no sensible person would go inside under those conditions. Fear for the safety of the occupant issuing the invitation, or of someone else inside, would be thought to justify entry, but the justification then would be the personal risk, the threats to life or limb, not the disputed invitation.

The visitor's reticence without some such good reason would show not timidity but a realization that when people living together disagree over the use of their common quarters, a resolution must come through voluntary accommodation, not by appeals to authority. Unless the people living together fall within some recognized hierarchy, like a household of parent and child or barracks housing military personnel of different grades, there is no societal understanding of superior and inferior, a fact reflected in a standard formulation of domestic property law, that "[e]ach cotenant . . . has the right to use and enjoy the entire property as if he or she were the sole owner, limited only by the same right in the other cotenants." . . .

Since the co-tenant wishing to open the door to a third party has no recognized authority in law or social practice to prevail over a present and objecting co-tenant, his disputed invitation, without more, gives a police officer no better claim to reasonableness in entering than the officer would have in the absence of any consent at all. Accordingly, in the balancing of competing individual and governmental interests entailed by the bar to unreasonable searches, the cooperative occupant's invitation adds nothing to the government's side to counter the force of an objecting individual's claim to security against the government's intrusion into his dwelling place. Since we hold to the "centuries-old principle of respect for the privacy of the home," *Wilson v. Layne*, 526 U.S. 603 (1999), "it is beyond dispute that the home is entitled to special protection as the center of the private lives of our people," *Minnesota v. Carter*, 525 U.S. 83 (1998). We have, after all, lived our whole national history with an understanding of "the ancient adage that a man's home is his castle [to the point that t]he poorest man may in his cottage bid defiance to all the forces of the Crown," *Miller v. United States*, 357 U.S. 301 (1958). . . .

So long as there is no evidence that the police have removed the potentially objecting tenant from the entrance for the sake of avoiding a possible objection, there is practical value in the simple clarity of complementary rules, one recognizing the co-tenant's permission when there is no fellow occupant on hand, the other according dispositive weight to the fellow occupant's contrary indication when he expresses it. For the very reason that *Rodriguez* held it would be unjustifiably impractical to require the police to take affirmative steps to confirm the actual authority of a consenting individual whose authority was apparent, we think it would needlessly limit the capacity of the police to respond to ostensibly legitimate opportunities in the field if we were to hold that reasonableness required the police to take affirmative steps to find a potentially objecting co-tenant before acting on the permission they had already received. There is no ready reason to believe that efforts to invite a refusal would make a difference in many cases, whereas every co-tenant consent case would turn into a test about the adequacy of the police's efforts to consult with a potential objector. Better to accept the formalism of distinguishing *Matlock* from this case than to impose a requirement, time-consuming in the field and in the courtroom, with no apparent systemic justification. The pragmatic decision to accept the simplicity of this line is, moreover, supported by the substantial number of instances in which suspects who are asked for permission to search actually consent, albeit imprudently, a fact that undercuts any argument that the police should try to locate a suspected inhabitant because his denial of consent would be a foregone conclusion.

This case invites a straightforward application of the rule that a physically present inhabitant's express refusal of consent to a police search is dispositive as to him, regardless of the consent of a fellow occupant. Scott Randolph's refusal is clear, and nothing in the record justifies the search on grounds independent of Janet Randolph's consent. The State does not argue that she gave any indication to the police of a need for protection inside the house that might have justified entry into the portion of the premises where the police found the powdery straw (which, if lawfully seized, could have been used when attempting to establish probable cause for the warrant issued later).

Nor does the State claim that the entry and search should be upheld under the rubric of exigent circumstances, owing to some apprehension by the police officers that Scott Randolph would destroy evidence of drug use before any warrant could be obtained.

☐ *Justice Stevens, concurring.*

At least since 1604 it has been settled that in the absence of exigent circumstances, a government agent has no right to enter a "house" or "castle" unless authorized to do so by a valid warrant. Every occupant of the home has a right—protected by the common law for centuries and by the Fourth Amendment since 1791—to refuse entry. When an occupant gives his or her consent to enter, he or she is waiving a valuable constitutional right. To be sure that the waiver is voluntary, it is sound practice—a practice some Justices of this Court thought necessary to make the waiver voluntary—for the officer to advise the occupant of that right. The issue in this case relates to the content of the advice that the officer should provide when met at the door by a man and a woman who are apparently joint tenants or joint owners of the property.

In the 18th century, when the Fourth Amendment was adopted, the advice would have been quite different from what is appropriate today. Given the then-prevailing dramatic differences between the property rights of the husband and the far lesser rights of the wife, only the consent of the husband would matter. Whether "the master of the house" consented or objected, his decision would control. Thus if "original understanding" were to govern the outcome of this case, the search was clearly invalid because the husband did not consent. History, however, is not dispositive because it is now clear, as a matter of constitutional law, that the male and the female are equal partners. *Reed v. Reed*, 404 U.S. 71 (1971).

In today's world the only advice that an officer could properly give should make it clear that each of the partners has a constitutional right that he or she may independently assert or waive. Assuming that both spouses are competent, neither one is a master possessing the power to override the other's constitutional right to deny entry to their castle. With these observations, I join the Court's opinion.

☐ *CHIEF JUSTICE ROBERTS, with whom Justice SCALIA joins, dissenting.*

The Court creates constitutional law by surmising what is typical when a social guest encounters an entirely atypical situation. The rule the majority fashions does not implement the high office of the Fourth Amendment to protect privacy, but instead provides protection on a random and happenstance basis, protecting, for example, a co-occupant who happens to be at the front door when the other occupant consents to a search, but not one napping or watching television in the next room. And the cost of affording such random protection is great, as demonstrated by the recurring cases in which abused spouses seek to authorize police entry into a home they share with a nonconsenting abuser.

The correct approach to the question presented is clearly mapped out in our precedents: The Fourth Amendment protects privacy. If an individual shares information, papers, or places with another, he assumes the risk that the other person will in turn share access to that information or those papers or places with the government. And just as an individual who has shared illegal plans or incriminating documents with another cannot interpose an objection when that other person turns the information over to the government, just because the individual happens to be present at the time, so too someone who shares a place with another cannot interpose an objection when that person decides to grant access to the police, simply because the objecting individual happens to be present.

A warrantless search is reasonable if police obtain the voluntary consent of a person authorized to give it. Co-occupants have "assumed the risk that one of their number might permit [a] common area to be searched." *United States v. Matlock*, 415 U.S. 164 (1974). Just as Mrs. Randolph could walk upstairs, come down, and turn her husband's cocaine straw over to the police, she can consent to police entry and search of what is, after all, her home, too.

In *Illinois v. Rodriguez*, 497 U.S. 177 (1990), this Court stated that "[w]hat [a person] is assured by the Fourth Amendment . . . is not that no government search of his house will occur unless he consents; but that no such search will occur that is 'unreasonable.'" One element that can make a warrantless government search of a home "'reasonable'" is voluntary consent. Proof of voluntary consent "is not limited to proof that consent was given by the defendant," but the government "may show that permission to search was obtained from a third party who possessed common authority over or other sufficient relationship to the premises." *Matlock*. Today's opinion creates an exception to this otherwise clear rule: A third-party consent search is unreasonable, and therefore constitutionally impermissible, if the co-occupant against whom evidence is obtained was present and objected to the entry and search.

This exception is based on what the majority describes as "widely shared social expectations" that "when people living together disagree over the use of their common quarters, a resolution must come through voluntary accommodation." But this fundamental predicate to the majority's analysis gets us nowhere: Does the objecting cotenant accede to the consenting cotenant's wishes, or the other way around? The majority's assumption about voluntary accommodation simply leads to the common stalemate of two gentlemen insisting that the other enter a room first. . . .

The common thread in our decisions upholding searches conducted pursuant to third-party consent is an understanding that a person "assume[s] the risk" that those who have access to and control over his shared property might consent to a search. In *Matlock*, we explained that this assumption of risk is derived from a third party's "joint access or control for most purposes" of shared property. And we concluded that shared use of property makes it "reasonable to recognize that any of the co-inhabitants has the right to permit the inspection in his own right."

In this sense, the risk assumed by a joint occupant is comparable to the risk assumed by one who reveals private information to another. If a person has incriminating information, he can keep it private in the face of a request from police to share it, because he has that right under the Fifth Amendment. If a person occupies a house with incriminating information in it, he can keep that information private in the face of a request from police to search the house, because he has that right under the Fourth Amendment. But if he shares the information—or the house—with another, that other can grant access to the police in each instance. . . .

The majority states its rule as follows: "[A] warrantless search of a shared dwelling for evidence over the express refusal of consent by a physically present resident cannot be justified as reasonable as to him on the basis of consent given to the police by another resident."

Just as the source of the majority's rule is not privacy, so too the interest it protects cannot reasonably be described as such. That interest is not protected if a co-owner happens to be absent when the police arrive, in the backyard gardening, asleep in the next room, or listening to music through earphones so that only his co-occupant hears the knock on the door. That the rule is so random in its application confirms that it bears no real relation to the privacy protected by the Fourth Amendment. What the majority's rule protects is not so much privacy as the good luck of a co-owner who just happens to be present at the door when the police arrive....

I respectfully dissent.

☐ *JUSTICE SCALIA, dissenting.*

It is not as clear to me as it is to Justice STEVENS that, at the time the Fourth Amendment was adopted, a police officer could enter a married woman's home over her objection, and could not enter with only her consent. Nor is it clear to me that the answers to these questions depended solely on who owned the house. It is entirely clear, however, that if the matter did depend solely on property rights, a latter-day alteration of property rights would also produce a latter-day alteration of the Fourth Amendment outcome—without altering the Fourth Amendment itself.

Justice STEVENS' attempted critique of originalism confuses the original import of the Fourth Amendment with the background sources of law to which the Amendment, on its original meaning, referred. From the date of its ratification until well into the 20th century, violation of the Amendment was tied to common-law trespass. On the basis of that connection, someone who had power to license the search of a house by a private party could authorize a police search. The issue of who could give such consent generally depended, in turn, on "historical and legal refinements" of property law. *United States v. Matlock*, 415 U.S. 164 (1974). As property law developed, individuals who previously could not authorize a search might become able to do so, and those who once could grant such consent might no longer have that power. But changes in the law of property to which the Fourth Amendment referred would not alter the Amendment's meaning: that anyone capable of authorizing a search by a private party could consent to a warrantless search by the police.

There is nothing new or surprising in the proposition that our unchanging Constitution refers to other bodies of law that might themselves change. The Fifth Amendment provides, for instance, that "private property" shall not "be taken for public use, without just compensation"; but it does not purport to define property rights....

B | *Exceptions to the Warrant Requirement*

In *Illinois v. Caballes* (2005) (excerpted below), the Court held that police could use drug-sniffing dogs around a car stopped for a routine traffic violation and that prosecutors could introduce evidence of contraband that was found as a result. In doing so, the majority reversed the state supreme court's ruling that such a search unconstitutionally enlarged the scope of permissible searches "without any specific and articulable facts" suggesting criminal activities. Justices Souter and Ginsburg dissented.

In its 2005–2006 term, the Court in a unanimous opinion in *Brigham City, Utah v. Stuart*, 126 S.Ct. 1943 (2006), also held that another exception to the Fourth Amendment requirement that police enter a homeowner's dwelling with a warrant or probable cause is "the need to assist persons who are seriously injured or threatened with such an injury." In Chief Justice Roberts's words: "Law enforcement officers may enter a home without a warrant to render emergency assistance to an injured occupant or to protect an occupant from imminent injury."

In addition, in *Samson v. California*, 126 S.Ct. 2193 (2006), the Court extended its ruling in *United States v. Knights*, 534 U.S. 112 (2001), holding that based on the "totality of circumstances" a warrantless search of a probationer's apartment was reasonable under the Fourth Amendment, to uphold warrantless and suspicionless searches of parolees. Writing for the Court, Justice Thomas ruled that suspicionless searches of parolees are reasonable based on the government's interests in monitoring parolees and protecting potential victims. Justices Stevens, Souter, and Breyer dissented.

Illinois v. Caballes
543 U.S. 405, 125 S.Ct. 834 (2005)

Illinois state trooper Daniel Gillette stopped Roy Caballes for speeding and radioed the police dispatcher to report the stop. A second trooper, Craig Graham overheard the transmission and immediately headed for the scene with his narcotics-detection dog. When they arrived, while Gillette was writing a ticket, Graham walked his dog around Caballes's car. The dog alerted at the trunk and the officers searched the trunk, found marijuana, and arrested Caballes. The entire incident lasted less than ten minutes. Caballes was convicted of a narcotics offense and sentenced to twelve years' imprisonment and a $256,136 fine. The trial judge denied Caballes's motion to suppress the seized evidence and held that the officers had not unnecessarily prolonged the stop and that the dog alert was sufficiently reliable to provide probable cause to conduct the search. Although an appellate court affirmed, the Illinois Supreme Court reversed, concluding that because the canine sniff was performed without any "'specific and articulable facts'" to suggest drug activity, the use of the dog "unjustifiably enlarg[ed] the scope of a routine traffic stop into a drug investigation." The state appealed that decision and the Supreme Court granted review.

The state supreme court's decision was reversed by a vote of six to two, with Chief Justice Rehnquist not participating. Justice Stevens delivered the opinion for the Court. Justices Souter and Ginsburg each filed dissenting opinions.

☐ *Justice STEVENS delivered the opinion of the Court.*

The question on which we granted *certiorari* is narrow: "Whether the Fourth Amendment requires reasonable, articulable suspicion to justify using a drug-detection dog to sniff a vehicle during a legitimate traffic stop." . . . Here, the initial seizure of respondent when he was stopped on the highway was based on probable cause, and was concededly lawful. It is nevertheless clear that a seizure that is lawful at its inception can violate the Fourth Amendment if its manner of execution unreasonably infringes interests protected by the Constitution. A seizure that is justified solely by the interest in issuing a warning ticket to the driver can become unlawful if it is prolonged beyond the time reasonably required to complete that mission. . . .

Official conduct that does not "compromise any legitimate interest in privacy" is not a search subject to the Fourth Amendment. We have held that any interest in possessing contraband cannot be deemed "legitimate," and thus, governmental conduct that only reveals the possession of contraband "compromises no legitimate privacy interest." This is because the expectation "that certain facts will not come to the attention of the authorities" is not the same as an interest in "privacy that society is prepared to consider reasonable." In *United States v. Place*, 462 U.S. 696 (1983), we treated a canine sniff by a well-trained narcotics-detection dog as "*sui generis*" because it "discloses only the presence or absence of narcotics, a contraband item." . . .

Accordingly, the use of a well-trained narcotics-detection dog—one that "does not expose noncontraband items that otherwise would remain hidden from public view"—during a lawful traffic stop, generally does not implicate legitimate privacy interests. In this case, the dog sniff was performed on the exterior of respondent's car while he was lawfully seized for a traffic violation. Any intrusion on respondent's privacy expectations does not rise to the level of a constitutionally cognizable infringement.

This conclusion is entirely consistent with our recent decision that the use of a thermal-imaging device to detect the growth of marijuana in a home constituted an unlawful search. *Kyllo v. United States*, 533 U.S. 27 (2001). Critical to that decision was the fact that the device was capable of detecting lawful activity—in that case, intimate details in a home, such as "at what hour each night the lady of the house takes her daily sauna and bath." The legitimate expectation that information about perfectly lawful activity will remain private is categorically distinguishable from respondent's hopes or expectations concerning the nondetection of contraband in the trunk of his car. A dog sniff conducted during a concededly lawful traffic stop that reveals no information other than the location of a substance that no individual has any right to possess does not violate the Fourth Amendment. . . .

☐ *Justice SOUTER, dissenting.*

I would hold that using the dog for the purposes of determining the presence of marijuana in the car's trunk was a search unauthorized as an incident of the speeding stop and unjustified on any other ground. . . .

At the heart both of [*United States v.*] *Place*, [462 U.S. 696 (1983)], and the Court's opinion today is the proposition that sniffs by a trained dog are *sui generis* because a reaction by the dog in going alert is a response to nothing but the presence of contraband. Hence, the argument goes, because the sniff can only reveal the presence of items devoid of any legal use, the sniff "does not implicate legitimate privacy interests" and is not to be treated as a search.

The infallible dog, however, is a creature of legal fiction. Although the Supreme Court of Illinois did not get into the sniffing averages of drug dogs, their supposed infallibility is belied by judicial opinions describing well-trained animals sniffing and alerting with less than perfect accuracy, whether owing to errors by their handlers, the limitations of the dogs themselves, or even the pervasive contamination of currency by cocaine. See, e.g., *United States v. Kennedy*, 131 F.3d 1371 (CA10 1997) (describing a dog that had a 71% accuracy rate); *United States v. Scarborough*, 128 F.3d 1373 (CA10 1997) (describing a dog that erroneously alerted 4 times out of 19 while working for the postal service and 8% of the time over its entire career); *United States v. Limares*, 269 F.3d 794 (CA7 2001) (accepting as reliable a dog that gave false positives between 7 and 38% of the time)....

Once the dog's fallibility is recognized, however, that ends the justification claimed in *Place* for treating the sniff as sui generis under the Fourth Amendment: the sniff alert does not necessarily signal hidden contraband, and opening the container or enclosed space whose emanations the dog has sensed will not necessarily reveal contraband or any other evidence of crime. This is not, of course, to deny that a dog's reaction may provide reasonable suspicion, or probable cause, to search the container or enclosure; the Fourth Amendment does not demand certainty of success to justify a search for evidence or contraband. The point is simply that the sniff and alert cannot claim the certainty that *Place* assumed, both in treating the deliberate use of sniffing dogs as *sui generis* and then taking that characterization as a reason to say they are not searches subject to Fourth Amendment scrutiny. And when that aura of uniqueness disappears, there is no basis in *Place*'s reasoning, and no good reason otherwise, to ignore the actual function that dog sniffs perform. They are conducted to obtain information about the contents of private spaces beyond anything that human senses could perceive, even when conventionally enhanced. The information is not provided by independent third parties beyond the reach of constitutional limitations, but gathered by the government's own officers in order to justify searches of the traditional sort, which may or may not reveal evidence of crime but will disclose anything meant to be kept private in the area searched. Thus in practice the government's use of a trained narcotics dog functions as a limited search to reveal undisclosed facts about private enclosures, to be used to justify a further and complete search of the enclosed area. And given the fallibility of the dog, the sniff is the first step in a process that may disclose "intimate details" without revealing contraband, just as a thermal-imaging device might do, as described in *Kyllo v. United States*, 533 U.S. 27 (2001).

It makes sense, then, to treat a sniff as the search that it amounts to in practice, and to rely on the body of our Fourth Amendment cases, including *Kyllo*, in deciding whether such a search is reasonable. As a general proposition, using a dog to sniff for drugs is subject to the rule that the object of enforcing criminal laws does not, without more, justify suspicionless Fourth Amendment intrusions. Since the police claim to have had no particular suspicion that Caballes was violating any drug law, this sniff search must stand or fall on its being ancillary to the traffic stop that led up to it. It is true that the police had probable cause to stop the car for an offense committed in the officer's presence, which Caballes concedes could have justified his arrest. There is no occasion to consider authority incident to arrest, however, for the police did nothing more than detain Caballes long enough to check his record and write a ticket. As a consequence, the reasonableness of the search must be assessed in relation to the actual delay the police chose to impose, and as Justice GINSBURG points out in her opinion, the Fourth Amendment consequences of stopping for a traffic citation are settled law. . . .

[I]n the case of the dog sniff, the dog does not smell the disclosed contraband; it smells a closed container. An affirmative reaction therefore does not identify a substance the police already legitimately possess, but informs the police instead merely of a reasonable chance of finding contraband they have yet to put their hands on. The police will then open the container and discover whatever lies within, be it marijuana or the owner's private papers. Thus, . . . both the certainty and the limit on disclosure that may follow are missing when the dog sniffs the car.

The Court today does not go so far as to say explicitly that sniff searches by dogs trained to sense contraband always get a free pass under the Fourth Amendment, since it reserves judgment on the constitutional significance of sniffs assumed to be more intrusive than a dog's walk around a stopped car. . . . For the sake of providing a workable framework to analyze cases on facts like these, which are certain to come along, I would treat the dog sniff as the familiar search it is in fact, subject to scrutiny under the Fourth Amendment.

☐ *Justice GINSBURG, with whom Justice SOUTER joins, dissenting.*

In *Terry v. Ohio*, [392 U.S. 1 (1968)], the Court upheld the stop and subsequent frisk of an individual based on an officer's observation of suspicious behavior and his reasonable belief that the suspect was armed. In a *Terry*-type investigatory stop, "the officer's action [must be] justified at its inception, and . . . reasonably related in scope to the circumstances which justified the interference in the first place." In applying *Terry*, the Court has several times indicated that the limitation on "scope" is not confined to the duration of the seizure; it also encompasses the manner in which the seizure is conducted. I would apply *Terry*'s reasonable-relation test, as the Illinois Supreme Court did, to determine whether the canine sniff impermissibly expanded the scope of the initially valid seizure of Caballes.

It is hardly dispositive that the dog sniff in this case may not have lengthened the duration of the stop. *Terry*, it merits repetition, instructs that any investigation must be "reasonably related in scope to the circumstances which justified the interference in the first place." The unwarranted and nonconsensual expansion of the seizure here from a routine traffic stop to a drug investigation broadened the scope of the investigation in a manner that, in my judgment, runs afoul of the Fourth Amendment. . . .

In my view, the Court diminishes the Fourth Amendment's force by abandoning the second *Terry* inquiry (was the police action "reasonably related in scope to the circumstances [justifying] the [initial] interference"). A drug-detection dog is an intimidating animal. Injecting such an animal into a routine traffic stop changes the character of the encounter between the police and the motorist. The stop becomes broader, more adversarial, and (in at least some cases) longer. Caballes—who, as far as Troopers Gillette and Graham knew, was guilty solely of driving six miles per hour over the speed limit—was exposed to the embarrassment and intimidation of being investigated, on a public thoroughfare, for drugs. Even if the drug sniff is not characterized as a Fourth Amendment "search," cf. *Indianapolis v. Edmond*, 531 U.S. 32 (2000); *United States v. Place*, 462 U.S. 696 (1983), the sniff surely broadened the scope of the traffic-violation-related seizure.

[T]oday's decision ... clears the way for suspicionless, dog-accompanied drug sweeps of parked cars along sidewalks and in parking lots. Nor would motorists have constitutional grounds for complaint should police with dogs, stationed at long traffic lights, circle cars waiting for the red signal to turn green.... The dog sniff in this case, it bears emphasis, was for drug detection only. A dog sniff for explosives, involving security interests not presented here, would be an entirely different matter. Detector dogs are ordinarily trained not as all-purpose sniffers, but for discrete purposes....

For the reasons stated, I would hold that the police violated Caballes's Fourth Amendment rights when, without cause to suspect wrongdoing, they conducted a dog sniff of his vehicle. I would therefore affirm the judgment of the Illinois Supreme Court.

■ THE DEVELOPMENT OF LAW

The National Security Agency's Warrantless Electronic Surveillance (reprise, in Vol. 1, Ch. 3, here)

F | *The Exclusionary Rule*

In a ruling related to the "inevitable discovery" exception to the Fourth Amendment's exclusionary rule that was upheld in *Nix v. Williams*, 467 U.S. 431 (1984) (excerpted in Vol. 2, Ch. 7), a bare majority of the Court held that a violation of the amendment's "knock-and-announce" rule, when executing a search warrant, does not trigger the exclusionary rule in *Hudson v. Michigan* (2006) (excerpted below). Justice Kennedy cast the pivotal vote and issued a concurring opinion. Justice Scalia delivered a plurality opinion for the Court's decision and Justice Breyer filed a dissent, which Justices Stevens, Souter, and Ginsburg joined.

Hudson v. Michigan
126 S.Ct. 2159 (2006)

Several Detroit, Michigan, police officers obtained a search warrant for Booker R. Hudson, Jr.'s house. When they arrived, they heard no noises and did not see any activity inside. Nonetheless, they forced their way into the house three to five seconds after announcing their presence at the door. Once inside, they found cocaine and a gun, for which Hudson was arrested. At his trial, Hudson's attorney sought to exclude the evidence against him on the ground that the search violated the Fourth Amendment "knock-and-announce" rule. The trial court ruled that that rule was violated, but held that the amendment's exclusionary rule did not require the suppression of the evidence against Hudson. That decision was eventually upheld by the Michigan state supreme court and Hudson appealed to the Supreme Court.

The state court's decision was affirmed by a vote of five to four, with Justice Kennedy casting the pivotal vote. Justice Scalia delivered the opinion for the Court. Justice Kennedy filed a concurring opinion. Justice Breyer filed a dissent, which was joined by Justices Stevens, Souter, and Ginsburg.

□ *Justice Scalia delivered the opinion of the Court.*

We decide whether violation of the "knock-and-announce" rule requires the suppression of all evidence found in the search....

The common-law principle that law enforcement officers must announce their presence and provide residents an opportunity to open the door is an ancient one. See *Wilson v. Arkansas*, 514 U.S. 927 (1995). Since 1917, when Congress passed the Espionage Act, this traditional protection has been part of federal statutory law. [I]n *Wilson*, we were asked whether the rule was also a command of the Fourth Amendment. Tracing its origins in our English legal heritage, we concluded that it was.

We recognized that the new constitutional rule we had announced is not easily applied. *Wilson* and cases following it have noted the many situations in which it is not necessary to knock and announce. It is not necessary when "circumstances presen[t] a threat of physical violence," or if there is "reason to believe that evidence would likely be destroyed if advance notice were given," or if knocking and announcing would be "futile," *Richards v. Wisconsin*, 520 U.S. 385 (1997). We require only that police "have a reasonable suspicion . . . under the particular circumstances" that one of these grounds for failing to knock and announce exists, and we have acknowledged that "[t]his showing is not high."

When the knock-and-announce rule does apply, it is not easy to determine precisely what officers must do. How many seconds' wait are too few? Our "reasonable wait time" standard, see *United States v. Banks*, 540 U.S. 31(2003), is necessarily vague.

Happily, these issues do not confront us here. From the trial level onward, Michigan has conceded that the entry was a knock-and-announce violation. The issue here is remedy. *Wilson* specifically declined to decide whether the exclusionary rule is appropriate for violation of the knock-and-announce requirement. That question is squarely before us now.

In *Weeks v. United States*, 232 U.S. 383 (1914), we adopted the federal exclusionary rule for evidence that was unlawfully seized from a home without a warrant in violation of the Fourth Amendment. We began applying the same rule to the States, through the Fourteenth Amendment, in *Mapp v. Ohio*, 367 U.S. 643 (1961).

Suppression of evidence, however, has always been our last resort, not our first impulse. The exclusionary rule generates "substantial social costs," *United States v. Leon*, 468 U.S. 897 (1984), which sometimes include setting the guilty free and the dangerous at large. . . .

In other words, exclusion may not be premised on the mere fact that a constitutional violation was a "but-for" cause of obtaining evidence. Our cases show that but-for causality is only a necessary, not a sufficient, condition for suppression. In this case, of course, the constitutional violation of an illegal manner of entry was not a but-for cause of obtaining the evidence. Whether that preliminary misstep had occurred or not, the police would have executed the warrant they had obtained, and would have discovered the gun and drugs inside the house. But even if the illegal entry here could be characterized as a but-for cause of discovering what was inside, we have "never held that evidence is 'fruit of the poisonous tree' simply because 'it would not have come to light but for the illegal actions of the police.'" *Segura v. United States*, 468 U.S. 796 (1984). Rather, but-for cause, or "causation in the logical sense alone," can be too attenuated to justify exclusion.

For this reason, cases excluding the fruits of unlawful warrantless searches, see, e.g., *Boyd v. United States*, 116 U.S. 616 (1886); *Weeks*; *Silverthorne Lumber Co. v. United States*, 251 U.S. 385 (1920); *Mapp* say nothing about the appropriateness of exclusion to vindicate the interests protected by the knock-and-announce requirement. Until a valid warrant has issued, citizens are entitled to shield "their persons, houses, papers, and effects" from the government's scrutiny. Exclusion of the evidence obtained by a warrantless search vindicates that entitlement. The interests protected by the knock-and-announce requirement are quite different—and do not include the shielding of potential evidence from the government's eyes.

One of those interests is the protection of human life and limb, because an unannounced entry may provoke violence in supposed self-defense by the surprised resident. Another interest is the protection of property. Breaking a house (as the old cases typically put it) absent an announcement would penalize someone who "'did not know of the process, of which, if he had notice, it is to be presumed that he would obey it. . . .'" *Wilson*. The knock-and-announce rule gives individuals "the opportunity to comply with the law and to avoid the destruction of property occasioned by a forcible entry." And thirdly, the knock-and-announce rule protects those elements of privacy and dignity that can be destroyed by a sudden entrance. It gives residents the "opportunity to prepare themselves for" the entry of the police. In other words, it assures the opportunity to collect oneself before answering the door.

What the knock-and-announce rule has never protected, however, is one's interest in preventing the government from seeing or taking evidence described in a warrant. Since the interests that were violated in this case have nothing to do with the seizure of the evidence, the exclusionary rule is inapplicable.

Quite apart from the requirement of unattenuated causation, the exclusionary rule has never been applied except "where its deterrence benefits outweigh its 'substantial social costs.'" The costs here are considerable. In addition to the grave adverse consequence that exclusion of relevant incriminating evidence always entails (viz., the risk of releasing dangerous criminals into society), imposing that massive remedy for a knock-and-announce violation would generate a constant flood of alleged failures to observe the rule. . . . The cost of entering this lottery would be small, but the jackpot enormous: suppression of all evidence, amounting in many cases to a get-out-of-jail-free card. Courts would experience as never before the reality that "[t]he exclusionary rule frequently requires extensive litigation to determine whether particular evidence must be excluded." Unlike the warrant or *Miranda* requirements, compliance with which is readily determined (either there was or was not a warrant; either the *Miranda* warning was given, or it was not), what constituted a "reasonable wait time" in a particular case, (or, for that matter, how many seconds the police in fact waited), or whether there was "reasonable suspicion". . . is difficult for the trial court to determine and even more difficult for an appellate court to review.

Another consequence of the incongruent remedy Hudson proposes would be police officers' refraining from timely entry after knocking and announcing. As we have observed, the amount of time they must wait is necessarily uncertain. If the consequences of running afoul of the rule were so massive, officers would be inclined to wait longer than the law requires—producing preventable violence against officers in some cases, and the destruction of evidence in many others. We deemed these consequences severe enough to produce our unanimous agreement that a mere "reasonable suspicion" that knocking and announcing "under the particular circumstances, would be dangerous or futile, or that it would inhibit the effective investigation of the crime," will cause the requirement to yield.

Next to these "substantial social costs" we must consider the deterrence benefits, existence of which is a necessary condition for exclusion. To begin with, the value of deterrence depends upon the strength of the incentive to commit the forbidden act. Viewed from this perspective, deterrence of knock-and-announce violations is not worth a lot. Violation of the warrant requirement sometimes produces incriminating evidence that could not otherwise be obtained. But ignoring knock-and-announce can realistically be expected to achieve absolutely nothing except the prevention of destruction of evidence and the avoidance of life-threatening resistance by occupants of the premises—dangers which, if there is even "reasonable suspicion" of their existence, suspend the knock-and-announce requirement anyway. Massive deterrence is hardly required.

It seems to us not even true, as Hudson contends, that without suppression there will be no deterrence of knock-and-announce violations at all. Of course even if this assertion were accurate, it would not necessarily justify suppression. Assuming (as the assertion must) that civil suit is not an effective deterrent, one can think of many forms of police misconduct that are similarly "undeterred." When, for example, a confessed suspect in the killing of a police officer, arrested (along with incriminating evidence) in a lawful warranted search, is subjected to physical abuse at the station house, would it seriously be suggested that the evidence must be excluded, since that is the only "effective deterrent"? And what, other than civil suit, is the "effective deterrent" of police violation of an already-confessed suspect's Sixth Amendment rights by denying him prompt access to counsel? Many would regard these violated rights as more significant than the right not to be intruded upon in one's nightclothes—and yet nothing but "ineffective" civil suit is available as a deterrent. And the police incentive for those violations is arguably greater than the incentive for disregarding the knock-and-announce rule.

We cannot assume that exclusion in this context is necessary deterrence simply because we found that it was necessary deterrence in different contexts and long ago. That would be forcing the public today to pay for the sins and inadequacies of a legal regime that existed almost half a century ago. Citizens whose Fourth Amendment rights were violated by federal officers could not bring suit until 10 years after *Mapp*, with this Court's decision in *Bivens v. Six Unknown Fed. Narcotics Agents*, 403 U.S. 388 (1971)....

Another development over the past half-century that deters civil-rights violations is the increasing professionalism of police forces, including a new emphasis on internal police discipline....

In sum, the social costs of applying the exclusionary rule to knock-and-announce violations are considerable; the incentive to such violations is minimal to begin with, and the extant deterrences against them are substantial—incomparably greater than the factors deterring warrantless entries when *Mapp* was decided. Resort to the massive remedy of suppressing evidence of guilt is unjustified.

A trio of cases—*Segura v. United States*, 468 U.S. 796 (1984); *New York v. Harris*, 495 U.S. 14 (1990); and *United States v. Ramirez*, 523 U.S. 65 (1998)—confirms our conclusion that suppression is unwarranted in this case....

For the foregoing reasons we affirm the judgment of the Michigan Court of Appeals.

☐ *Justice KENNEDY, concurring in part and concurring in the judgment.*

Two points should be underscored with respect to today's decision. First, the knock-and-announce requirement protects rights and expectations linked to ancient principles in our constitutional order. The Court's decision should not be interpreted as suggesting that violations of the requirement are trivial or beyond the law's concern. Second, the continued operation of the exclusionary rule, as settled and defined by our precedents, is not in doubt. Today's decision determines only that in the specific context of the knock-and-announce requirement, a violation is not sufficiently related to the later discovery of evidence to justify suppression....

Our system, as the Court explains, has developed procedures for training police officers and imposing discipline for failures to act competently and lawfully. If those measures prove ineffective, they can be fortified with more detailed regulations or legislation. Supplementing these safeguards are civil remedies, such as those available under [U.S. Code] Section 1983, that provide restitution for discrete harms. These remedies apply to all violations, including, of course, exceptional cases in which unannounced entries cause severe fright and humiliation....

Today's decision does not address any demonstrated pattern of knock-and-announce violations.... Even then, however, the Court would have to acknowledge that extending the remedy of exclusion to all the evidence seized following a knock-and-announce violation would mean revising the requirement of causation that limits our discretion in applying the exclusionary rule. That type of extension also would have significant practical implications, adding to the list of issues requiring resolution at the criminal trial questions such as whether police officers entered a home after waiting 10 seconds or 20.

In this case the relevant evidence was discovered not because of a failure to knock-and-announce, but because of a subsequent search pursuant to a lawful warrant. The Court in my view is correct to hold that suppression was not required. . . .

☐ *Justice BREYER, with whom Justice STEVENS, Justice SOUTER, and Justice GINSBURG join, dissenting.*

In *Wilson v. Arkansas*, 514 U.S. 927 (1995), a unanimous Court held that the Fourth Amendment normally requires law enforcement officers to knock and announce their presence before entering a dwelling. Today's opinion holds that evidence seized from a home following a violation of this requirement need not be suppressed.

As a result, the Court destroys the strongest legal incentive to comply with the Constitution's knock-and-announce requirement. And the Court does so without significant support in precedent. At least I can find no such support in the many Fourth Amendment cases the Court has decided in the near century since it first set forth the exclusionary principle in *Weeks v. United States*, 232 U.S. 383 (1914).

Today's opinion is thus doubly troubling. It represents a significant departure from the Court's precedents. And it weakens, perhaps destroys, much of the practical value of the Constitution's knock-and-announce protection.

This Court has set forth the legal principles that ought to have determined the outcome of this case in two sets of basic Fourth Amendment cases. I shall begin by describing that underlying case law.

The first set of cases describes the constitutional knock-and-announce requirement, a requirement that this Court initially set forth only 11 years ago in *Wilson v. Arkansas*. In *Wilson*, tracing the lineage of the knock-and-announce rule back to the 13th century, we wrote that "[a]n examination of the common law of search and seizure leaves no doubt that the reasonableness of a search of a dwelling may depend in part on whether law enforcement officers announced their presence and authority prior to entering."

We noted that this "basic principle" was agreed upon by "[s]everal prominent founding-era commentators," and "was woven quickly into the fabric of early American law" via state constitutions and statutes. We further concluded that there was "little doubt that the Framers of the Fourth Amendment thought that the method of an officer's entry into a dwelling was among the factors to be considered in assessing the reasonableness of a search or seizure."

And we held that the "common-law 'knock and announce' principle forms a part of the reasonableness inquiry under the Fourth Amendment." Thus, "a search or seizure of a dwelling might be constitutionally defective if police officers enter without prior announcement."

The second set of cases sets forth certain well-established principles that are relevant here. They include: *Boyd v. United States*, 116 U.S. 616 (1886). In this seminal Fourth Amendment case, decided 120 years ago, the Court wrote, in frequently quoted language, that the Fourth Amendment's prohibitions apply "to all invasions on the part of the government and its employees of the sanctity of a man's home and the privacies of life. It is not the breaking of his doors, and the rummaging of his drawers, that constitutes the essence of the offence; but it is the invasion of his indefeasible right of personal security, personal liberty and private property."

Weeks, decided 28 years after *Boyd*, originated the exclusionary rule. The Court held that the Federal Government could not retain evidence seized unconstitutionally and use that evidence in a federal criminal trial. The Court pointed out that "[i]f letters and private documents" could be unlawfully seized from a home "and used in evidence against a citizen accused of an offense, the protection of the Fourth Amendment declaring his right to be secure against such searches and seizures is of no value, and . . . might as well be stricken from the Constitution." . . .

Wolf v. Colorado, 338 U.S. 25 (1949), and *Mapp v. Ohio*, 367 U.S. 643 (1961). Both of these cases considered whether *Weeks*' exclusionary rule applies to the States. In *Wolf*, the Court held that it did not. In *Mapp*, the Court overruled *Wolf*. Experience, it said, showed that alternative methods of enforcing the Fourth Amendment's requirements had failed. The Court consequently held that "all evidence obtained by searches and seizures in violation of the Constitution is, by that same authority, inadmissible in a state court." "To hold otherwise," the Court added, would be "to grant the right but in reality to withhold its privilege and enjoyment."

Reading our knock-and-announce cases, in light of this foundational Fourth Amendment case law, it is clear that the exclusionary rule should apply. For one thing, elementary logic leads to that conclusion. We have held that a court must "conside[r]" whether officers complied with the knock-and-announce requirement "in assessing the reasonableness of a search or seizure." *Wilson*. The Fourth Amendment insists that an unreasonable search or seizure is, constitutionally speaking, an illegal search or seizure. And ever since *Weeks* (in respect to federal prosecutions) and *Mapp* (in respect to state prosecutions), "the use of evidence secured through an illegal search and seizure" is "barred" in criminal trials. . . .

Why is application of the exclusionary rule any the less necessary here? Without such a rule, as in *Mapp*, police know that they can ignore the Constitution's requirements without risking suppression of evidence discovered after an unreasonable entry. As in *Mapp*, some government officers will find it easier, or believe it less risky, to proceed with what they consider a necessary search immediately and without the requisite constitutional (say, warrant or knock-and-announce) compliance. . . .

To argue, as the majority does, that new remedies, such as Section 1983 actions or better trained police, make suppression unnecessary is to argue that *Wolf*, not *Mapp*, is now the law. (The Court recently rejected a similar argument in *Dickerson v. United States*, 530 U.S. 428 (2000).) To argue that there may be few civil suits because violations may produce nothing "more than nominal injury" is to confirm, not to deny, the inability of civil suits to deter violations. And to argue without evidence (and despite myriad reported cases of violations, no reported case of civil damages, and Michigan's concession of their nonexistence) that civil suits may provide deterrence because claims may "have been settled" is, perhaps, to search in desperation for an argument. Rather, the majority, as it candidly admits, has simply "assumed" that, "[a]s far as [it] know[s], civil liability is an effective deterrent," support-free assumption that *Mapp* and subsequent cases make clear does not embody the Court's normal approach to difficult questions of Fourth Amendment law. . . .

Neither can the majority justify its failure to respect the need for deterrence, as set forth consistently in the Court's prior case law, through its claim of "substantial social costs"—at least if it means that those "social costs" are somehow special here. The only costs it mentions are those that typically accompany any use of the Fourth Amendment's exclusionary principle: (1) that where the constable blunders, a guilty defendant may be set free (consider *Mapp* itself); (2) that defendants may assert claims where Fourth Amendment rights are uncertain (consider the Court's qualified immunity jurisprudence), and (3) that sometimes it is difficult to decide the merits of those uncertain claims. In fact, the "no-knock" warrants that are provided by many States, by diminishing uncertainty, may make application of the knock-and-announce principle less "cost[ly]" on the whole than application of comparable Fourth Amendment principles, such as determining whether a particular warrantless search was justified by exigency. The majority's "substantial social costs" argument is an argument against the Fourth Amendment's exclusionary principle itself. And it is an argument that this Court, until now, has consistently rejected....

There is perhaps one additional argument implicit in the majority's approach. The majority says, for example, that the "cost" to a defendant of "entering this lottery," i.e., of claiming a "knock-and-announce" violation, "would be small, but the jackpot enormous"—namely, a potential "get-out-of-jail-free card." It adds that the "social costs" of applying the exclusionary rule here are not worth the deterrence benefits. Leaving aside what I believe are invalid arguments based on precedent or the majority's own estimate that suppression is not necessary to deter constitutional violations, one is left with a simple unvarnished conclusion, namely, that in this kind of case, a knock-and-announce case, "[r]esort to the massive remedy of suppressing evidence of guilt is unjustified." Why is that judicial judgment, taken on its own, inappropriate? Could it not be argued that the knock-and-announce rule, a subsidiary Fourth Amendment rule, is simply not important enough to warrant a suppression remedy? Could the majority not simply claim that the suppression game is not worth the candle?

The answer, I believe, is "no." That "no" reflects history, a history that shows the knock-and-announce rule is important. That "no" reflects precedent, precedent that shows there is no pre-existing legal category of exceptions to the exclusionary rule into which the knock-and-announce cases might fit. That "no" reflects empirical fact, experience that provides confirmation of what common sense suggests: without suppression there is little to deter knock-and-announce violations.

There may be instances in the law where text or history or tradition leaves room for a judicial decision that rests upon little more than an unvarnished judicial instinct. But this is not one of them. Rather, our Fourth Amendment traditions place high value upon protecting privacy in the home. They emphasize the need to assure that its constitutional protections are effective, lest the Amendment "'sound the word of promise to the ear but break it to the hope.'" They include an exclusionary principle, which since *Weeks* has formed the centerpiece of the criminal law's effort to ensure the practical reality of those promises. That is why the Court should assure itself that any departure from that principle is firmly grounded in logic, in history, in precedent, and in empirical fact. It has not done so. That is why, with respect, I dissent.

9

THE RIGHTS TO COUNSEL AND OTHER PROCEDURAL GUARANTEES

A | *The Right to Counsel*

In a five to four ruling, in *United States v. Gonzalez-Lopez*, 126 S.Ct. 2557 (2006), the Court held that the Sixth Amendment guarantees the right to have a paid counsel of the defendant's choosing and that the violation of that right entails a reversal of the defendant's conviction. Justice Scalia delivered the opinion of the Court. Justice Alito filed a dissent, which Chief Justice Roberts and Justices Kennedy and Thomas joined.

B | Plea Bargaining and the Right to Effective Counsel

■ THE DEVELOPMENT OF LAW

Rulings on Plea Bargaining and Effective Counsel

CASE	VOTE	RULING
Florida v. Nixon, 543 U.S. 175 (2004)	8:0	Writing for the Court, Justice Ginsburg held that the Sixth Amendment was not violated by an attorney's confessing his client's guilt in a gruesome murder case, without the client's consent, in order to maintain his credibility with the jury and to subsequently argue for a life-time sentence, rather than the imposition of the death penalty. Justice Ginsburg noted that "In a capital case, counsel must consider in conjunction both the guilt and penalty phases in determining how best to proceed."

D | The Right to an Impartial Jury Trial

In *Apprendi v. New Jesery*, 530 U.S. 466 (2000), the Court struck down a state law permitting judges to hand down longer sentences for "hate crimes" based on the "preponderance of evidence" standard. A bare majority ruled that enhanced sentences may be imposed only by a jury and on the basis of the stricter "beyond a reasonable doubt" standard. That ruling was then extended in *Ring v. Arizona*, 536 U.S. 584 (2002), and in *Blackely v. Washington*, 542 U.S. 296 (2004). In *Blackely*, a bare majority struck down a state sentencing system for permitting judges to make findings that increase a defendant's sentence beyond the ordinary range for violating the Sixth Amendment right to a jury trial. Writing for the Court, Justice Scalia reaffirmed that "any fact that increases the penalty for a crime beyond the prescribed statutory maximum must be submitted to a jury and proved beyond a reasonable doubt." Dissenting Justice O'Connor warned that "Over 20 years of sentencing reform are all but lost," and specifically in jeopardy were the 1987 federal mandatory sentencing guidelines, setting mandatory minimum sentences and adopted as part of the war on crime and to ensure the nationwide application of federal criminal law. Justice O'Connor proved prophetic because in *United States v. Booker*, 543 U.S. 220 (2005) a bare majority ruled that the federal guidelines violate the Sixth Amendment because federal judges may impose enhanced sentences based on facts that a jury did not consider.

The Court was badly fragmented in *Booker*, however, and two opinions for the Court were delivered for different bare majorities. On the one hand, Justice Stevens, joined by Justices Scalia, Souter, Thomas, and Ginsburg, ruled that federal judges are no longer bound by the guidelines. On the other hand, Justice Breyer, joined by Chief Justice Rehnquist and Justices O'Connor, Kennedy, and Ginsburg, held that the guidelines should still be consulted and that judges' sentences are subject to reversal if appellate courts find them unreasonable and defendants deserve longer or shorter sentences. The federal guidelines, in the words of Justice Breyer, who helped write them, serve to "avoid excessive sentencing disparities while maintaining flexibility sufficient to individualize sentences where necessary." Justice Ginsburg cast the crucial fifth vote for both opinions but issued no separate opinion. Justices Stevens, Scalia, Thomas, and Breyer, each filed dissenting opinions.

The Court also reaffirmed its ruling in *Batson v. Kentucky*, 476 U.S. 79 (1986) (excerpted in Vol. 2, Ch. 9) that racial discrimination in the use of preemptory challenges in jury selection is impermissible in *Miller-El v. Dretke*, 545 U.S. 231 (2005). In *Miller-El* the prosecution had "shuffled" 10 of the 11 eligible blacks in the jury pool so as to exclude them from the jury. Writing for the majority, Justice Souter underscored that "when the government's choice of jurors is tainted with racial bias" it jeopardizes "the very integrity of the courts." Dissenting Justice Thomas, joined by Chief Justice Rehnquist and Justice Scalia, argued that practically all of the prosecution's preemptory strikes of blacks could be explained on nonracial grounds. In a related decision, *Johnson v. California*, 543 U.S. 499 (2005), the Court in an eight to one ruling, with Justice Thomas dissenting, held that the California supreme court's standard for showing racial bias, namely, that discrimination was "more likely than not," was too strict under *Batson*. Writing for the Court, Justice Stevens held that defendants need show only a "reasonable inference" of racial bias in the use of preemptory challenges and jury selection.

F | The Right to Be Informed of Charges and to Confront Accusers

In *Davis v. Washington*, 126 S.Ct. 2266 (2006), the Court held that statements made during a 911 call may be introduced at trial without affording the defendant the opportunity to confront the accuser because such statements are not "testimonial" and thus not subject to the Sixth Amendment's confrontation clause. Writing for the Court, Justice Scalia ruled that statements made in a 911 call were not "testimonial" because they were made in reporting an immediate emergency demanding police assistance, whereas statements made by a victim to police at the crime scene are "testimonial" and may not be introduced at a trial unless the defendant has the opportunity to confront the witness.

10

CRUEL AND UNUSUAL PUNISHMENT

B | *Capital Punishment*

Overturning *Stanford v. Kentucky*, 492 U.S. 361 (1989), which upheld the execution of minors convicted of murder under the age of eighteen but older than sixteen, a bare majority of the Court held that the execution of minors violates the Eighth Amendment in *Roper v. Simmons* (excerpted below). The ruling affects approximately seventy death row inmates.

Roper v. Simmons
543 U.S. 551, 125 S.Ct. 1183 (2005)

At the age of 17, Christopher Simmons committed murder. About nine months later, after he had turned 18, he was tried and sentenced to death. Before the murder, in chilling, callous terms he talked about his plan, discussing it for the most part with two friends, then aged 15 and 16. Simmons proposed to commit burglary and murder by breaking and entering, tying up a victim, and throwing the victim off a bridge. Simmons assured his friends they could "get away with it" because they were minors. Simmons was later charged with burglary, kidnapping, stealing, and murder. Because Simmons was 17 at the time of the crime, he was outside the criminal jurisdiction of Missouri's juvenile court system. He was tried as an adult, convicted, and sentenced to death. The Missouri Supreme Court affirmed. But, after those proceedings, the U.S.

Supreme Court held that the Eighth and Fourteenth Amendments prohibit the execution of a mentally retarded person. *Atkins v. Virginia*, 536 U.S. 304 (2002). Simmons then filed a new petition for state postconviction relief, arguing that the reasoning of *Atkins* established that the Constitution prohibits the execution of a juvenile who was under 18 when the crime was committed. The Missouri Supreme Court agreed and held that since *Stanford v. Kentucky*, 492 U.S. 361 (1989), upholding the execution of minors who commit murders, "a national consensus has developed against the execution of juvenile offenders, as demonstrated by the fact that eighteen states now bar such executions for juveniles, that twelve other states bar executions altogether, that no state has lowered its age of execution below 18 since *Stanford*, that five states have legislatively or by case law raised or established the minimum age at 18, and that the imposition of the juvenile death penalty has become truly unusual over the last decade."

The state supreme court's decision was affirmed by a five to four vote. Justice Kennedy delivered the opinion for the Court. Justice Stevens filed a concurring opinion. Justices O'Connor and Scalia filed dissenting opinions; Chief Justice Rehnquist and Justice Thomas joined the latter's dissent.

☐ *Justice KENNEDY delivered the opinion of the Court.*

This case requires us to address, for the second time in a decade and a half, whether it is permissible under the Eighth and Fourteenth Amendments to the Constitution of the United States to execute a juvenile offender who was older than 15 but younger than 18 when he committed a capital crime. In *Stanford v. Kentucky*, 492 U.S. 361 (1989), a divided Court rejected the proposition that the Constitution bars capital punishment for juvenile offenders in this age group. We reconsider the question....

The prohibition against "cruel and unusual punishments," like other expansive language in the Constitution, must be interpreted according to its text, by considering history, tradition, and precedent, and with due regard for its purpose and function in the constitutional design. To implement this framework we have established the propriety and affirmed the necessity of referring to "the evolving standards of decency that mark the progress of a maturing society" to determine which punishments are so disproportionate as to be cruel and unusual. *Trop v. Dulles*, 356 U.S. 86 (1958).

In *Thompson v. Oklahoma*, 487 U.S. 815 (1988), a plurality of the Court determined that our standards of decency do not permit the execution of any offender under the age of 16 at the time of the crime. The plurality opinion explained that no death penalty State that had given express consideration to a minimum age for the death penalty had set the age lower than 16. The plurality also observed that "[t]he conclusion that it would offend civilized standards of decency to execute a person who was less than 16 years old at the time of his or her offense is consistent with the views that have been expressed by respected professional organizations, by other nations that share our Anglo-American heritage, and by the leading members of the Western European community."

Bringing its independent judgment to bear on the permissibility of the death penalty for a 15-year-old offender, the *Thompson* plurality stressed that "[t]he reasons why juveniles are not trusted with the privileges and responsibilities of an adult also explain why their irresponsible conduct is not as morally reprehensible as that of an adult." According to the plurality, the lesser culpability of offenders under 16 made the death penalty inappropriate as a form of retribution, while the low likelihood that offenders under 16 engaged in "the kind of cost-benefit analysis that attaches any weight to the possibility of execution" made the death penalty ineffective as a means of deterrence....

The next year, in *Stanford v. Kentucky*, 492 U.S. 361 (1989), the Court, over a dissenting opinion joined by four Justices, referred to contemporary standards of decency in this country and concluded the Eighth and Fourteenth Amendments did not proscribe the execution of juvenile offenders over 15 but under 18. The Court noted that 22 of the 37 death penalty States permitted the death penalty for 16-year-old offenders, and, among these 37 States, 25 permitted it for 17-year-old offenders. These numbers, in the Court's view, indicated there was no national consensus "sufficient to label a particular punishment cruel and unusual." A plurality of the Court also "emphatically reject[ed]" the suggestion that the Court should bring its own judgment to bear on the acceptability of the juvenile death penalty.

The same day the Court decided *Stanford*, it held that the Eighth Amendment did not mandate a categorical exemption from the death penalty for the mentally retarded. *Penry v. Lynaugh*, 492 U.S. 302 (1989). In reaching this conclusion it stressed that only two States had enacted laws banning the imposition of the death penalty on a mentally retarded person convicted of a capital offense.

Three Terms ago the subject was reconsidered in *Atkins* [*v. Virginia*, 536 U.S. 304 (2002)]. We held that standards of decency have evolved since *Penry* and now demonstrate that the execution of the mentally retarded is cruel and unusual punishment. The Court noted objective indicia of society's standards, as expressed in legislative enactments and state practice with respect to executions of the mentally retarded. When *Atkins* was decided only a minority of States permitted the practice, and even in those States it was rare. On the basis of these indicia the Court determined that executing mentally retarded offenders "has become truly unusual, and it is fair to say that a national consensus has developed against it."

The inquiry into our society's evolving standards of decency did not end there. The *Atkins* Court neither repeated nor relied upon the statement in *Stanford* that the Court's independent judgment has no bearing on the acceptability of a particular punishment under the Eighth Amendment. Instead we returned to the rule, established in decisions predating *Stanford*, that "'the Constitution contemplates that in the end our own judgment will be brought to bear on the question of the acceptability of the death penalty under the Eighth Amendment.'" Mental retardation, the Court said, diminishes personal culpability even if the offender can distinguish right from wrong. The impairments of mentally retarded offenders make it less defensible to impose the death penalty as retribution for past crimes and less likely that the death penalty will have a real deterrent effect. Based on these considerations and on the finding of national consensus against executing the mentally retarded, the Court ruled that the death penalty constitutes an excessive sanction for the entire category of mentally retarded offenders, and that the Eighth Amendment "'places a substantive restriction on the State's power to take the life' of a mentally retarded offender."

Just as the *Atkins* Court reconsidered the issue decided in *Penry*, we now reconsider the issue decided in *Stanford*. The beginning point is a review of objective indicia of consensus, as expressed in particular by the enactments of legislatures that have addressed the question. This data gives us essential instruction. We then must determine, in the exercise of our own independent judgment, whether the death penalty is proportionate punishment for juveniles.

The evidence of national consensus against the death penalty for juveniles is similar, and in some respects parallel, to the evidence *Atkins* held sufficient to demonstrate a national consensus against the death penalty for the mentally retarded. When *Atkins* was decided, 30 States prohibited the death penalty for the mentally retarded. This number comprised 12 that had abandoned the death penalty altogether, and 18 that maintained it but excluded the mentally retarded from its reach. By a similar calculation in this case, 30 States prohibit the juvenile death penalty, comprising 12 that have rejected the death penalty altogether and 18 that maintain it but, by express provision or judicial interpretation, exclude juveniles from its reach. *Atkins* emphasized that even in the 20 States without formal prohibition, the practice of executing the mentally retarded was infrequent. Since *Penry*, only five States had executed offenders known to have an IQ under 70. In the present case, too, even in the 20 States without a formal prohibition on executing juveniles, the practice is infrequent. Since *Stanford*, six States have executed prisoners for crimes committed as juveniles. In the past 10 years, only three have done so: Oklahoma, Texas, and Virginia. . . .

Petitioner cannot show national consensus in favor of capital punishment for juveniles but still resists the conclusion that any consensus exists against it. Petitioner supports this position with, in particular, the observation that when the Senate ratified the International Covenant on Civil and Political Rights (ICCPR), Dec. 19, 1966, it did so subject to the President's proposed reservation regarding Article 6(5) of that treaty, which prohibits capital punishment for juveniles. This reservation at best provides only faint support for petitioner's argument. First, the reservation was passed in 1992; since then, five States have abandoned capital punishment for juveniles. Second, Congress considered the issue when enacting the Federal Death Penalty Act in 1994, and determined that the death penalty should not extend to juveniles. The reservation to Article 6(5) of the ICCPR provides minimal evidence that there is not now a national consensus against juvenile executions.

As in *Atkins*, the objective indicia of consensus in this case—the rejection of the juvenile death penalty in the majority of States; the infrequency of its use even where it remains on the books; and the consistency in the trend toward abolition of the practice—provide sufficient evidence that today our society views juveniles, in the words *Atkins* used respecting the mentally retarded, as "categorically less culpable than the average criminal."

A majority of States have rejected the imposition of the death penalty on juvenile offenders under 18, and we now hold this is required by the Eighth Amendment. . . .

Three general differences between juveniles under 18 and adults demonstrate that juvenile offenders cannot with reliability be classified among the worst offenders. First, as any parent knows and as the scientific and sociological studies respondent and his *amici* cite tend to confirm, "[a] lack of maturity and an underdeveloped sense of responsibility are found in youth more often than in adults and are more understandable among the young. These qualities often result in impetuous and ill-considered actions and decisions."

The second area of difference is that juveniles are more vulnerable or susceptible to negative influences and outside pressures, including peer pressure. . . . The third broad difference is that the character of a juvenile is not as well formed as that of an adult. The personality traits of juveniles are more transitory. . . .

Once the diminished culpability of juveniles is recognized, it is evident that the penological justifications for the death penalty apply to them with lesser force than to adults. We have held there are two distinct social purposes served by the death penalty: "'retribution and deterrence of capital crimes by prospective offenders.'" *Atkins*. As for retribution, we remarked in *Atkins* that "[i]f the culpability of the average murderer is insufficient to justify the most extreme sanction available to the State, the lesser culpability of the mentally retarded offender surely does not merit that form of retribution." The same conclusions follow from the lesser culpability of the juvenile offender. . . .

As for deterrence, it is unclear whether the death penalty has a significant or even measurable deterrent effect on juveniles, as counsel for the petitioner acknowledged at oral argument. . . .

These considerations mean *Stanford v. Kentucky* should be deemed no longer controlling on this issue. . . .

Our determination that the death penalty is disproportionate punishment for offenders under 18 finds confirmation in the stark reality that the United States is the only country in the world that continues to give official sanction to the juvenile death penalty. This reality does not become controlling, for the task of interpreting the Eighth Amendment remains our responsibility. Yet at least from the time of the Court's decision in *Trop*, the Court has referred to the laws of other countries and to international authorities as instructive for its interpretation of the Eighth Amendment's prohibition of "cruel and unusual punishments."

As respondent and a number of *amici* emphasize, Article 37 of the United Nations Convention on the Rights of the Child, which every country in the world has ratified save for the United States and Somalia, contains an express prohibition on capital punishment for crimes committed by juveniles under 18. United Nations Convention on the Rights of the Child, Art. 37, (entered into force Sept. 2, 1990). . . .

It is proper that we acknowledge the overwhelming weight of international opinion against the juvenile death penalty, resting in large part on the understanding that the instability and emotional imbalance of young people may often be a factor in the crime. The opinion of the world community, while not controlling our outcome, does provide respected and significant confirmation for our own conclusions.

The Eighth and Fourteenths forbid imposition of the death penalty on offenders who were under the age of 18 when their crimes were committed.

☐ *Justice STEVENS, with whom Justice GINSBURG joins, concurring.*

Perhaps even more important than our specific holding today is our reaffirmation of the basic principle that informs the Court's interpretation of the Eighth Amendment. If the meaning of that Amendment had been frozen when it was originally drafted, it would impose no impediment to the execution of 7-year-old children today. See *Stanford v. Kentucky*, 492 U.S. 361 (1989) (describing the common law at the time of the Amendment's adoption). The evolving standards of decency that have driven our construction of this critically important part of the Bill of Rights foreclose any such reading of the Amendment. In the best tradition of the common law, the pace of that evolution is a matter for continuing debate; but that our understanding of the Constitution does change from time to time has been settled since JOHN MARSHALL breathed life into its text....

☐ *Justice SCALIA, with whom THE CHIEF JUSTICE and Justice THOMAS join, dissenting.*

The Court ... proclaims itself sole arbiter of our Nation's moral standards—and in the course of discharging that awesome responsibility purports to take guidance from the views of foreign courts and legislatures. Because I do not believe that the meaning of our Eighth Amendment, any more than the meaning of other provisions of our Constitution, should be determined by the subjective views of five Members of this Court and like-minded foreigners, I dissent....

Words have no meaning if the views of less than 50% of death penalty States can constitute a national consensus. Our previous cases have required overwhelming opposition to a challenged practice, generally over a long period of time. In *Coker v. Georgia*, 433 U.S. 584 (1977), a plurality concluded the Eighth Amendment prohibited capital punishment for rape of an adult woman where only one jurisdiction authorized such punishment. The plurality also observed that "[a]t no time in the last 50 years ha[d] a majority of States authorized death as a punishment for rape." In *Ford v. Wainwright*, 477 U.S. 399 (1986), we held execution of the insane unconstitutional, tracing the roots of this prohibition to the common law and noting that "no State in the union permits the execution of the insane." In *Enmund v. Florida*, 458 U.S. 782 (1982), we invalidated capital punishment imposed for participation in a robbery in which an accomplice committed murder, because 78% of all death penalty States prohibited this punishment. Even there we expressed some hesitation, because the legislative judgment was "neither 'wholly unanimous among state legislatures,' ... nor as compelling as the legislative judgments considered in *Coker*." By contrast, agreement among 42% of death penalty States in *Stanford*, which the Court appears to believe was correctly decided at the time was insufficient to show a national consensus....

The Court's reliance on the infrequency of executions, for under-18 Murderers credits an argument that this Court considered and explicitly rejected in *Stanford*. That infrequency is explained, we accurately said, both by "the undisputed fact that a far smaller percentage of capital crimes are committed by persons under 18 than over 18," and by the fact that juries are required at sentencing to consider the offender's youth as a mitigating factor. Thus, "it is not only possible, but overwhelmingly probable, that the very considerations which induce [respondent] and [his] supporters to believe that death should never be imposed on offenders under 18 cause prosecutors and juries to believe that it should rarely be imposed." *Stanford*. . . .

Of course, the real force driving today's decision is . . . the Court's "own judgment" that murderers younger than 18 can never be as morally culpable as older counterparts. The Court claims that this usurpation of the role of moral arbiter is simply a "retur[n] to the rul[e] established in decisions predating *Stanford*." That supposed rule—which is reflected solely in *dicta* and never once in a holding that purports to supplant the consensus of the American people with the Justices' views—was repudiated in *Stanford* for the very good reason that it has no foundation in law or logic. If the Eighth Amendment set forth an ordinary rule of law, it would indeed be the role of this Court to say what the law is. But the Court having pronounced that the Eighth Amendment is an ever-changing reflection of "the evolving standards of decency" of our society, it makes no sense for the Justices then to prescribe those standards rather than discern them from the practices of our people. On the evolving-standards hypothesis, the only legitimate function of this Court is to identify a moral consensus of the American people. By what conceivable warrant can nine lawyers presume to be the authoritative conscience of the Nation? . . .

Though the views of our own citizens are essentially irrelevant to the Court's decision today, the views of other countries and the so-called International community take center stage.

The Court begins by noting that "Article 37 of the United Nations Convention on the Rights of the Child, which every country in the world has ratified save for the United States and Somalia, contains an express prohibition on capital punishment for crimes committed by juveniles under 18." The Court also discusses the International Covenant on Civil and Political Rights (ICCPR), which the Senate ratified only subject to a reservation that reads: "The United States reserves the right, subject to its Constitutional restraints, to impose capital punishment on any person (other than a pregnant woman) duly convicted under existing or future laws permitting the imposition of capital punishment, including such punishment for crime committed by persons below eighteen years of age." Unless the Court has added to its arsenal the power to join and ratify treaties on behalf of the United States, I cannot see how this evidence favors, rather than refutes, its position. That the Senate and the President—those actors our Constitution empowers to enter into treaties, see Art. II, Sec. 2—have declined to join and ratify treaties prohibiting execution of under-18 offenders can only suggest that our country has either not reached a national consensus on the question, or has reached a consensus contrary to what the Court announces. . . .

More fundamentally, however, the basic premise of the Court's argument—that American law should conform to the laws of the rest of the world—ought to be rejected out of hand. In fact the Court itself does not believe it. In many significant respects the laws of most other countries differ from our law—including not only such explicit provisions of our Constitution as the right to jury trial and grand jury indictment, but even many interpretations of the Constitution prescribed by this Court itself. The Court-pronounced exclusionary rule, for example, is distinctively American. When we adopted that rule in *Mapp v. Ohio*, 367 U.S. 643 (1961), it was "unique to American Jurisprudence." Since then a categorical exclusionary rule has been "universally rejected" by other countries, including those with rules prohibiting illegal searches and police misconduct, despite the fact that none of these countries "appears to have any alternative form of discipline for police that is effective in preventing search violations." England, for example, rarely excludes evidence found during an illegal search or seizure and has only recently begun excluding evidence from illegally obtained confessions.... The European Court of Human Rights has held that introduction of illegally seized evidence does not violate the "fair trial" requirement in Article 6, Sec. 1, of the European Convention on Human Rights....

And let us not forget the Court's abortion jurisprudence, which makes us one of only six countries that allow abortion on demand until the point of viability. Though the Government and *amici* in cases following *Roe v. Wade*, 410 U.S. 113 (1973), urged the Court to follow the international community's lead, these arguments fell on deaf ears.

The Court's special reliance on the laws of the United Kingdom is perhaps the most indefensible part of its opinion. It is of course true that we share a common history with the United Kingdom, and that we often consult English sources when asked to discern the meaning of a constitutional text written against the backdrop of 18th-century English law and legal thought. If we applied that approach today, our task would be an easy one. As we explained in *Harmelin v. Michigan*, 501 U.S. 957 (1991), the "Cruell and Unusuall Punishments" provision of the English Declaration of Rights was originally meant to describe those punishments "'out of [the Judges'] Power'"—that is, those punishments that were not authorized by common law or statute, but that were nonetheless administered by the Crown or the Crown's judges. Under that reasoning, the death penalty for under-18 offenders would easily survive this challenge. The Court has, however—I think wrongly—long rejected a purely originalist approach to our Eighth Amendment, and that is certainly not the approach the Court takes today. Instead, the Court undertakes the majestic task of determining (and thereby prescribing) our Nation's current standards of decency. It is beyond comprehension why we should look, for that purpose, to a country that has developed, in the centuries since the Revolutionary War—and with increasing speed since the United Kingdom's recent submission to the jurisprudence of European courts dominated by continental jurists—a legal, political, and social culture quite different from our own....

The Court should either profess its willingness to reconsider all these matters in light of the views of foreigners, or else it should cease putting forth foreigners' views as part of the reasoned basis of its decisions. To invoke alien law when it agrees with one's own thinking, and ignore it otherwise, is not reasoned decision making, but sophistry....

To add insult to injury, the Court affirms the Missouri Supreme Court without even admonishing that court for its flagrant disregard of our precedent in *Stanford*. Until today, we have always held that "it is this Court's prerogative alone to overrule one of its precedents." That has been true even where "'changes in judicial doctrine' ha[ve] significantly undermined" our prior holding, and even where our prior holding "appears to rest on reasons rejected in some other line of decisions." Today, however, the Court silently approves a state-court decision that blatantly rejected controlling precedent....

Allowing lower courts to reinterpret the Eighth Amendment whenever they decide enough time has passed for a new snapshot leaves this Court's decisions without any force—especially since the "evolution" of our Eighth Amendment is no longer determined by objective criteria. To allow lower courts to behave as we do, "updating" the Eighth Amendment as needed, destroys stability and makes our case law an unreliable basis for the designing of laws by citizens and their representatives, and for action by public officials. The result will be to crown arbitrariness with chaos.

■ THE DEVELOPMENT OF LAW
Other Recent Rulings on Capital Punishment

CASE	VOTE	RULING
Brown v. Sanders, 126 S.Ct. 884 (2006)	5:4	Writing for the majority, Justice Scalia held that a death row inmate is not entitled to federal habeas corpus relief when a state defines the aggravating circumstances for imposing capital punishment and a jury imposes a death sentence based on four of those factors, two of which were subsequently invalidated by a state supreme court that nonetheless upheld the sentence. Justice Scalia noted that California's list of sentencing factors was not limited to discrete factors but included the general "circumstances of the crime." Justices Stevens, Souter, Ginsburg, and Breyer dissented.
Oregon v. Guzek, 126 S.Ct. 1226 (2006)	9:0	Writing for the Court, Justice Breyer held that states may limit the introduction of innocence-related evidence at the sentencing stage of a capital case to that presented at the original trial and to bar the introduction of such new evidence.
Kansas v. Marsh, 126 S.Ct. 2516 (2006)	9:0	Writing for the Court, Justice Thomas upheld Kansas's law permitting a death sentence when the aggravating and mitigating factors are equally weighted, overturning a state supreme court ruling to the contrary. In an impassioned dissent, joined by Justices Stevens, Ginsburg, and Breyer, Justice Souter deemed the state's law "morally absurd" and contended that the majority's decision repudiated "decades of precedent aimed at eliminating freakish capital sentencing."

11

THE RIGHT OF PRIVACY

A | *Privacy and Reproductive Freedom*

In her last major opinion, Justice O'Connor wrote for a unanimous Court in *Ayotte v. Planned Parenthood of Northern New England* (excerpted below), holding that lower courts went too far in striking down the entirety of New Hampshire's restrictive abortion law, requiring minors to obtain parental notice. That law provides an exception for when a teenager's life is at stake, but does not make a general health exception, for psychological reasons and non-emergency situations. The opinion, however, did not clarify whether abortion restrictions must include a general health exception in non-emergency situations, or whether the constitutionality of abortion laws should be judged by a different standard than other laws.

In its 2006–2007 term, the Court will consider two appeals of appellate courts' decisions holding unconstitutional the Partial-Birth Abortion Ban Act of 2003 in *Gonzales v. Carhart* (No. 05-380) and *Gonzales v. Planned Parenthood Federation of America* (No. 05-1382). That act was signed into law by President George W. Bush in response to the invalidation of similar state laws in *Stenberg v. Carhart*, 530 U.S. 914 (2000) (excerpted in Vol. 2, Ch. 11). In that case the Court held that a Nebraska statute was vague and failed to provide an exception from its ban on so-called partial-birth or late-term abortions for when a woman's health is endangered. Based on that precedent the U.S. Court of Appeals for the Eighth Circuit invalidated the 2003 federal law in *Carhart v. Gonzales*, 413 F. 3d 791 (2005); subsequently two other federal appellate courts enjoined the enforcement of the law. At issue is whether the law is invalid because it lacks a health exception from the ban on late-term abortions after 20 weeks of a pregnancy, and how broad that exception must be; in other words, must an exception be made not only to save a woman's life but also for psychological or other reasons.

In *Gonzales v. Planned Parenthood Federation of America*, the Court will consider the government's appeal of a decision of the U.S. Court of Appeals for the Ninth Circuit that affirmed a district court's decision and enjoining the enforcement of the 2003 law. The district court held that the partial-birth ban act was unconstitutional on three grounds: (1) the law imposed an undue burden on a woman's right to terminate her pregnancy before viability; (2) the law was unconstitutionally vague; and (3) the law failed to provide an exception for when a woman's health is in danger. The district court also enjoined the enforcement of the entire act as a remedy. The appellate court affirmed on all grounds and the Bush administration appealed.

Notably, in *Stenberg v. Carhart*, the Court split five to four with Justice O'Connor casting the pivotal vote, and joining Justices Stevens, Souter, Ginsburg, and Breyer; Chief Justice Rehnquist and Justices Scalia, Kennedy, and Thomas dissented. The case presents a challenge to the first federal law banning a particular abortion procedure since the 1973 landmark ruling in *Roe v. Wade* (excerpted in Vol. 2, Ch. 11). The appeals also present the first abortion cases since the appointments of Chief Justice Roberts and Justice Alito.

Ayotte v. Planned Parenthood of Northern New England
126 S.Ct. 961 (2006)

In 2003, New Hampshire enacted the Parental Notification Prior to Abortion Act, prohibiting physicians from performing an abortion on a pregnant minor until 48 hours after written notice to her parent or guardian. The law allows for three circumstances in which a doctor may perform an abortion without notifying the minor's parent. First, notice is not required if "[t]he attending abortion provider certifies in the pregnant minor's record that the abortion is necessary to prevent the minor's death and there is insufficient time to provide the required notice." Second, a person entitled to receive notice may certify that he or she has already been notified. Finally, a minor may petition a judge to authorize her physician to perform an abortion without parental notification. The judge must so authorize if he or she finds that the minor is mature and capable of giving informed consent, or that an abortion without notification is in the minor's best interests. The law, however, does not explicitly permit a physician to perform an abortion in a medical emergency without parental notification. A doctor and three clinics that offer reproductive health services challenged the constitutionality of the law. A federal district court declared the law unconstitutional on the ground that it was invalid for failing "to comply with the constitutional requirement that laws restricting a woman's access to abortion must provide a health exception." It also found that the law's judicial bypass would not operate expeditiously enough in medical emergencies. The Court of Appeals for the First Circuit affirmed, based on *Stenberg v. Carhart* (2000), *Planned Parenthood of Southeastern Pa. v. Casey* (1992), and *Roe v. Wade* (1973) [all excerpted in Vol. 2, Ch. 11]. The state appealed and the Supreme Court granted review.

The appellate court's decision was vacated and remanded. Justice O'Connor delivered the opinion for a unanimous Court.

☐ *Justice O'CONNOR delivered the opinion of the Court.*

We do not revisit our abortion precedents today, but rather address a question of remedy: If enforcing a statute that regulates access to abortion would be unconstitutional in medical emergencies, what is the appropriate judicial response? We hold that invalidating the statute entirely is not always necessary or justified, for lower courts may be able to render narrower declaratory and injunctive relief. New Hampshire has maintained that in most if not all cases, the Act's judicial bypass and the State's "competing harms" statutes should protect both physician and patient when a minor needs an immediate abortion. But the District Court and Court of Appeals found neither of these provisions to protect minors' health reliably in all emergencies. And New Hampshire has conceded that, under our cases, it would be unconstitutional to apply the Act in a manner that subjects minors to significant health risks.

We turn to the question of remedy: When a statute restricting access to abortion may be applied in a manner that harms women's health, what is the appropriate relief? Generally speaking, when confronting a constitutional flaw in a statute, we try to limit the solution to the problem. We prefer, for example, to enjoin only the unconstitutional applications of a statute while leaving other applications in force, or to sever its problematic portions while leaving the remainder intact.

Three interrelated principles inform our approach to remedies. First, we try not to nullify more of a legislature's work than is necessary, for we know that "[a] ruling of unconstitutionality frustrates the intent of the elected representatives of the people." It is axiomatic that a "statute may be invalid as applied to one state of facts and yet valid as applied to another." *Dahnke-Walker Milling Co. v. Bondurant*, 257 U.S. 282 (1921). Accordingly, the "normal rule" is that "partial, rather than facial, invalidation is the required course," such that a "statute may ... be declared invalid to the extent that it reaches too far, but otherwise left intact." *Brockett v. Spokane Arcades, Inc.*, 472 U.S. 491 (1985).

Second, mindful that our constitutional mandate and institutional competence are limited, we restrain ourselves from "rewrit[ing] state law to conform it to constitutional requirements" even as we strive to salvage it. Third, the touchstone for any decision about remedy is legislative intent, for a court cannot "use its remedial powers to circumvent the intent of the legislature." *Califano v. Westcott*, 443 U.S. 76 (1979).

In this case, the courts below chose the most blunt remedy—permanently enjoining the enforcement of New Hampshire's parental notification law and thereby invalidating it entirely. That is understandable, for we, too, have previously invalidated an abortion statute in its entirety because of the same constitutional flaw. In *Stenberg*, we addressed a Nebraska law banning so-called "partial birth abortion" unless the procedure was necessary to save the pregnant woman's life. We held Nebraska's law unconstitutional because it lacked a health exception. But the parties in *Stenberg* did not ask for, and we did not contemplate, relief more finely drawn. In the case that is before us, however, we agree with New Hampshire that the lower courts need not have invalidated the law wholesale....

There is some dispute as to whether New Hampshire's legislature intended the statute to be susceptible to such a remedy. New Hampshire notes that the Act contains a severability clause providing that "[i]f any provision of this subdivision or the application thereof to any person or circumstance is held invalid, such invalidity shall not affect the provisions or applications of this subdivision which can be given effect without the invalid provisions or applications." Respondents, on the other hand, contend that New Hampshire legislators preferred no statute at all to a statute enjoined in the way we have described. Because this is an open question, we remand for the lower courts to determine legislative intent in the first instance....

12

THE EQUAL PROTECTION OF THE LAWS

A | *Racial Discrimination and State Action*

In *Johnson v. California*, 543 U.S. 499 (2005), the Court held that the "strict scrutiny" test applies in cases of racially segregated prison cells, but declined to decide whether California's prison policy of segregating inmates failed to satisfy that test. Writing for the Court, Justice O'Connor observed: "By perpetuating the notion that race matters, racial segregation of inmates may exacerbate the very patterns of violence that it is said to counteract. In the prison context, when the government's power is at its apex, we think that searching judicial review of racial classifications is necessary to guard against invidious discrimination." In a separate opinion, joined by Justices Souter and Breyer, Justice Ginsburg agreed but indicated that the use of racial classifications may be permissible in order to wipe out "entrenched discrimination and its after-effects." Justice Stevens dissented and contended that the majority should have gone farther and struck down California's policy. In a separate dissent joined by Justice Scalia, Justice Thomas countered that the majority should have deferred to California prison officials in managing their prison populations, observing that "The Constitution has always demanded less within the prison walls."

B | *Racial Discrimination in Education*

In its 2006–2007 term, the Court will consider two challenges to race-based school admissions policies in public elementary and secondary schools, in *Parents Involved in Community Schools v. Seattle School District No. 1* (No. 05-908) and *Meredith v. Jefferson County Board of Education* (No. 05-915). These are the first major cases dealing with efforts to achieve integrated public schools since *Freeman v. Pitts*, 503 U.S. 467 (1992) (excerpted in Vol. 2, Ch. 12), which signaled lower courts to withdraw from court-ordered mandated efforts to achieve racially integrated schools and to return control to local school districts. But, these cases present challenges to local school board race-based policies aimed at maintaining integrated schools. Both involve school district policies aimed at addressing *de facto* segregation as a result of housing patterns and the resegregation of public schools. Both arose from claims the policies violate the Fourteenth Amendment and constitute unconstitutional affirmation action. As such, they present the first opportunity for the Court to reconsider the controversy over affirmative action since the University of Michigan undergraduate recruitment program was invalidated by a six to three vote in *Gratz v. Bollinger*, 539 U.S. 244 (2003) (excerpted in Vol. 2, Ch. 12); and the University of Michigan Law School's program was upheld by a five to four vote in *Grutter v. Bollinger*, 539 U.S. 306 (2003) (excerpted in Vol. 2, Ch. 12), with Justice O'Connor casting the pivotal vote in holding that race may be a factor, though not the predominate factor, in admissions in order to achieve diverse student bodies. Notably, the cases also are the first to present these issues since Chief Justice Roberts filled the seat of the late Chief Justice Rehnquist, and Justice Alito replaced Justice O'Connor on the bench.

Seattle School District No. 1 presents a challenge to a policy of giving, under certain circumstances, racial preferences in school assignments. Under the program, students may indicate their preference for a high school, but the district assigns students to each school with a goal of having about forty percent white students and sixty percent racial minorities in order to offset racially segregated housing patterns. If too many white students apply for the same school, priority is given to students with a sibling at the school. Otherwise, racial preference is used as a "tiebreaker" in school assignments. A federal district court upheld the program as narrowly tailored to achieving the school district goal of integrated schools. The Court of Appeals for the Ninth Circuit affirmed that decision.

Meredith v. Jefferson County Board of Education involves a challenge to a different kind of race-based student school assignments. In Louisville, Kentucky, Jefferson County, like other areas around the country, was increasingly racially isolated due to housing patterns. In order to maintain an integrated school system, the county adopted guidelines aimed at assuring that fifteen to fifty percent of each school enrolled African Americans. The county provided for both traditional and special, nontraditional magnet schools. Any student could apply to the traditional schools, but only students from certain designated residential areas could apply to particular nontraditional magnet schools, which offer more opportunities and resources. The policy was challenged by a white family whose son was not assigned to a nontraditional magnet school located across the street from their house. A federal district court rejected their claim that the policy of assigning students to nontraditional magnet schools amounted to a quota system, since there was no fixed criterion, and that the county had a compelling interest in achieving and maintaining racial balance in all of its schools. However, the court found that the guidelines for student assignments to traditional schools were not narrowly tailored because, unlike nontraditional schools, the assignment process placed applicants on different racial tracks. The Court of Appeals for the Sixth Circuit affirmed and its decision was appealed.

C | *Affirmative Action and Reverse Discrimination*

The Court will consider *Parents Involved in Community Schools v. Seattle School District No. 1* (No. 05-908) and *Meredith v. Jefferson County Board of Education* (No. 05-915) in its 2006–2007 term. Both involve challenges to race-based policies for the assignment of students in primary and secondary schools. Both are discussed in Section B of this chapter.

D | Nonracial Classifications and the Equal Protection of the Law

(4) Alienage and Age

■ THE DEVELOPMENT OF LAW
Rulings on the Classification of Aliens

CASE	VOTE	RULING
Jama v. Immigration and Customs Enforcement, 543 U.S. 335 (2005)	5:4	Writing for the Court, Justice Scalia held that a refugee living in the United States may be deported after a criminal conviction to the home country, even without the consent of that country's government. Justices Souter, Stevens, Ginsburg, and Breyer dissented.
Clark v. Martinez, 543 U.S. 371 (2005)	7:2	Writing for the Court, and drawing on the ruling in *Zadvydas v. Davis*, U.S. 678 (2001), holding that aliens may be detained for six months as "reasonably necessary" to effectuate their removal, Justice Scalia held that inadmissible aliens may be held six months or longer, as "reasonably necessary," even if they may not be returned to their home country. Chief Justice Rehnquist and Justice Thomas dissented.

Index of Cases

Cases printed in boldface are excerpted on the page(s) printed in boldface.

A(FC) and others (FC) v. Secretary of State for the Home Department, 34
Agins v. City of Tiburon, 100
Alden v. Maine, 3
American Trucking Associations, Inc. v. Michigan Public Service Commission, 58
Apprendi v. New Jersey, 158
Arizona v. Rumsey, 82
Atkins v. Virginia, 162–165
Auer v. Robbins, 52, 54
Ayotte v. Planned Parenthood of Northern New England, 170, **171–173**

Balderas v. Texas, 69
Bates v. Dow Agrosciences, 56
Batson v. Kentucky, 159
Beard v. Banks, 112
Berman v. Parker, 90, 93–96, 98–100
Bivens v. Six Unknown Fed. Narcotics Agents, 153
Blackely v. Washington, 158
BMW v. Gore, 103
Board of Ed. of Westside Community Schools (Dist. 66) v. Mergens, 109
Board of Education of Independent School District No. 92 of Pottawatomie City v. Earls, 3
Board of Regents of State Colleges v. Roth, 104
Boyd v. United States, 151, 154–155
Boy Scouts of America v. Dale, 109–110
Brigham City, Utah v. Stuart, 145
Brockett v. Spokane Arcades, Inc., 172
Brown v. Legal Foundation of Wash., 97
Brown v. Sanders, 169

Buckley v. Valeo, 74, 80–84, 86–89
Bush v. Gore, 4

Calder v. Bull, 96
Califano v. Westcott, 172
Cantwell v. Connecticut, 133
Carhart v. Gonzales, 170
Central Virginia Community College et al. v. Katz, 58
Chevron U.S.A. Inc. v. Natural Resources Defense Council, Inc., 52–54
Church of the Lukumi Babalu Aye, Inc. v. Hialeah, 130, 135
City of Boerne v. Flores, 39, 114–115, 137
Clark v. Martinez, 177
Cleburne v. Cleburne Living Center, Inc., 95
Clingman v. Beaver, 89
Coker v. Georgia, 166
Connick v. Myers, 75
County of Allegheny v. American Civil Liberties Union, Greater Pittsburgh Chapter, 113, 125, 131
Cutter v. Wilkinson, 113, **114–117**

Dahnke-Walker Milling Co. v. Bondurant, 172
Davis v. Bandemer, 62–63
Davis v. Washington, 160
Deck v. Mississippi, 104
Dickerson v. United States, 155

Edwards v. Aguillard, 120
Elk Grove Unified School District v. Newdow, 116, 123

Employment Division, Department of
    Human Resources of Oregon v. Smith,
    114–115
Engel v. Vitale, 119–120
Enmund v. Florida, 166
Epperson v. Arkansas, 129
Everson v. Board of Ed. of Ewing, 124,
    129, 133
Ex parte Milligan, 15
Ex parte Quirin, 15–17, 23–24, 27

Federal Election Comm'n v. Colorado
    Republican Federal Campaign Comm.,
    88
Florida v. Nixon, 158
Ford v. Wainwright, 166
Freeman v. Pitts, 175
Freytag v. C.I.R., 36

Garcetti v. Ceballos, 74–80
Georgia v. Ashcroft, 66, 73
Georgia v. Randolph, 139–144
Gibbons v. Ogden, 44
Gonzales v. Carhart, 170
Gonzales v. O Centro Espirita Beneficente
    Uniao do Vegetal, 39, 137
Gonzales v. Oregon, 38, **50–55**
Gonzales v. Planned Parenthood Federation
    of America, 170–171
Gonzales v. Raich, 38, **39–50**, 51,
    54–55
Good News Club v. Milford Central School,
    119
Granholm v. Heald, 57
Gratz v. Bollinger, 175
Grutter v. Bollinger, 3, 175

Hamdan v. Rumsfeld, 11–27
Hamdi v. Rumsfeld, 15, 22–23
Harmelin v. Michigan, 168
Hawaii Housing Authority v. Midkiff, 90,
    92–96, 98–99
Hobbie v. Unemployment Appeals Comm'n.
    of Fla., 115
Holder v. Hall, 73
Hudson v. Michigan, 149, **150–156**
Hunt v. Cromartie, 3
Hunt v. McNair, 119

Hurley v. Irish-American Gay, Lesbian and
    Bisexual Group of Boston, Inc., 108

Illinois v. Caballes, 144, **145–149**
Illinois v. Rodriguez, 140–141, 143
Indianapolis v. Edmond, 149
Ireland v. United Kingdom, 31

Jama v. Immigration and Customs
    Enforcement, 177
Johanns v. Livestock Marketing Association,
    111
Johnson v. California, 159, 174
Johnson v. De Grandy, 65–68
Johnson v. Eisentrager, 25
Jones v. Flowers, 104
Joseph Burstyn v. Wilson, 111

Kansas v. Marsh, 169
Karcher v. Daggett, 63, 68
**Kelo v. City of New London,
    Connecticut**, 90, **91–100**
Kyllo v. United States, 146–147

Lawrence v. Texas, 4
**League of United Latin American
    Citizens v. Perry**, 59, **60–74**
Lee v. Weisman, 120, 123
Lemon v. Kurtzman, 118–119, 122, 124,
    129–130
Lingle v. Chevron, 100
Locke v. Davey, 117
Lynch v. Donnelly, 119, 134

Mapp v. Ohio, 151, 153, 155–156, 167
Marsh v. Chambers, 118–119, 134–135
**McCreary County v. American Civil
    Liberties Union of Kentucky**, 4, 113,
    120, 122–123, **128–136**
McGowan v. Maryland, 119, 130
Medtronic, Inc. v. Lohr, 53
Meredith v. Jefferson County Board of
    Education, 175–176
Michigan v. Summers, 138
Mid-Con Freight Systems, Inc. v. Michigan
    Public Service Commission, 57
Miller v. Johnson, 66
Miller v. United States, 141

Index of Cases

Miller-El v. Dretke, 159
Minnesota v. Carter, 141
Minnesota v. Olson, 140
Monongahela Nav. Co. v. United States, 97
Muehler v. Mena, 138

Nevada Department of Human Resources v. Hibbs, 3
New State Ice Co. v. Liebmann, 46
New York v. Harris, 153
New York v. United States, 3
Nixon v. Shrink Missouri Government PAC, 84–86, 88
Nix v. Williams, 149
NLRB v. Jones & Laughlin Steel Corp., 41, 45
Northern Insurance Co. v. Chatham County, Georgia, 58

Oregon v. Guzek, 169

Padilla v. Hanft, 10
Parents Involved in Community Schools v. Seattle School District No. 1, 175–176
Penn Central Transportation Co. v. New York, 100
Penry v. Lynaugh, 163–164
Perez v. United States, 41, 43–44
Phillip Morris USA v. Williams, 103
Pickering v. Board of Education of Township High School Dist. 205, Will Cty., 75–76, 78–80
Planned Parenthood of Southeastern Pennsylvania v. Casey, 3, 172
Printz v. United States, 3, 49
PruneYard Shopping Center v. Robins, 108

Randall v. Sorrell, 80–89
R.A.V. v. St. Paul, 108
Reed v. Reed, 142
Reid v. Covert, 16
Richards v. Wisconsin, 150
Ring v. Arizona, 158
Roe v. Wade, 3, 168, 171–172
Roper v. Simmons, 161–168
Rumsfeld v. Forum for Academic and Institutional Rights, 105–110
Rumsfeld v. Padilla, 10

Samson v. California, 145
Schlesinger v. Councilman, 14, 20
School Dist. of Abington Township v. Schempp, 118–120, 122, 127, 129
Segura v. United States, 151, 153
Seminole Tribe of Florida. v. Florida, 3
Shaw v. Hunt (Shaw II), 66
Shaw v. Reno, 66
Sherbert v. Verner, 124
Shreveport Rate Cases, 45
Silverthorne Lumber Co v. United States, 151
Skidmore v. Swift & Co., 52
Smith v. Maryland, 32
Stanford v. Kentucky, 161–168
State Farm Automobile Insurance v. Campbell, 103
Stenberg v. Carhart, 4, 170–173
Stone v. Graham, 113, 120, 124–126, 129, 131
Strickley v. Highland Boy Gold Mining Co., 93

Tennessee v. Lane, 3
Terry v. Ohio, 148
Thompson v. Oklahoma, 162–163
Thornburg v. Gingles, 65–67
Torcaso v. Watkins, 127
Town of Castle Rock v. Gonzales, 104
Trop v. Dulles, 162, 165

United States v. Banks, 150
United States v. Booker, 159
United States v. Carolene Products Co., 100
United States v. Coombs, 44
United States v. Georgia, 58
United States v. Gonzalez-Lopez, 157
United States v. Grubbs, 138
United States v. International Business Machines Corp., 82
United States v. Kennedy, 147
United States v. Knights, 145
United States v. Leon, 151
United States v. Limares, 147
United States v. Lopez, 3, 40–41, 43, 45–48, 50
United States v. Matlock, 140–141, 143–144

United States v. Mead Corp., 52
United States v. Morrison, 3, 40, 43, 45–48
United States v. Place, 146–147, 149
United States v. Ramirez, 153
United States v. Scarborough, 147
United States v. United Foods, 111
United States v. United States District Court, 33

Van Orden v. Perry, 113, **117–128**
Vieth v. Jubelirer, 61–63, 69–73

Wallace v. Jaffree, 118, 129–130, 133
Washington v. Glucksberg, 51

Weeks v. United States, 151, 154–155
West Virginia Bd. of Ed. v. Barnette, 107–108
Whitman v. American Trucking Assns., Inc., 53
Wickard v. Filburn, 40–44, 49
Wilson v. Arkansas, 150–151, 154–155
Wilson v. Layne, 141
Wolf v. Colorado, 155
Wooley v. Maynard, 107–108

Zadvydas v. Davis, 177
Zelman v. Simmons-Harris, 119, 135
Zorach v. Clauson, 134

Other Books by David M. O'Brien

Storm Center:
The Supreme Court in American Politics
7th ed.

Constitutional Law and Politics:
Vol. 1. *Struggles for Power and Governmental Accountability*
Vol. 2. *Civil Rights and Civil Liberties*
6th ed.

Animal Sacrifice and Religious Freedom:
Church of Lukumi Babalu Aye v. City of Hialeah

Judicial Roulette

What Process Is Due?
Courts and Science-Policy Disputes

The Public's Right to Know:
The Supreme Court and the First Amendment

Privacy, Law, and Public Policy

Judges on Judging: Views from the Bench
2nd ed. (editor)

To Dream of Dreams:
Religious Freedom and Constitutional Politics in Postwar Japan
(with Yasuo Ohkoshi)

Abortion and American Politics
(with Barbara H. Craig)

Judicial Independence in the Age of Democracy:
Critical Perspectives from Around the World
(edited with Peter Russell)

The Politics of Technology Assessment:
Institutions, Processes and Policy Disputes
(edited with Donald Marchand)

Views from the Bench:
The Judiciary and Constitutional Politics
(edited with Mark Cannon)

The Politics of American Government
3d ed.
(with Stephen J. Wayne, G. Calvin Mackenzie, and Richard Cole)

Government by the People
21st ed.
(with David B. Magleby, Paul Light, James MacGregor Burns,
J. W. Peltason, and Thomas E. Cronin)